Writing and Gender

Writing and Gender

Virginia Woolf's Writing Practice

Sue Roe

HARVESTER WHEATSHEAF
ST. MARTIN'S PRESS

First published 1990 by
Harvester Wheatsheaf
66 Wood Lane End, Hemel Hempstead
Hertfordshire HP2 4RG
A division of
Simon & Schuster International Group

and in the USA by
St. Martin's Press, Inc.,
175 Fifth Avenue,
New York,
NY 10010

Typeset in 10½/12½pt Garamond
by Keyboard Services, Luton

Printed and bound in Great Britain by
BPCC Wheatons Ltd, Exeter

Library of Congress Cataloging in publication data
applied for
ISBN 0-312-05766-0

British Library Cataloguing in Publication Data

Roe, Sue, *1956–*
    Writing and gender: Virginia Woolf's writing practice.
    1. Authors, English 20th century Biography
    I. Title
    823.912

    ISBN 0-7108-1038-5
    ISBN 0-7108-1101-2 pbk

1 2 3 4 5   94 93 92 91 90

To Johnny

Contents

Acknowledgements

In writing this book I have been grateful for the invaluable encouragement and sensitive criticism I have received from those who read early and/or later drafts and encouraged me to proceed. They are Bernard Sharratt; Janet Montefiore; Hermione Lee; Graham Clarke; Nicki Jackowska; Susan Sellers; Coral Ann Howells; Stephen Plaice, and the Harvester reader who wished to remain anonymous.

My thanks are also due to Lola L. Szladits, Curator of the Berg Collection of the New York Public Library, Astor, Lenox and Tilden Foundations, for whose generous help I was most grateful during my three week visit to the Berg Collection.

I should like here to thank also Bet Inglis, of the Manuscript Section, University of Sussex Library, for her generous assistance during each of my visits there.

Sue Burnham typed an entire draft with careful and patient attention, and I should like here to express my grateful thanks to her.

My parents gave their inimitable support at important moments, and to them I am sincerely grateful. Likewise, my brother David.

John Spiers gave me consistent and enthusiastic support in beginning, pursuing and completing the work and continued at all times to believe that I would one day complete the project. For all his devoted and inspiring support I am indebted to him.

The Author gratefully acknowledges also the Henry W. and Albert A. Berg Collection, The New York Public Library, Astor, Lenox and Tilden Foundations and Professor Quentin Bell, for permission to quote from unpublished sources. Also the Executors of the Virginia Woolf Estate and The Hogarth Press for permission to quote from Virginia Woolf's published texts. Also Harcourt Brace Jovanovich for permission to quote the following extracts from Virginia Woolf's work in copyright: Excerpts from *Orlando*, copyright 1928 by Virginia Woolf and renewed 1956 by Leonard Woolf, reprinted by permission of Harcourt Brace Jovanovich, Inc; excerpts from *To the Lighthouse* by Virginia Woolf, copyright 1927 by Harcourt Brace Jovanovich, Inc., and renewed by Leonard Woolf, reprinted by permission of the publisher; excerpts from *Moments of Being* by Virginia Woolf, copyright © 1976 by Quentin Bell and Angelica Garnett, reprinted by permission of Harcourt Brace Jovanocich, Inc; excerpts from *Between the Acts* by Virginia Woolf, copyright 1941 by Harcourt Brace Jovanovich, Inc., and renewed 1969 by Leonard Woolf, reprinted by permission of the publisher; excerpts from *The Diary of Virginia Woolf*, Volume III, copyright © 1978 by Quentin Bell and Angelica Garnett, reprinted by permission of Harcourt Brace Jovanovich, Inc; excerpts from *The Diary of Virginia Woolf*, Volume V, copyright © 1984 by Quentin Bell and Angelica Garnett, reprinted by permission of Harcourt Brace Jovanovich, Inc.

Abbreviations

(Full details of publication are given in footnotes and bibliography)

AWD	*A Writer's Diary*, edited by Leonard Woolf
BA	*Between the Acts*
Bell, I; II	*Virginia Woolf: A Biography*, by Quentin Bell
CDB	*The Captain's Death Bed*
CR	*The Common Reader*
CS	*Congenial Spirits: The Letters of Virginia Woolf*, selected and edited by Joanne Trautmann Banks
CW	*Contemporary Writers*
D, I–V	*The Diary of Virginia Woolf*, edited by Anne Olivier Bell
DoM	*The Death of the Moth*
HH	*A Haunted House, and Other Stories*
JR	*Jacob's Room*
L, I–VI	*The Letters of Virginia Woolf*, edited by Nigel Nicolson
M	*Melymbrosia*, An Early Version of *The Voyage Out*, edited with an introduction by Louise A. DeSalvo
MB	*Moments of Being*: unpublished autobiographical writings, edited with an introduction and notes by Jeanne Schulkind
Mrs D	*Mrs Dalloway*
N&D	*Night and Day*
O	*Orlando*
P	*The Pargiters*: the novel-essay portion of *The Years*, edited with an introduction by Mitchell A. Leaska
PH	*Pointz Hall*: the earlier and later typescripts of *Between the Acts*, edited with an introduction, annotations and an afterword by Mitchell A. Leaska
RF	*Roger Fry: A Biography*
ROO	*A Room of One's Own*

TG	*Three Guineas*
TL	*To the Lighthouse*
TL Draft	*To the Lighthouse*: the original holograph draft, transcribed and edited by Susan Dick
VO	*The Voyage Out*
W	*The Waves*
W Drafts	*The Waves*: the two holograph drafts, transcribed and edited by J. W. Graham
W&W	*Virginia Woolf: Women and Writing*, edited by Michèle Barrett
Y	*The Years*

Introduction

I AM A LITTLE BOY AND ADRIAN IS A GIRL I HAVE SENT YOU
SOME CHOCOLATES GOOD BYE VIRGINIA   (CS, p. 2)

In her earliest attempts to write – before she even learned to join up her
letters – Virginia Stephen was already experimenting with forms of
gender definition. It must be left to the reader to speculate on the
precise implications of this early letter to George Duckworth: the
confusion he seems to have inspired is noteworthy in the light of later,
by now well-known and ubiquitously cited events involving the Duckworth brothers.[1] But if the writing may here be ominous in one respect,
it also reflects a generosity of spirit, a playful inventiveness and a sense
of form which the young Virginia was to carry over into adulthood as
features of her writing practice.

By the time she reached her twenties, the woman who was to become
Virginia Woolf had already lived an entire, nightmarish narrative of
tragic and traumatic events which had succeeded in severely disrupting
any sense of stable identity and had challenged at a fundamental level
her confidence in the reliability of relationships with others.[2] She was
by now proposing to 'found a colony where there shall be no marrying
– unless you happen to fall in love with a symphony of Beethoven – no
human element at all, except what comes through Art – . . .' (CS, p. 6),
and trying her hand at written compositions of a somewhat 'bloodless'
kind. She '[ran] to a book as a child to its mother', she admitted in a
letter to Violet Dickinson, and had decided that 'the flesh' could only
be but 'a cumbersome illustration' (CS, p. 36).

The writing projects she initiated during her early twenties reflected
her state of mind. She had formed plans, for example, to collaborate
with Jack Hills on a play which was to show 'a man and woman – . . .
never meeting – . . . but all the time you'll feel them come nearer . . . –
but when they almost meet – only a door between – you see how they

1

just miss – . . .' (Bell, I, p. 125). Her plans never came to fruition, though the positioning of Clarissa and Septimus within *Mrs Dalloway* could be seen as a later development of this idea.

She was also writing at this time brief sketches describing landscape, and recounting pseudo-dramatic events such as 'Terrible Tragedy in a Duckpond'[3] in a flat, schoolgirlish style which, as she herself was aware, were hardly masterpieces in the making. She showed such pieces to the family friend, Madge Vaughan (who, since the death of Julia Stephen had, together with Violet Dickinson, become something of a mother figure), and Madge responded with some healthy criticism. Virginia defended her work against this, insisting that she knew that what she had written was 'very narrow', and was sure she could explain why this was so 'from *external* reasons; such as education, way of life etc.' but added that the 'vague and dream like world, without love, or heart, or passion, or sex' which she depicted in her writing was the only 'world' she really cared about. 'It seems to me better to write of the things I do feel,' she added, 'than to dabble in things I frankly dont understand in the least. That is the kind of blunder – in literature – which seems to me ghastly and unpardonable' (*CS*, p. 26). Like the painters with whom she was later to feel a common bond – Roger Fry, Duncan Grant and, of course, her sister, Vanessa Bell – she was even at this embryonic stage in her writing practice fiercely adamant that her subject matter should evolve out of the possibilities and observe the limitations of her medium (in the case of a writer, of course, language itself; the writer 'herself') and that the voice she was beginning to develop should be authentically her own.

By the time she married Leonard Woolf, she had already begun on the project which was to become her first full-length novel, *The Voyage Out*, in which she was to bear out her early resolutions by exploring the inner life of a heroine whose senses were aroused only by Beethoven Sonatas. And she gives in her correspondence a strong impression of having married only on condition that her changed circumstances would further her opportunities to develop her writing: 'L.', for whom she felt (at least, physically) 'no more than a rock' thought her writing 'the best part of her'.[4] She approved, moreover, of the register office wedding, which seemed to effect her transformation into a married woman with admirable succinctness: 'You stand up and repeat two sentences, and then sign your name' (*L*, II, p. 3). But a different name did not necessarily denote a changed state. She '[found] the climax immensely exaggerated', she reported from her honeymoon: 'Except for a sustained good humour . . . due to the fact that every twinge of anger is at once visited upon my husband, I might be still Miss S.' (*L*, II, pp. 6–7). In this letter (to Ka Cox) she again conveys a mixture of confusion, resilience and a somewhat ragged, raw process of negotiation: with her husband, but primarily with herself.

She became a celibate wife, enjoying a marriage which gave her security, companionship with a devoted husband and a busy and stimulating social life, and confining to her writing practice the struggle to create a gendered identity. Her first fictional heroine, Rachel Vinrace, suffered the effects of the constraints on her creator's imagination. Woolf drafted this difficult novel, ostensibly about the heroine's rite of passage into womanhood, seven agonising times, and as many times attempted to solve the problem of Rachel's sexual inertia. But the trouble was (as Woolf herself dimly perceived) that she needed to depict for Rachel a psychological transition which she was simply unable to imagine. (She had meant, she later told Vanessa, to introduce some 'tupping', but 'somehow it seemed out of the picture' (*L*, II, p. 394).)

Virginia Woolf's writing practice, then, began thus. In the light of these beginnings, her achievements are extraordinary. Today, she has become every feminist reader's favourite subject: the 'mother' we think back through and precursor of 'women's writing'. She can always provide the feminist *mot juste*; has always seen it all, been through it all, before. She has been so readily and so ubiquitously appropriated to the feminist literary Cause that it sometimes seems as though every feminist insight has its origin somewhere in the work of Virginia Woolf. Her novels are constantly seen as guiding examples of the subversion in fiction of patriarchal structures, and most feminist criticism of her work gives the impression of a mind dealing determinedly with revisionary insights into the question of sexual difference. Where problems relating to gender are critically discussed, they are usually seen as biographical, rather than as problems intrinsically to do with the practice of writing. In recent years, Woolf's fiction has been read in the light of various different aspects of literary theory, but it is difficult, as Gayatri Spivak has candidly admitted, to apply such perspectives other than reductively.[5]

It is equally difficult to reconcile the outspoken Virginia Woolf, capable of parodying women's political dilemmas and urging the assumption of women's independence, with the creative artist who produced vivid, but largely abstract work such as 'Kew Gardens' or 'A Haunted House'. If her critics have tended to concentrate on one aspect of Virginia Woolf or the other – the feminist revolutionary or the 'aesthete' –[6] this may well be because her writing about gender has tended to be either ignored, or regarded as politically inspired and, in her fiction, fully formed. But if it is difficult for her readers to reconcile Woolf's aesthetic 'flights of the mind' with her more uncompromising pronouncements on the politics of gender, it would have been considerably more difficult for the creative artist, who cannot use language to 'summarise' a position or to offer a conclusive point of view, to reconcile fine writing with politically and personally problematic ideas. In this book I suggest that, far from resolving problems as it were on Virginia Woolf's behalf, or drawing conclusions she herself was unable to draw, it might be possible to make a more judicious appraisal of the difficulties, the agonies and the subtleties of Woolf's thinking on the issue of gender by charting her ongoing and complex attempts to construct a gendered identity within her writing practice.

I began by suggesting, partly in jest, that it might be possible to begin to detect the origins of Virginia Woolf's thinking about gender in her childhood correspondence. It is as good a place to start as any, but such a suggestion must also draw attention to the difficulty of applying any kind of historical perspective to a process that can never be seen as having an indisputable point of origin. Woolf herself was very much aware of this problem, and tackled it with tenacity and originality in her biography of Roger Fry, in the course of which she faced the problem of assembling 'the facts' of his life into a narrative suggestive of the particular vagaries of Fry's vision and personality. Her attempt to evoke, rather than simply describe, the connections between the 'life' and the 'work' felt like 'tethered and literal rubbish-heap grubbing' (*L*, VI, p. 404) and this ambitious project was, she felt, 'the worst of all [her] life's experiences' (*D*, V, p. 234). 'Only one subject seemed to escape his insatiable curiosity,' she writes, towards the end of the book and with discernible exasperation, 'and that was himself' (*RF*, p. 252): it was impossible to give a cohesive portrait of a practising artist, but perhaps she might have achieved more if she had written in more detail about the execution of the painter's work. As it is, her ambitiously Freudian attempts to write an evocative rather than a descriptive biography do give a unique insight, despite some obvious shortcomings, into the demands of the creative practices of both biographer and subject.

There is a sense in which, as Woolf herself discovered in writing 'Roger', creative practice never 'begins at the beginning', and the point of origination is constantly shifting, rather than consistently suggesting a stable or fixed starting point. In attempting to highlight aspects of creative practice it has to be remembered that the writer not only consistently draws on, but is always simultaneously in the process of constructing the subjective identity 'behind' the work. In investigating the writing practice of Virginia Woolf we have at least some of the 'facts' of her life at our disposal, but any analysis of the ways in which these were, at any given stage, transposed into new artistic forms can only be partial. The process of 'translating' material into art changes the nature of the material, and the raw material can only be regarded as significant in terms of its place within the work: the business of tracing images and events back into their 'original' place within the lived experience of Virginia Woolf can only ever be part of the process of criticism. Even an analysis of the subtle ways in which Woolf moved imagery backwards and forwards, using images to negotiate between different 'selves', can never tell the whole 'story', but such an analysis may take us closer to an understanding of the ideas and influences which Woolf brought into play in the course of her ongoing struggle (which she herself would not have regarded as having any clear narrative 'line' or 'shape') to construct a gendered identity within fiction.

To begin, then, if not 'at the beginning', at least with an aspect of Woolf's project which has come to seem fundamental: 'the history of Virginia Woolf' was, during her own lifetime, at least, a shrouded and unwritten story. Her biographers and critics have pieced it together so that it has come to seem to have coherence, but it was not until the end of her life and of her writing career, when she turned to the writing of 'A Sketch of the Past', that she began to construct an autobiographical story which reflects the links for her between gender and composition. To the extent that she drew on aspects of her own history in constructing her novels, she did so tentatively and with great caution. Her history, such as it was, was a narrative composed of shocks, intrusions and bereavements, and she had reacted by becoming, at least to some extent, emotionally anaesthetised. The events which, when she described them in 'A Sketch of the Past', were to come to have a charged, creative significance, lay for many years under wraps.

The history of Virginia Woolf was as much the product as the source of her writing practice, and if the atmosphere of her early prose had an ascetic, 'screened' quality and seemed to render the author of the text

non-commital and obscure, it can with hindsight be seen to reflect, in
quality if not in subject matter, the atmosphere of her 'own' story. The
'extraordinarily inert, incantatory rhythm of the prose, and the remotely reminiscent nature of the image' which Wilfrid Mellers noted,
for example, in his review of *The Years*,[7] is suggestive of much more
when applied to Woolf's writing practice than when taken simply as a
criticism of her text.

The *techniques* of her writing practice were of paramount importance to Woolf at all times, and she knew that it was only by finding the
right 'shape' or 'mould' for a book that she could bring her material as
vibrantly as possible into play. Throughout her writing practice she
was determined (as I show in Part I) that her writing should never lapse
into autobiography. She was highly suspicious of her own 'story' and
took great pains, as her writing practice developed, to excise it, delete it,
keep it out. She was always anxious to use writing 'as an art, not as a
method of self expression' and with this as her goal, almost anything, if
it interested or appealed to her, might evolve into an originating image
or idea. Just prior to beginning *Jacob's Room*, for example, she went to
see an exhibition of Negro carvings, and 'dimly [saw] that something in
their style might be written, and also that if I had one on the mantelpiece I should be a different sort of character – less adorable, as far as I
can make out, but somebody you wouldn't forget in a hurry' (*L*, II,
p. 429). Again, here, the desire is to construct a self, but a self which
would be constructed in – and in the process of – *writing*: it is 'the
writing "I" ', as she later came to refer to it, which she here resolves to
make memorable.

For reasons such as these, I decline in this book to set Virginia Woolf
in any fixed 'historical context', preferring instead to chart the steadily
developing context which she herself developed through her writing
practice. My primary concern, in attempting to isolate Woolf's process
of constructing and reconstructing gender identity within her writing
practice, is not only with her own developing 'theories' with regard to
both sexuality and language, but also with the problem that in the final
analysis a fixed and dependable reference point for the construction of
gender was precisely what she lacked.

The fundamental questions always needed to be asked, and asked
again. How *does* an artist adjust perspective? How might she
evolve an appropriate form? How might it be possible to evoke colour

and light in writing? How does a woman writer resist sexual censorship (for Woolf, particularly, in the contexts of a Victorian
upbringing and a celibate marriage)? These were questions Virginia
Woolf constantly needed to pose, and to which she constantly sought
new answers by trying out new sketches, new phrases, new designs,
new techniques. The practices of the Post-Impressionist painters
fascinated her, but their theories could not be directly transposed into
her medium. In the process of examining such issues she faced the
challenge of drawing on aspects of herself while keeping other aspects
firmly at bay.

In charting some of the details of this always complex, always
fascinating, always idiosyncratic process I pay particular attention to
that last question – how does a woman writer resist sexual censorship –
since from the earliest stages of her writing practice Woolf was determined to solve this problem. As a celibate woman attempting to write
about sexuality, she developed a tendency to draw a veil or a pane of
glass over 'things [she] frankly [didn't] understand in the least', and this
became a feature of her style.

For most of her writing life she felt – like Mary Carmichael, the
novelist she invents in *A Room of One's Own*– 'encumbered with that
self-consciousness in the presence of "sin" which is the legacy of our
sexual barbarity' (*ROO*, p. 88). "Sin", when committed by a woman
writer, amounts simply to the capacity to think about sexuality, but
even this imprecise definition gives little idea of the full extent of the
vacuousness of the term, since the activity is only definable in terms of
its failure to achieve expression. The censorship of women's vitality has
come about, she claims in *A Room of One's Own*, not only through
lack of education and the prohibition of access to professional resources,
but also through a subtle and insidious practice of male elitism which
has long ensured that women function 'as looking-glasses possessing
the magic and delicious power of reflecting the figure of man at twice its
natural size' (*ROO*, p. 37). She is thinking here, no doubt, about her
mother and the anti-Suffrage attitudes which prevailed in the household of her childhood, and which she was furious to find still dominating
the evolution of her 'writing "I"' decades later.

In her writing of the 1930s (in *Three Guineas*, *The Years* and shorter
pieces such as 'Professions for Women') she was to define more fully
the subtle context of censorship – imposed by 'the figure of man' –
within which she saw women artists as being constrained to work. In
'Professions for Women' she personified the censor in the figure of the
'Angel in the House', whose function it is to edit the thoughts of women

novelists even as they write, by reminding them that they are in a male world and so 'must charm, must conciliate, must – . . . – tell lies if they are to succeed' (*DoM*, p. 151). Under her influence it is impossible for a woman writer to express 'the truth about human relations, morality, sex' (*ibid.*) because she makes it impossible to sustain an original thought. If anyone were to tell the truth about female desire, she reminds the hapless novelist, 'men . . . would be shocked' (*DoM*, p. 152): it was a fairly forcible disincentive, given the violent and tyrannical male reactions to shock which dominated Woolf's memories of her adolescence.

It took a long time for Virginia Woolf to begin to identify some of the more tangible sources of self-censorship within her own writing. For much of her writing practice she worked delicately and painstakingly within a dimly perceived framework of constraints on self-expression, rather than in reaction against this, and her writing – perhaps as a result of this – often has a veiled or glassy quality. She eventually gave up, in *The Voyage Out*, on her attempt to write a novel about 'the things people don't say' because she had no real way of identifying such things, and she only resumed this struggle after she had proved to herself, in *Jacob's Room*, that she could write a 'crepuscular' novel about the dynamics of desire. (Significantly, she was delighted with her achievement in *Jacob's Room* without ever admitting to herself the implications – or even the nature – of what she had achieved there.)

When in *Mrs Dalloway* she went further, working with the attempt to identify the very timbre of a woman's voice, she again pulled herself back into the old constraints. She had wanted to expose the social system which had edited out the dark side, or 'black heart' of her own creativity (and she reveals there, though cursorily, the obtuseness of contemporary psychiatry, culling examples directly from her own experience) but she could only do this by marginalising her subject: the plight of the traumatised Septimus, like the frisson of an old memory, only fleetingly touches Clarissa.

In composing her later novels, she came to realise that her *own* process of self censorship – which undoubtedly took her Victorian upbringing as its model – was more powerful than she had hitherto grasped. She by now passionately wanted to write freely in fiction about the lack of education for women and the restrictions of 'chastity', but the constraints which she wished so fervently to describe in fiction were uncomfortably similar to those which operated to restrict her in her own writing practice.

The importance of the 'atmosphere' of a work of art[8] again enters in here: in *Three Guineas* she could be content to write in a tone of powerful stridency which muddied her argument and earned her charges of naivetée, but she was nevertheless satisfied that she had been passionately – even 'violently' – outspoken. However, when she turned, in writing *The Years*, back to the problem of transposing such convictions into artistic form, she still could not quite say what it was she meant: the *techniques* of art were more demanding, and seemed more pressing, than those of polemic.

There is, running through Virginia Woolf's entire process of composition, an imagery suggestive of a subverted feminity which surfaces despite the strain of its needing to be drawn on whilst at the same time being held in check. In Part I of this book, I look at some of the techniques of Woolf's writing practice; in Part II, I highlight the way in which this particular imagery emerged, in the process of composing each of her later novels, each time in a different shape and form. Woolf was struggling at all times with a delicate and subtle process which necessitated a kind of regulated remembering: she had to be careful not to release too many painful memories too soon, especially *because* she was always determined to avoid writing autobiography. She was a novelist: she wanted to tell new stories, not simply to capitalise on the old ones, and it is *this* determination, as much as any self-consciousness about the nature of her own story, which is a determining factor in the process of composition.

The old stories gradually became easier to identify, but the links between the development of her art and the gradual piecing together of her own history – which took place, at different levels, simultaneously – were at all times extremely subtle and absolutely pliable: she continued to want to denounce rather than exploit the idea of art as a means of self-revelation. We now have access to some graphic and revealing accounts of her repressive childhood and traumatic adolescence. But though the 'facts' of Woolf's own life are invaluable in suggesting how and why she developed such a subtle process of censoring herself, they cannot offer us a direct route into something else. That is, the particular version of this process which translates itself into the language and imagery of her writing practice, ensuring that there would always be things she would find it impossible to say in this medium. Gradually, she evolved an imagery evocative of, but not identical to, that of her own fragmented sense of origination, but – by its very nature – it is not always an easy 'story' to expose for critical analysis. I seek in this book not to identify a hidden subject matter, but rather to demonstrate the ways in which Woolf's highly complicated sense of veiled and sheltered femininity encouraged a particular style of composition, enabling her to hover in the vicinity of, linger with and then glance off, some of the things she had thought she would never be able to say.

In a sense, Virginia Woolf's writing practice may be regarded as the activity which gradually and painfully freed her from the effects of her debilitating history, though this was not the reason why she embarked on it. She wanted to be an artist. As is the case with many writers, it offered her a creative route back to her own 'origins' and enabled her to lay claim to her own insights. An analysis of this complex process offers glimpses of a creative female subject in the process of construction: in this case, a complex and idiosyncratic character who, in her writing, refuses to be paralysed or petrified, but is determined to construct for herself instead a vital new identity, to invent a subject uninhibited by the constraints imposed by history or by others.

The novels of Virginia Woolf, as I suggest in Part II of this book, always tell a complicated network of different stories, always offer a number of interpretations of the same story; Virginia Woolf's writing practice, drawing on and transposing her own 'stories', can tell yet another story. This time it is a story not about 'the history of women' (though Woolf on a number of occasions attempted such a thing); nor about 'sexual difference' as it has elsewhere been defined; nor even about the 'life-story' of Virginia Woolf. Her writing practice constructs the narrative of an attempt, not to make a particular shape or to tell a particular story, but rather to forge a language which could both reflect and enable the construction of gendered identity within a work of art. As the creator of such a narrative – and largely as the result of the courage and stamina she consistently brought to each new attempt – Virginia Woolf became an important and influential artist, and a woman who hardly seems likely to be forgotten in a hurry.

Part I

Virginia Woolf's Writing Practice

. . . To use writing as an art, not as a method of self-expression.
(*ROO*, p. 79)

Virginia Woolf's
Writing Practice

Reading

In her struggle to construct frameworks for her thinking, Virginia Woolf used the process of writing as a way of shaping meaning: language did not immediately express but rather gave her access to the insights her work reflects; she built the scenes of her novels around images dependent for their significance on coincidence and continuity; invented for her characters phrases and modes of behaviour which screened as well as reflected meaning. Because she worked in this way, her definitions of gender – which were always in flux, never static – function as an integral part of, and element within, the development of her aesthetic. It thus becomes possible to identify her feminism as issuing from her writing practice: forged by writing, rather than consolidated within it. In the light of this, Woolf's feminism might be found to be linked more closely with her writing problems than with her perception of external conditions or events, and even to influence her constant stylistic experimentation, her switches from a poetic to a more realist prose, and back again.

In order, then, to dig deeply into the nature of her thinking about gender, it becomes necessary to attempt to define her aesthetic: to identify a system which, even if it is never identifiable as a conclusive formulation in her writing, can be discerned in the forms in which it comes into play within her writing *practice*. She broke with representation, creating new forms of the novel. She was an experimentalist, inventing ways of saying things the novel had not, hitherto, been equipped to say. She abandoned the realist techniques characteristic of her predecessors, finding ways of structuring her work which were analogous with the new experiments taking place in the realm of contemporary painting. Such are the typical critical reactions to Woolf's work.[1] How might it be possible to analyse the ways in which she was able to achieve these things; to identify and to define her aesthetic? And, to examine the ways in which her aesthetic strategy might be connected with her individual and idiosyncratic style of feminist thinking? If it were possible to offer an analysis of the construction of Virginia Woolf's aesthetic, to identify and describe significant stages in her writing process, then perhaps the implications of these procedures for her feminism might be brought to light.

She identified, in her reading, aspects of her own writing methods. She tended to see in others' work the problems she herself was grappling with, which is perhaps why her own criticism tends to be impressionistic and subjective; why she characteristically identifies problems rather than passing value judgements.[2] She consistently identified, in her reading, paradoxes and anomalies of style and structure, and, particularly in her criticism written in the 1920s, needed to identify the importance of a break with realism and a challenge to the centrality and coherence of the human subject, issues which she took over as being essential in her own work. In her reading of the work of the Elizabethans, the Greeks, the nineteenth century Russian and the contemporary English novelists, she sought consistently to identify a force directed against the current of plot and narrative continuity, placing, instead, an emphasis on isolated moments and on the private epiphanies of feeling and emotion depicted in the interstices of life and of narrative continuum.

She conceived of narrative structure as to some extent a constraint, and went so far as to urge the importance of a literature capable of conveying an emotional and psychological power inexpressible in words. In 'Craftsmanship' (originally conceived as a radio broadcast entitled 'Words Fail Me') she expressed her sense that the English language was no longer equipped to suggest the nuances of emotional and psychological insight which she saw as belonging to contemporary life;[3] in 'On Not Knowing Greek', she identified 'an ambiguity' at the heart of the Greek language 'which is the mark of the highest poetry; we cannot know exactly what it means . . . The meaning is just on the far side of language' (*CR*, 1, pp. 31–2).

She identified this ability to describe the 'rapid flight of the mind' which was for her suggested by the works of the Greeks as a poetic one, and on one occasion wished that she herself were able to write poetry: 'It is a great pity that I am a prose writing and not a poetic animal. Then I could express my feelings, gratitude, contentment, spiritual joy, physical comfort, friendship, appreciation – . . .' (*L*, I, p. 441). The *simultaneity* of emotions expressed in poetry was a goal for her: she conceived of the human mind as functioning simultaneously on a number of levels, and thus praised Dorothy Richardson's ability to register in the mind of her heroine 'one after another, and one on top of another, words, cries, shouts, notes of a violin, . . .' (*W&W*, p. 189).

It seemed difficult to identify the source of this achievement. She tried, in writing about Turgenev's work, to identify the reasons for her impression that in his novels 'the form is in one sense so perfect, in another so broken. They are about Russia in the fifties and sixties of the last century, and yet they are about ourselves at the present moment' (*CDB*, p. 55). 'A novelist, of course,' she added, 'lives so much deeper down than a critic that his statements are apt to be contradictory and confusing; they seem to break in process of coming to the surface, and do not hold together in the light of reason' (*ibid.*).

Without this proviso, she quotes this advice to a young poet: 'Trouver, en la cherchant, une expression *propre* est impossible: elle doit couler de source' (*ibid.*), placing the emphasis, for her, on writing as *process*: a process of excavation and emergence which, like Aeschylus' poetic power, refuses to be constrained by language.

The language of explanation, then, was regarded by Woolf as ill-equipped to describe either fiction itself, or the process of writing it. One important facet of her reading is her emphasis on the connection between the structure of fiction and the process of writing: if the writer's mind seemed impossible to pin down to a stable definition, so too, importantly, did the mind of the ficitious character. She criticised her direct predecessors (Bennett, Wells and Galsworthy) for their assumption that a human subject could be depicted in terms of material minutiae, and in 'An Unwritten Novel' and 'Mr Bennett and Mrs Brown,' she considered instead the possibility that the life of a human subject cannot be depicted solely through accurate observation, suggesting instead that fiction should take on the challenge of somehow reflecting its own limitations in this respect. In 'Modern Fiction' she attempted to distinguish between her predecessors' treatment of character and her own, focusing, in the process, on the necessary change in perspective required by the modern novelist. Again, as in her writing on Turgenev, what is notable is her conception of the presence of the writer in his or her work: 'if a writer were a free man and not a slave, if he could write what he chose, not what he must, if he could base his work upon his own feeling and not upon convention, there would be no plot, no comedy, no tragedy, no love interest or catastrophe in the accepted style, . . .' (*CR*, 1, pp. 149–51).

She sought, then, a complete break with representation, recognising that traditional narrative was incapable of expressing a fluid, rather than an artificially stable subject; and in her own work began to develop a lyricism which would run counter to the narratives of observation and exegesis favoured by her predecessors. It is clear from her Diary entries of the time, and from her letters to Clive Bell and particularly to Roger Fry, that the Post-Impressionist movement which preoccupied the contemporary painters with whom she was in daily contact influenced her conception of the novel. In her biography of Roger Fry, she was later to note Fry's attention to the novel: his dissatisfaction with most literature, and his expectation that the novel, particularly in France, was capable of attending to the rhythms and methods of its own procedures in ways which the Post-Impressionist painters were beginning to explore. For Fry, the novelist Gerald Brenan was one of the first to have fully explored the connections between writing and painting: 'I mean,' he explained, 'he believes that everything must come out of the *matière* of his prose and not out of the ideas and emotions he describes' (*RF*, pp. 208–9). In a letter to Woolf, Fry had written that she herself seemed to him to share with only the French novelists this relationship with her '*matière*' and the ability to evoke it in her fiction[4] – it is the same relationship as that identified by Woolf in her essay on Turgenev.

However, Woolf encountered again the problem of how to convey this relationship in explicatory language when she attempted, in her biography of Fry, to identify a *method* for such procedures. She acknowledged the link, and Fry's preoccupation with the link, between writing and painting, but resorted to metaphor when constrained to describe the shared process of psychological excavation. Fry, she emphasised there, read books 'by the light of [the Post-Impressionist movement]'. She likened him to a water-diviner who 'seemed to have tapped some hidden spring sunk beneath the incrustations that had blocked it. The twig turned vigorously and unexpectedly in streets, in galleries, but also in front of the bookcase' (*RF*, p. 149). She is struggling, here, to convey some notion of breaking through a barrier or releasing a block comparable, for her, with the barriers implicitly erected by the method of realist representation; but she is characteristically unable to analyse the implications of this insight: her own writing becomes, here, clumsy and obscure.

She nowhere offers, in *Roger Fry*, a theory of Post-Impressionism, but it is clear from isolated instances in her work and from the drafts of her later fiction that the changes in notions of perspective which the painters were working on affected her profoundly, and the Post-Impressionists undoubtedly echoed and confirmed her in her conviction that traditional methods of representation were no longer adequate to express the workings of the subjective consciousness. In this respect, she stressed the similarities between the creative mind – weighing past against present moments – and that of contemporary politics which offered new sources of reinterpretation. She stressed, too, particularly in 'Modern Fiction', the fragmentation of the human subject resultant on contemporary and political changes, and thus the importance for the contemporary novelist of recognising a need to re-focus attention on the introspective, rather than the social or material, life of his or her characters.

The notion of the artist's recourse to the unconscious mind was vital to her, but she expressed it, at least in her critical writing, as a problem of perspective: the problem facing the modern novelist was, she advocated, that of finding ways of visualising and transcribing new *foci* of attention:

> [the writer] has to have the courage to say that what interests him is no longer 'this' but 'that': out of 'that' alone must he construct his work. For the moderns 'that', the point of interest, lies very likely in the dark places of psychology. (*CR*, 1, p. 156)

At this point everything promises to come together for the contemporary reader. It is clear that Woolf was working in her reading, her writing on the novel and in her sympathy with what the painters were doing, with a notion of the unconscious mind as a reserve for creative ideas and as a potential source of new material. The alternative perspectives of the unconscious would offer new structures and patterns of thinking and seeing and would represent an alternative view of the subjective mind, in contrast with the character-portraits offered by her predecessors. But though Freud's ideas were by this stage widely known in the circles in which she moved, and though the Hogarth Press published his works, she seems to have resisted until much later any detailed investigation into his theories. She sensed the importance of the unconscious, both as a reserve for the creative process and as a potential area of new subject matter, but her explorations into this area were fragmented, unstructured and improvisational,[5] as though – here again – it was a matter of letting her material 'couler de source'.

.She had already, as early as 1919, discerned in the work of Dorothy Richardson a concern with 'the dark places', and her review of Richardson's *The Tunnel* offered a description of the consciousness of Richardson's central character as a clear alternative to the preoccupations of the nineteenth century novelists. In Richardson's work, she noted, ' "him" and "her" are cut out', leaving instead, 'denuded, unsheltered, unbegun and unfinished, the consciousness of Miriam Henderson, the small sensitive lump of matter, half transparent and half opaque, which endlessly reflects and distorts the variegated procession, and is, we are bidden to believe, the source beneath the surface, the very oyster within the shell.'[6] The mind is seen by her, as early as 1919, as a reflector, with a capacity to offer a distorted perspective similar to those being explored by the Post-Impressionists. 'Art', Fry had announced, 'is significant deformity' (*RF*, p. 169).

In her review of Richardson's later novel, *Revolving Lights*, Woolf identified Richardson's concern with psychological introspection and the resultant new emphases of her subject matter as capable of producing a specifically feminine text. The result of her concern with 'the dark places' was to have devised a *method* which might be identified as specific to a women's writing and designed especially to describe the workings of the female consciousness:

> She has invented, or, if she has not invented, developed and applied to her
> own uses, a sentence which we might call the psychological sentence of the
> feminine gender . . . Other writers of the opposite sex have used sentences
> of this description and stretched them to the extreme. But there is a
> difference. Miss Richardson has fashioned her sentence consciously, in
> order that it may descend to the depths and crannies of Miriam
> Henderson's consciousness. It is a woman's sentence . . .   (*W&W*, p. 191)

She fails in this review to quote any sentence of Richardson's in demonstration of her argument, but identifies in her sentence an elasticity – it is a sentence capable of 'suspending the frailest particles' – and, in her method, attention to a change in the novelist's perspective. The plot, as defined by the Edwardians, was emphatically not Dorothy

Richardson's concern: 'A man might fall dead at [Miriam's] feet (it is not likely), and Miriam might feel that a violent-coloured ray of light was an important element in her consciousness of the tragedy. If she felt it, she would say it' (*W&W*, pp. 191–2).

In the medium of painting, it might very well be that a violent-coloured ray of light would be the most instrumental factor in focusing an onlooker's perception of a tragedy. But for the medium of fiction, despite the character's new ability to be outspoken about her priorities, this perspective posed a problem, and Woolf herself felt that despite the importance of Richardson's method as representing a clear alternative to the methods of nineteenth century narrative, Richardson's text referred the reader to its methods 'too didactically' (*W&W*, p. 192).

She had, though, in her earlier review of *The Tunnel*, quoted a passage from Richardson's work in order to demonstrate her concern with the structure of the mind as an oyster within its shell, and her portrayal of the mind in the process of receiving impressions: this passage might serve as an example of Richardson's 'psychological sentence of the feminine gender'. The passage illustrated, for Woolf, Richardson's disregard for the 'story' in favour of a method of describing 'impressions as they flicker through Miriam's mind, waking incongruously other thoughts, and plaiting incessantly the many-coloured and innumerable threads of life': in this frame of mind, Richardson writes,

> Coming events cast *light*. It is like dropping everything and walking backward to something you know is there. However far you go out you come back . . . I am back now where I was before I began trying to do things like other people. I left home to get here.
>
> (*W&W*, pp 189–90)

In addition to privileging light and colour, Richardson incorporates into her sentence a notion of moving backwards as well as forwards in time, and a suggestion that meaning might be determined by the retrieval, in present reality, of something prior to, but connected with, now. In addition, the subjective consciousness acquires an extra dimension: that of a dream-like level of consciousness which offers a new way of substantiating meaning, so that the narrative seems here to be functioning, at least to some extent, on a symbolic level.

By contrast, Woolf was to offer in her work of 1928, *A Room of One's Own*, an example of the 'man's sentence' prevalent at the beginning of the nineteenth century, in comparison with which the implications of the 'psychological sentence of the feminine gender' invented by Dorothy Richardson become clear. The 'man's sentence', suggested Woolf, might run something like this:

> The grandeur of their works was an argument with them, not to stop short,
> but to proceed. They could have no higher excitement or satisfaction than
> in the exercise of their art and endless generation of truth and beauty.
> Success prompts to exertion; and habit facilitates success.   (*ROO*, p. 77)

The 'man's sentence', in contrast to Dorothy Richardson's, re-generates itself in a repetitive, circular narrative line. It reflects the male pomposity and the arrogance of the male ego elsewhere described in *A Room of One's Own* and *Three Guineas*, and argues proudly for its own self-perpetuation, inscribing no access to the sources of its argument. Rather, its justification is in its completeness, and its perpetuation is its own reward.

But whilst a painter might be capable of registering simultaneously and one on top of another the fragments of sense impression that together constituted Dorothy Richardson's composition, the novel still seemed to Woolf to demand a clear narrative shape, if such impressions were to take on significance. A violent-coloured ray of light described in a narrative would of itself lack the powers of organisation it would be capable of taking on in a painting. And though Woolf felt the power of Richardson's capacity to recognise and to delve into some of the 'dark places' of her character's psychology, she had to admit, in the final analysis, to wishing for some more conventional representation of the heroine's mind: 'the figures of other people on whom Miriam casts her capricious light are vivid enough', she judged, 'but their sayings and doings never reach that degree of significance which we, perhaps unreasonably, expect.' Sometimes it even seemed that the realist mode would be capable of evoking more. 'But it must be admitted that we are exacting', she admonished herself, in conclusion. 'We want to be rid of realism, to penetrate without its help into the regions beneath it, and further require that Miss Richardson shall fashion this new material into something which has the shapeliness of the old accepted forms' (*W&W*, pp. 190–1).

'We are asking too much; . . .' she went on. Nevertheless, this is as succinct a summary as she ever drew up of the task she set herself.

Writing

How did she go about it? She focused, in her own narrative, on experiments with time, perceiving that new temporal perspectives might offer ways of making new structural contrasts in narrative and, by the time she wrote *Mrs Dalloway*, feeling that the process of recollection was an important aspect of her attempt to forge a theory of a female aesthetic. The notes she made on the first page of the first draft of *Mrs Dalloway* testify to her attempt to define a female aesthetic in her description of a woman's voice, which was, she noted:

> a vibration in the core of the sound so that each word, or note, comes
> fluttering, alive, yet with some reluctance to inflict its vitality, some grief
> for the past which holds it back, some impulse nevertheless to glide into the
> recesses of the heart.[7]

A female aesthetic, then, would be linked with time, as it is in *To the Lighthouse*, where Lily Briscoe's review of the past, in Part Three of the novel, enables her to confront her own sexuality. The invention of Mrs Dalloway's memories, mid-way through the writing of that novel, saved Woolf's central character from becoming too 'tinselly' and, in a Diary entry for June 1923, while *Mrs Dalloway* was in progress, she revealed a sense that the writing process brought her own past, or unconscious time, at some level into play:

> Often now I have to control my excitement – as if I were pushing through a
> screen; or as if something beat fiercely close to me. What this portends I
> don't know. It is a general sense of the poetry of existence that overcomes
> me. Often it is connected with the sea & St. Ives.   (*D*, II, p. 246)

Her sense of the past as a reserve, capable of throwing up images from which narratives might be spun, was a sense she shared with Proust – for Woolf he was by 'far the greatest modern novelist' (*L*, III, p. 385) – but she also shared with him a conviction that the images which emerged in this way held implications which *could* be retrieved, but not by the analysis of the intellect. She wrote to Gerald Brenan that

> beauty, which you say I sometimes achieve, is only got by grinding all the
> flints together; by facing what must be humiliation – the things one can't
> do –   (*L*, II, p. 599)

The process of recollection had, she thought, 'something sexual in it' (*L*, III, p. 525); experimentation with the notion of time might offer a way of working with new narrative perspectives and new ways of constructing character. Visual and aural beauty might be achieved, but only in fragments; her own recollections might be used as a source of new material, but only unconsciously.

How, then, did she set about filtering these fragmented insights into the writing process? An investigation of her writing about her *own* writing, and of the draft stages of her novels, suggests that she tended to adopt a procedure, or series of stages, which enabled her to steer a path through these questions and to tap her own unconscious mind with extreme caution. Using the images of her own recollection in a regulated way, she kept a slight distance from her material whilst using herself as a source. The tension which came to be discernible as a hallmark of her writing process, the balance to be maintained, was between the danger of letting her own nightmares swamp and overpower her, and using them as a creative reserve. 'We all live,' she wrote to Gerald Brenan, 'those of us who feel or reflect, with recurring cataclysms of horror, starting up in the night in agony . . .' (*ibid*): the challenge of the writing process entailed, for her, using those seemingly empty spaces as a source, without succumbing to the horror.

On occasion, she lacked the power to regulate the images which emerged. Indeed, when she first began writing she lacked sufficient experience to know how to frame the images which obsessed her, and the writing of *The Voyage Out* took on a nightmarish quality which she had, then, to find a way of disciplining. Writing to Ethel Smyth in 1930, she recalled this phase of her 'writer's life':

> After being ill and suffering every form and variety of nightmare and
> extravagant intensity of perception – . . . I was so tremendously afraid of
> my own insanity that I wrote *Night and Day* mainly to prove to my own
> satisfaction that I could keep entirely off that dangerous ground. I wrote it,
> lying in bed, allowed to write for only one half hour a day. And I made
> myself copy from plaster casts, partly to tranquillise, partly to learn
> anatomy.   (*L*, IV, p. 231)

The drafts of *The Voyage Out* reveal the agony of being unable to *finish* a work which came to be a vehicle for her own nightmares and anxieties. What also happened, as the letter to Ethel Smyth reveals, was that Woolf was unable to extricate *herself*: an over-engagement with unstructured writing made her physically and emotionally ill and she was forced, then, to adopt external strategies for composition which resulted in an over-structured and unspontaneous work.

The initial stage of the writing procedure which she came to adopt in the face of these problems necessitated, to some extent, however, a state of submission to seemingly unrelated images which floated up: a sinking down into some unstructured realm of synaesthetic experience during which visual and aural images emerged, fraught with a significance the source of which was, at this stage, inaccessible to her. At this stage, the *shape* which was to emerge could not concern her. She noted, in the early stages of *The Voyage Out*'s composition:

Whether my conception is solid is a vastly important matter to me, but at the same time, almost impersonal. I mean to stand at my desk this autumn and work doggedly, . . . without lifting the lid off the pot, . . . (*L*, I, p. 361)

In these initial stages of the writing process, it was even as though the sensations she was dealing with bore little resemblance to language. She disagreed with Vita Sackville-West, for whom beginning to write was a question of finding the *mot juste*:

> As for the *mot juste*, you are quite wrong . . . it is all rhythm. . . . A sight, an emotion, creates this wave in the mind, long before it makes words to fit it; and in writing (such is my present belief) one has to recapture this, and set this working (which has nothing apparently to do with words) and then, as it breaks and tumbles in the mind, it makes words to fit it . . .
>
> (*L*, III, p. 247)

She 'rocked' herself into writing, she noted in her Diary (*D*, II, p. 193). Even when, in the much later stages of her writing career, she came to advocate, and to some extent to master, a combination of introspection and attention to externality, she still needed, in the initial stages of the writing process, to 'dig': to surrender herself to a process of unconscious excavation. It seemed to others, for example, that in *Orlando* she had achieved a desirable combination of spontaneity and rhythm with a deft and fluid story-telling, but to Virginia Woolf herself *Orlando* was a work which had been written entirely with the surface of her imagination: in her next book, she resolved to retrieve some access to her own psychological reserves. She hoped, in what was to become *The Waves*, to combine the 'inner & the outer' (*D*, III, pp. 209–10) but nevertheless needed as a first priority to attend to the quality of the single moment before concerning herself with any kind of formal or narrative structure. Moreover, there was a strong sense in which she saw herself as the carrier or vehicle of the novel, which would make its own time: 'As for my next book,' she recorded, prior to beginning *The Waves*, 'I am going to hold myself from writing it till I have it impending in me: grown heavy in my mind like a ripe pear; pendant, gravid, asking to be cut or it will fall . . .'. The idea that she can produce something 'whole' is again associated, for her, with the idea of writing poetry: 'Why admit anything to literature', she adds, 'that is not poetry – by which I mean saturated?' (*D*, III, pp. 209–10).

By 1928, though, she had learned, even in this initial stage, to discern the signals of the succeeding stage of her writing process. The desire to slough off realism altogether was still strong, but she had earlier learned that some means of keeping this process of 'saturation' in check was crucial if the novel were not to become impossibly abstract. After spending a season copying from plaster casts, she had devised a shape for the novel which followed *Night and Day – Jacob's Room –* in which 'one thing should open out of another' (*D*, II, p. 13), following on from the experiments in perspective which she had practised in such stories as 'A Mark on the Wall', in which the 'story', such as it was, unfolded in a process of free association instigated by the sustained observation of a single image. This new, kaleidoscopic form afforded her a sense of freedom from narrative constraints, but was only fully achievable in *Jacob's Room* because Jacob's untimely death in Flanders gave credibility to the novel's untimely and abrupt ending and to Woolf's depiction of a character left suspended and in fragments. When R. C. Trevelyan criticised *Jacob's Room*, Woolf defended it as an experiment, and admitted its shortcomings:

> Of course, the effect of breaking with strict representation is very
> unsettling, and many things were not controlled as they should have been.
> It is true, I expect, that the characters remain shadowy for the most part;
> but the method was not so much at fault as my ignorance of how to use it
> psychologically.   (*L*, II, p. 588)

Her method was not exactly *at fault*: she retained, throughout her writing career, her experiments with perspective and her refusal to conform to conventional notions of narrative time. But it required some adaptations if she was to be able to create credible characters – that her characters were 'puppets' was one criticism levelled against her.[8] It became clear that she needed to devise ways of *shaping* narrative in order to demonstrate new psychological perspectives, a way of presenting juxtapositions in a more structured way than the linear progress of *Jacob's Room* had allowed.

And so, beginning with *Mrs Dalloway*, she began to *design* her novels, sketching out narrative shapes and the relationships between characters and events, in a process which she was to continue to adopt, usually in the stages following the primary 'saturation'. During this second stage of the writing process, some of the images for which she had dug, or which had seemingly floated up of their own accord, became concrete, representing tangible sources for the characters she was about to create. One of her early draft notes for *The Waves*, for instance, records the supposition 'That lives are waves, . . . by which life is maintained; a rounding off which has nothing to do with events.'[9] Resolving to net some of the images which were emerging for that novel, she resolved to 'attack this angular shape in my mind' (*D*, III, p. 219). After a period of immersion, she was ready to organise herself, and did so by sketching out the relations between, at this stage, seemingly arbitrary, objective images:

> Every morning I write a little sketch . . . I am not saying, . . . that these sketches have any relevance. Yet perhaps it might be done in that way . . . islands of light – islands in the stream that I am trying to convey: life itself going on. The current of the moths flying strongly this way. A lamp & a flower pot in the centre.   (*D*, III, pp. 229–30)

She began, at this stage in the process, with 'character'. *Mrs Dalloway* was planned as 'an advance upon Jacob. The human soul will be treated more seriously: one must emphasize character' (*L*, II, p. 569). But her characters were conceived, at least initially, as having diagrammatic rather than 'human' relationships. The design for *Mrs Dalloway*, she noted in her notebook, was to be:

> . . . something like this –
>
> Mrs D. comes along.
> (as in past chapter:)
> We then go on to a general statement, introducing Septimus.
> They are linked together by the aeroplane.
> We then return to Mrs D. alone in her drawing room and settle into her.[10]

Planning *To the Lighthouse*, she followed the same procedure, noting that the novel was to be:

> All character – *not* a view of the world.
> Two blocks joined by a corridor.

She drew the diagram, then proceeded:

> Topics that may come in:
> How her beauty is to be conveyed by the impression that she makes on all these people.[11]

She *blocked* her novels, then, aligning subjective content with diagrammatic form, ranging the canvas with figures which would be brought to life individually once the novel had taken shape, and this device became for her a feature of the process of imagining. It enabled her to introduce formal discipline without relinquishing her resistance to authorial over-intrusion. And, just as she had struggled to find a way of relinquishing the kind of authorial control exercised by the nineteenth century novelists, so she resisted, too, the temptation to become over-concerned with the novel's form. She had observed this temptation at work much earlier, when in the early stages of her writing career (on 29 July 1918) she had been taken to the studio of the painter,

Mark Gertler, '& shown his solid "unrelenting" teapot.' She had noted in her Diary at the time that,

> Form obsesses him. He sees a lamp as an imminent dominant
> overwhelming mass of matter. Ever since he was a child the solidity & the
> shapes of objects have tortured him. I advised him, for arts sake, to keep
> sane; to grasp, & not exaggerate, & put sheets of glass between him and his
> matter. (*D*, I, pp. 175–6)

When later she came to sketch out her novels, she followed her own advice, working, at this stage in the process, from the shapes and masses of objects as starting points for narrative structure,[12] maintaining always a distance between the material and herself. For the painters, one way of overcoming the problem of form was by *centering* a line or shape. Roger Fry had argued in 'An Essay on Aesthetics' that in a painting the relationship between a central line and the frame of the picture was the key factor in determining perspective, 'so that the eye rests willingly within the bounds of the picture.'[13] Woolf echoed this advice when she explained to Fry the function of the central image in *To the Lighthouse*: she meant *nothing* by the lighthouse, she said: 'One has to have a central line down the middle of the book to hold the design together (*L*, III, p. 385–7). But she also protested that she had not thought the psychological implication of this through: 'I saw that all sorts of feelings would accrue to this, but I refused to think them out, and trusted that people would make it the deposit for their own emotions – . . .' (*ibid.*).

'I can't manage Symbolism except in this vague, generalised way', she concluded: 'directly I'm told what a thing means, it becomes hateful to me' (*ibid.*). Her diagrams did not offer her psychological analogues; there were no 'Symbolic' forms. But the process of designing the images which were beginning to emerge released in her the ability to begin to make up phrases, to devise fragments of dialogue, which would enable some of the connections between form and imagery to begin to emerge. The idea of using the aeroplane as a diagrammatic link between Mrs Dalloway and Septimus is followed in Woolf's notebook by a note reminding her that 'It is to be psychology' and immediately by another idea: 'Can one admit rhapsodies?'[14]

The psychology of the novel would be ascertained by the voices of the *characters*, rather than by the authorial voice but also, in *Mrs Dalloway*, by incidental street noises: a note on page three of her notebook reads,

'Eleven o'clock strikes', then, 'This is the aeroplane hour . . .'. The striking of the hour performs the same unifying function as the aeroplane: it 'Covers both Septimus and Rezia in Regents Park and Clarissa['s] reflections' (*ibid.*). The structure of *Mrs Dalloway* was to be aural as well as formal. She noted on page four of the notebook, 'No chapters. Possible choruses', and she held on to the idea of a chorus – presumably with the function of the Greek chorus in mind[15] – for six months, after which she decided that they were not convincing, and that the dialogue between characters would after all have to bear the weight of the novel's psychological significance. Characters who would be important in this respect, though, might still nevertheless be outsiders, since it was clear that she was still reluctant to move too far from the new perspectives, the psychological fragmentation, and the 'break with representation' which she had achieved in *Jacob's Room*. She still wanted, she noted, 'the effect of real life.'[16]

Two months later, she picked up again the idea of a possible chorus of onlookers or subsidiary characters,[17] and an additional note made at this stage suggests that incidental sounds might also be employed to indicate an emerging theme of dislocation. 'Psychology' becomes, in *Mrs Dalloway*, indicative of some complexity of feeling suggestive of estrangement – Septimus cannot embody his own sensations without feeling as if he will be completely destroyed by them – and a single aural effect might be instrumental in evoking this, as a note in the notebook suggests ('The barrel organ! Beauty of an impersonal kind is still real. But human beings betray each other . . . Then what remains?').[18]

In her drafts for the later work, *The Waves*, she also introduced incidental sounds, along with voices, when she came to the stage of devising phrases for her characters. The flying moths and static flower-pot which she had designed as the novel's centrepiece initially acted as the dual image at the centre of her canvas: this sketch would incorporate the 'two different currents' – narrative continuity, and attention to the moment, (*D*, III, p. 229) – and the walls of the schoolroom in which her characters were seated would constitute the picture's frame. But as soon as she began to make up phrases, the moths revealed a propensity to explore beyond the framework, flying outside the confines of the schoolroom to explore the outer walls and – as Woolf was eventually to discover – revealing the weakness of the original centrepiece as a unifying image. This particular novel went through copious drafts, and a whole wealth of imagery was gradually discarded, as Woolf was forced, at the phrase-making stage, to *empty* her images of meaning in order to return to the initial stage and let her images re-emerge informally. The moth threatened to disturb the equilibrium of her idea by dominating the design and, itself, taking over the writing:

> An enormous moth had settled on the bare plaster wall . . . As the wings
> . . . quivered, the purple crescent on [. . .] the dark border [on the lower
> wings . . .] . . . made a mysterious hieroglyph. . . .[19]

In this novel, the stages of image-making and phrase-making become fused, but not, nevertheless, without the centrepiece's having been arrived at, even if it was later discarded.

Phrases emerge, in *The Waves* as in *Mrs Dalloway*, together with *sounds* – 'faint rustlings, faint stirrings, . . . And then . . . some bird pattered out a few irrelevant bars . . . of . . . sound . . .' (*W Drafts*) – but because the formal design had failed to work, visual and aural images become confused, and the pressure to discern a narrative design is again brought to bear:

> Sight and sound interrupted each other, as if the mind of a very old person,
> man or woman, had gone back to the dawn of memory; without being able
> to finish any sentence; without being sure in what order things came;
> without attempting to make a coherent story.   (*ibid.*, I, p. 2)

In this novel, voices are suggestive of stories, but they refuse to *tell* them: just as the children in the first draft listen to the voice of their teacher without properly hearing or being able to interpret his words, so this suggestiveness of voice, and its capacity for inducing distraction, is seen by Woolf as she drafts her novel as something obscurely all-pervasive:

> in the same way, a thousand other children listened to their masters voice as
> it read, with clear rules of conviction; or the mumble of some deep inner
> disillusion; . . . they sneered across the aisle . . . or felt the thrill of some
> heroic visage its strangeness, its seductiveness; . . .   (*ibid.*, I, p. 20)

Throughout the drafts of *The Waves*, the lyrical phrases which constitute the characters' speech go on reflecting this initial fault in the composition, so that characters, perspective, whole histories are sketched and discarded, as is the lonely mind, a persona originally adopted by Woolf as a way of interjecting an authorial but nevertheless anonymous – thus unintrusive – voice. It might have been, this novel, a history of the world in six different voices, pieced together in synaesthetic imagery; but lacking a design, Woolf ran the risk of having devised a play for voices which lacked dramatic form, composed of empty, sterile phrases. It was a problem discerned by the lonely mind, even in the very early stages of the novel's composition:

I am telling myself the story of the world from the beginning. I am not
concerned with the single life, but with lives together. I have [. . .] am trying
to find, in the folds of the past – . . . such fragments as time having broken
the perfect vessel; [. . .] still keeps safe; [. . .] The perfect vessel? But it was
not by any means made of durable stuff.   (*ibid.*, I, p. 9)

It is the vessel, then – the 'container' – of the subject which is frail. If,
as Woolf had noted on beginning to plan *The Waves*, the subject is to be
given a kind of birth – she had felt it 'gravid, impending' – then the
lonely mind is here referring to the writing self: a particular version of
the self which has to be unearthed and rediscovered, and then rendered,
perhaps, fit to act as the 'receptacle' for the work of art. There is, here,
too, a notion of perfection being strived after. If Stravinsky had declared,
'I am the vessel through which *Le Sacré* passed', Woolf is here describing
the lonely mind struggling with the same notion, but Woolf's vessel,
unlike Stravinsky's, is not a passive container: it needs to be 'perfected'
in order to be fit to produce the work: not only the work but the self
capable of producing the work needs to be perfected, and constantly re-
defined. A cryptic continuation of this note by the lonely mind suggests
a need to refine further this notion: 'For it was only', the lonely mind
records, 'when the thing had happened that one could [. . .] & the
violence of the shock was over that one could [. . .] understand, or [. . .]
really; live; . . .' (*ibid.*). The need to survive some shock is introduced
here, but not embellished.

The Waves went through two extensive and copious drafts and
occupied twenty-two notebooks before Woolf devised the final, published draft, in which Bernard's phrase-making predominates and the
chanting in six voices is interspersed with Interludes. In devising the
Interludes, Woolf was making one last attempt to frame a perspective
for her characters' phrases, and the Interludes might be viewed as a
series of paintings depicting various stages in the development of a day,
and the attendant changes in landscape and seascape which would
symbolise the developing stages of the characters' lives. But in resorting
to this method she was unable to achieve a satisfactory integration of
her design with her phrase-making, and the writing process discernible
in the drafts of *The Waves* is in fact illustrative of what happened when
she elected *not* to follow the stages of her writing process which in her
other novels worked for her, and which she perfected in *To the
Lighthouse*.

By the time she came to begin the second draft, she had abandoned the moth and the flowerpot and had begun, this time, with a series of speeches in which the characters each describe their perception of an object. They see 'A purple ball hanging'; 'a vast slab of pale yellow'; 'a slope with purple vallies' (Draft II, p. 402): as though she had resorted, at this stage, to conflating two stages of the writing process, and each character now discerned a different design in his or her phrase. But she could not work with six different designs, and the flower suddenly re-emerges in the section of the draft dealing with Percival's death, in a speech by Jinny:

> The flower stands before us,
> the flower with six sides;
> the flower seen
> simultaneously. . . .   (Draft II, p. 646 verso)

The flower stands, perhaps, on the table at which they are seated; but by this stage the characters' histories are too far flung for it to sustain a capacity to centre them and it is soon afterwards bequeathed to Bernard, who employs it as an intermediate image of childhood in a story which takes up the lonely mind's reference to a moment of significant shock:

> Take a flower, an ordinary red flower seen for a moment in a garden; laid
> like pure light upon like colour burning upon caverns of blackness. next
> moment & [sic] clap in the back of the head – terrific – for which reason the
> flower is remembered.   (Draft II, p. 658)

Again, the context for this moment of shock is not given, and its significance is left unexplained.

Not having been able to light upon a design, Woolf's perspective in this novel remains confused and ever-changing, and she is at pains to find a way of distinguishing between her characters. It is consistently unclear whether she is attempting to devise six stories – or histories – or whether she is attempting to demonstrate the inappropriateness of this endeavour to the actual structures of human life. For Bernard, attempting to draw together the threads of the novel, the presence of an audience offers the possibility of centering and designing a self: 'so that if I had a pencil & a sheet of paper I could draw the design of my life, [. . .] and it would be seen that those innumerable scenes depend from a thin black line which is what I call (provisionally) myself' (Draft II, p. 657).

But that line would have to be seen against a perspective, and such perspectives as Woolf needs to incorporate into the text of *The Waves* can only be depicted in phrases. She discerned perspective in momentary static scenes, as she noted in one of her notebooks for *The Waves*, but was defeated in this novel by the necessity, which she could not find a way of meeting, of transposing scenes into narrative. Moreover, since she had not found a design, she was unable to decide on a backdrop:

> The perspective against wh. one sees life –
> is it the stars, or the woods at Elvedon
> or the British Empire?
> I have never been able to 'see' for long:
> hence I only make phrases.   (Draft II, p. 765)

She was still aware, of course, that she was trying to re-shape the novel – 'That the novel changed when the perspective changed' (*ibid.*) – but she still had nothing definitive, at this late stage in the drafting of *The Waves*, to say on the matter: 'I'm not a preacher' (*ibid.*).

She was to attempt, in the final draft, to *interpose* perspective, but the Interludes fail to act as frames, except for what they themselves contain, and even the fundamental questions of whether she wanted a speaker, no speaker or six speakers; whether these were individual lives or simply separate illusions of a common, corporate life, remained unsolved. As a result, her speakers are continually pre-occupied with questions relating to the novel's composition, as in Rhoda's speech, from Draft II:

> & What emerges? Something that we have made. Square & oblong: placed
> on top of each other: a perfect dwelling place. Very little is left outside. One
> thing is imposed on top of another; The structure has become visible. What
> is inchoate out there (the people passing) is here explained. (Draft II, p. 578)

But the explanation continually changes: the centre of *The Waves* is ever-shifting, and one of the last notes made prior to the drafting of the final draft suggests that Woolf was as far as ever from having made any kind of decision about the focus of the novel: 'Far far away I hear the fall of the waves on the beach. Sometimes I think I have escaped identity: that I am free' (*ibid.*, p. 768).

***

In drafting *Between the Acts*, Woolf again used the idea of a centrepiece, but this time with a more obvious design function and in a more specifically domestic setting, as though this time she were determined to put her house in order. From the very earliest stage of the drafting of this novel, a control and an organisation are effected which had not been in evidence since the drafting of *To the Lighthouse*. She begins with a lamp on the table in a room of the house ánd, as in *To the Lighthouse*, explores the idea of the light it casts as a central focus. The lamp here functions as a pure image, releasing phrases which act not as potential speeches but simply as a way of engendering ideas and perspectives. The image is precise: the lamp is an oil lamp, and it gives out a steady, presiding light, so that 'all its parts now visible, not evanescent and vanishing . . . immortality broods; and death disappears; and the moment is for ever; . . . [it] surveys the whole unembarrassed by the part; . . .'.[20] The image of the oil lamp thus releases some of the imagery of *The Waves* but this time it reflects a simultaneous capacity to effect unity and suggests an ability to make a decision about the disparate fragments which will compose the day, to find a perspective which will eventually effect an ending, drawing the day to its conclusion or close.

Having drawn, as it were, a circle round the image of the lamp, Woolf can then pan out from it into the garden, where four of the characters are seated in a circle in deck chairs, and she thus uses this method of – as it were – adjusting her lens to draft descriptions of different parts of the house and grounds. Sections of the early draft are headed, for example, 'The Garden'; 'At the Table'; 'The Terrace'; 'The Library';[21] and with the house as a structure or frame, Woolf can then go on to compose her novel in phrases of description, dialogue or soliloquy, much of which was retained by her throughout two drafts and into the third, published draft.[22]

With the first three stages of the writing process successfully effected Woolf was able, in *Between the Acts*, to effect a fourth stage, in which a focus on the present moment could take place alongside and within the framework of a narrative continuity which is based, in this novel, on the history of the house. The first draft contains the moment – retained in the published novel – in which Isa interrupts her father-in-law in his reflections. The interruption disturbs him, 'But it was his own fault. Since he had persisted in living all these years, stretching finer and finer the thread of life from twenty-two to seventy-four, it was not for him to complain, . . .' (*PH*, p. 53). Isa, whose presence in the room interrupts his memories of the past, represents to him regeneration and continuity, in contrast with her own perspective, which privileges the present moment, which she seeks to excavate and explore: 'The moor is dark,' she said [to herself], 'the moor is dark beneath the moon. The rapid dews of dusk have drunk the last sweet breath of heaven . . . I have ordered the fish', she continued, . . . (*PH*, p. 53).

The moment contains a recognition of the need for continuity and perpetual renewal, and also for a timetable; musings about the past produce momentary images: old men in clubs; old men in rooms. In this novel, the present moment is contained in the narrative of the household and there is usually a narrative – a history – to be discerned as the source of momentary reflection.

As a result of this structural integration *Between the Acts* depicts the generation of time and the family, juxtaposing family life with variations on the orthodox relations between the sexes: it represents the conventions and it renews them. Virginia Woolf was able, by providing a framework for events, to investigate the implications not only of key events in the life of the household but also what was going on in the interstices of narrative event: what happened between the acts. In this final novel, she even incorporated a metaphor for its own structure: the village pageant in which phases of history are parodied and some of the mechanics of Miss La Trobe's composition are still in evidence. The risk of 'sticking' at the phrase-making stage is parodied by the stiff and contrived style of Miss La Trobe's characters' speeches and by the formal chaos of the pageant. *Between the Acts* can be read as both a model and a parody of Virginia Woolf's writing process.

The successive stages of the writing process were not necessarily undertaken by Woolf consciously. After a hundred and twenty draft pages of *Pointz Hall*, for instance, she was still not able to identify the formal structure, though she was aware that it did already have a quality of coherence and unity. 'I rush to it for relief after a long pressure of Fry facts', she noted. 'But I think I see a whole somewhere – it was simply seized, one day, . . . as a dangling thread: no notion what page came next. And then they came' (*D*, V, p. 193).

The stages were present, however, in the drafts of each of her novels. She needed to go through them again each time she wrote, but each time she resolved some problems and encountered others, and in some of the novels one or sometimes two stages of the process took precedence and seemed to characterise her writing methods for that particular novel, as in *The Voyage Out*, which seemed to remain at the 'saturation' stage, and *The Waves*, in which images and phrases became and seemed to remain entangled.

It is possible to offer a sketch of Woolf's writing method as she worked on her novels, from *The Voyage Out* to *Between the Acts*, which echoes to some extent the procedure adopted for each individual novel. At certain points in her writing career, she can be seen to have mastered a new stage of the process. Thus, the 'saturation' stage which absorbed her in the writing of *The Voyage Out* gave way to a preoccupation with design embarked on in the stories and pursued through *Jacob's Room*, to be developed in *Mrs Dalloway* and perfected in *To the Lighthouse*. The tendency to make up phrases, which she had been able to do since she began *The Voyage Out*, found itself a perfectly conducive character in Mrs Ramsay, predominated in the writing of *The Waves*, and was then parodied in *Between the Acts* through the medium of the pageant, allowing Woolf sufficient distance from it to have found a structure which acted as a context or vessel for it, between the acts.

The three novels missing from this schema are *Orlando*, *Night and Day* and *The Years*, each being works which offered Woolf a respite from the usual writing process, but none of which enabled her to solve the problems she encountered in the course of her usual procedure. In *Orlando* she parodied existing narrative structures and achieved unorthodoxy through pastiche, in *Night and Day* and *The Years* she began with her subject matter, rather than allowing it to emerge through the writing process: *Night and Day* was an extraordinarily mannered, if, in its own way, parodic, exploration of the issues of female independence and women's suffrage which borrows – and parodies – narrative styles from Jane Austen and was written, specifically, to offer Woolf a break from the strains of her natural writing process. *The Years* began from a decision to examine 'the sexual life of women' and was originally designed as an 'essay-novel' in which she planned to intersperse factual with fictional material, and was clearly an attempt to get to grips with not only the structure which had eluded her in *The Years*, but also the subject matter which had not, after all, emerged in the novel.

For, as the preceding analysis of Virginia Woolf's writing practice reveals, the issue of a *woman* writing is scarcely present in the process of composition. There are two exceptions: the attempt to analyse the particular timbre of a woman's voice, recorded on page one of the drafts of *Mrs Dalloway*, and a very early note belonging to the series of diary entries leading up to the beginnings of her composition of *The Waves*. Significantly, this entry follows a note recording the knowledge that in *To the Lighthouse* she seemed to have perfected her method, and so felt she had nothing left to say: what followed was an image which seemed to float up in an entirely disconnected way, yet it presages a preoccupation which was to go on absorbing her throughout the drafts of *The Moths*:

> I am now and then haunted by some semi mystic very profound life of a woman, which shall all be told on one occasion; & time shall be utterly obliterated; future shall somehow blossom out of the past.   (*D*, III, p. 118)

'One incident', she went on, '– say the fall of a flower – might contain it.' Her theory was, she added, that 'the actual event practically does not exist – nor time either.' Again, the stress is on process, and on something coming into being, rather than on anything identifiably static. Such a process, moreover, would imply the active participation of the writer in a similar re-forging of the self: she finds it impossible to take up a fixed position in relation to this idea, or to view it with any degree of objectivity: 'But I don't want to force this' (*ibid.*).

The image of the flower was to re-emerge, as I have noted, as a centrepiece in the early drafts of *The Moths*, and though Woolf at no point in the novel that was to become *The Waves* effects its fall, a later Diary entry situates it in time and records the early link made by her between the image of the flower and the idea of a female persona. In addition, the entry reveals Woolf's preoccupations while preparing these initial drafts with anonymity, with gender, and with a time scheme which can be seen to hark back to her early idea to identify gender through the timbre of Mrs Dalloway's voice. The 1929 entry for *The Moths* records this set of specific preoccupations:

> The flower can always be changing. But there must be more unity between each scene than I can find at present. Autobiography it might be called. How am I to make one lap, or act, . . . more intense than another; if there are only scenes? One must get the sense that this is the beginning: this the middle; that the climax – . . . two different currents – the moths flying along; the flower upright in the centre; a perpetual crumbling & renewing of the plant. In its leaves she might see things happen. But who is she? I am very anxious that she should have no name . . . Of course I can make her think backwards & forwards; I can tell stories. But thats not it. Also I shall do away with exact place & time. Anything may be out of the window –
> . . .   (*D*, III, pp. 229–30)

The significance of this entry as an example of Woolf's formal pre-occupations is clear: the attempt to provide 'two different currents' reflects her consistent attempt to provide an engagement with the single moment, contrasted with her efforts, nevertheless, to devise a narrative structure. But in this instance, her subject matter becomes an issue.

Moreover, she is identifying here not only a preoccupation with gender, an attempt to usher in a specifically female observer or participant (it is not entirely clear which), but also a clear link between the *construction* of a female persona, and the composition of the novel as a whole.

It is clear that 'she' will need to be constructed from nothing: Woolf has no preconceptions about the nature or status of this character within the writing. She is to be entirely anonymous: to 'have no name'; to be an observer, to offer a perspective, and yet still to be very close to the centre of the composition. She will see things happen in the leaves of the plant: leaves, clearly, with a certain quality of transparency, like the 'leaf showing the light through' which was the most beautiful thing Virginia Woolf could imagine, when asked as a child to name such a thing.

'Autobiography it might be called', this as yet mysterious text with the changing flower at its centre. But autobiography suggests to Woolf a developing narrative and she is working, here, only with indeterminate, indistinguishable 'scenes'. Of course, 'she' could think both forwards and backwards, as the reading of Proust's work enabled Woolf to do whenever she felt hypnotised, suspended (*D*, III, p. 209); and, of course, as she had enabled Mrs Dalloway to do. Despite the obvious attempt at disinterestedness or anonymity, it is clear that she is allowing some of her own deep-seated preoccupations to enter into the record of her thoughts about her writing; allowing *herself* to begin to filter through. She seems to be allowing her *own* voice, here, to have some say, and yet still holding herself back, refusing to be partial: 'Anything might be out of the window – . . .'.

Soon, she was resolving to hold back yet more, and recording in her Diary, 'I now begin to see *The Moths* rather too clearly, or at least strenuously, for my comfort' (*D*, III, p. 236). The image of the sea was filtering in, and she needed to resist the temptation to infiltrate memories of her own childhood: 'I think it will begin like this: dawn; the shells on the beach; . . . voices of cock & nightingale; . . . all the children at a long table – lessons . . . this shall be Childhood; but it must not be *my* childhood; . . ., the sense of unreality; things oddly proportioned' (*ibid.*).

The notion of somehow going back to the beginning, of tracing this sudden vague, creative impulse to its source, produces specific synaesthetic effects: the sound of shells on a beach; the contrasting voices of cock and nightingale – evocative of night and day – and childhood. There is a strong sense that Woolf is here taking *herself* back to the beginning. But the recognition that she is doing so produces a rapid elision, or bid for something less specific: 'Well, all sorts of characters are to be there . . .'. Still, she is aware that she *is* writing about childhood, though again she checks herself: 'but it must not be *my* childhood' – 'must not be' is an instruction to herself, rather than an observation.

The entire process revealed in this passage bears very close comparison with the note she had made concerning the specifically female quality of Mrs Dalloway's voice, which would betray 'a vibration in the core of the sound so that each word, or note, comes fluttering, alive, yet with some reluctance to inflict its vitality, some grief for the past which holds it back, some impulse nevertheless to glide into the recesses of the heart' (*op. cit.*). In addition, it recalls the Diary entry for June 1923, written while *Mrs Dalloway* was in progress: 'Often now I have to control my excitement – as if I were pushing through a screen or as if something beat fiercely close to me . . . It is a general sense of the poetry of existence that overcomes me. Often it is connected with the sea . . .' (*op. cit.*).

The entry suggests that it may be all the more significant that Woolf seems to have *dis*engaged, in the three of her novels concerned overtly with feminist issues and/or female sexuality, from the stages of her normal writing procedure, focusing instead on external issues culled from history and other literature, and parodying other writing styles – though there is no reason to suppose that this distinction suggests anything in the way of a conscious planning on her part. The entry begins to suggest that she had no basis from which to explore or construct a 'psychological sentence of the feminine gender': moving forwards produced only disconnected images; moving backwards highlighted some tendency to *screen* what might have been the beginnings of a sudden desire to chart, one day, 'some semi mystic very profound life of a woman', which nevertheless should 'all be told on one occasion'. The source of this potential story seemed in some sense to lie in a retrieval of the imagery of childhood, but memories of childhood came accompanied by a sense of 'unreality; things oddly proportioned'.

The confusion and lack of direction parodied by Woolf in *A Room of*

One's Own might in some measure be traced to this inability to identify a starting point from which to think about the female sex, 'this organism that has been under the shadow of the rock these million years' (*ROO*, p. 84). She is at pains, in that text, to identify what she sees as a dislocation of the female subject as a side-effect of male power and influence in the spheres of education, politics and even writing, reading the letter 'I' as 'a straight dark bar, a shadow' (p. 98) marring the page of the male novelist, and failing to identify, even in its shadow, a female 'I': 'all is shapeless as mist. Is that a tree? No, it is a woman. But . . . she has not a bone in her body, I thought, watching Phoebe, for that was her name, coming across the beach' (p. 98). '"I"', she warns the reader on the second page, 'is only a convenient term for somebody who has no real being' (p. 6), when applied to a woman; and an attempt to construct a specifically female text results in a formless saturation in unrelated images from which it is clear that 'she' is unlikely to emerge. Her advice to women writers advocates the kind of excavation of one's own consciousness which she identified as the key to Dorothy Richardson's method, but her own version of it is as unsatisfactory and as indisciplined as she ultimately finds Richardson's to be: 'Above all,' she advises, '. . . you must illumine your own soul with its profundities and its shallows, and its vanities and its generosities, and say what your beauty means to you or your plainness, and what is your relation to the ever-changing and turning world of gloves and shoes . . . For in imagination I had gone into a shop . . .' (*ROO*, p. 89). Again, the distractions take over.

She encountered a similar problem when reading of the lives of other women. Reading the autobiography of Beatrice Webb, she identified structures and directions which she felt to be lacking in her own life, and regretted that, unlike Mrs Webb, she was unable to define her life in terms of 'causes'. She experienced instead, she noted, 'Great excitability & search after something . . .'. Yet she had 'some restless searcher in me. Why is there not a discovery in life?' she asked herself, 'Something one can lay hands on & say "This is it?"' (*D*, III, p. 62). That this unfulfilled search might have something to do with her own sexuality is now specifically suggested here, though it might well be significant that the possibility of envisaging something satisfactory, achieved, came a moment later, from imagining 'the moon which is risen over Persia' (*ibid.*), where Vita was soon to arrive.[23]

This sense of holding something back, the stress on anonymity and the feeling that the self – the 'I' – was fragmented or unfocused, was something Woolf continually experienced, particularly after having completed a novel, when she was often haunted by the sense that something had been left out, or unaccounted for. The fragmentation or dislocation of the self was, however, a sense she drew on in the course of the writing process: if she could somehow concentrate on or contain that sense of fragmentation, then the images would continue to emerge. This mood, as I have shown, represented for her an important initial stage of the writing process, but it also necessitated a screening or separation of an aspect of herself. Early in her writing career, she recorded the incompatibilities of writing and the surface life: 'I disliked so much', she noted, 'the irruption of Sydney – one must become externalised; very, very concentrated, all at one point, not having to draw upon the scattered parts of one's character, living in the brain. Sydney comes and I'm Virginia; when I write I'm merely a sensibility' (*D*, II, p. 193).

There was a sense, at this stage in the process, that she was in some way submerged, letting go; but at the same time her sense of control, of holding back, was very strong: she was 'very, very concentrated, all at one point, *not* having to draw upon the scattered parts . . .' (*ibid.*, emphasis mine). Initially, as her very early Diary entries for *The Voyage Out* reveal, she had hoped to forge a life-style in which the scattered parts would somehow coalesce; her marriage to Leonard Woolf was to have helped her in this respect. When she became engaged, she nurtured high hopes for marriage as a context for her writing, and Leonard encouraged her in these, as an early letter to Violet Dickinson reveals: 'L. wants me to say,' she wrote, 'that if I cease to write when married, I shall be divorced' (*L*, I, p. 502).

Later, however, the oscillation between 'Virginia' and the writing sensibility became more troublesome. After finishing *To the Lighthouse* she retreated to Rodmell for a while, and allowed herself to 'plunge into deep waters'. While writing, she noted, she was always 'curbing and controlling this odd immeasurable soul. When it expands, . . . one goes down into the well & nothing protects one . . . I exist however. I am. Then I ask myself what am I?' (*L*, III, p. 112). Within her novels she depicts similar attempts, by her characters, to question identity, so that this process is by no means perceived by her to relate exclusively to the writing process, but it is significant that it is only when she is *not* 'submerged' in her writing practice that she gives herself the freedom to attend to the question of her own identity in quite this way.

In the final stages of her life, she became increasingly preoccupied with, and hampered by, the notion that something was being 'left out': that there was some facet of herself which might have been a source of creativity or origination, but which was being screened or resisted. This feeling filtered into the process of writing *Between the Acts* in a way that eventually broke her. Despite her having, in this novel, mastered fairly soon a balance between phrases and a structure, despite having integrated her 'diagram' of the novel in a way that was to allow her to achieve, finally, a narrative structure which would contain evocations of isolated moments, the kind of dislocation evident in the drafts of *The Waves* was again to haunt and torment her, and this time she was unable to find any way of distancing herself from it. Having sent her final (now the published) draft of *Between the Acts* to John Lehmann for his comments, she almost immediately wrote to him in a panic asking to retract it: the novel was a disaster, she felt, and nowhere near finished. Before he had an opportunity to return it, she committed suicide.

The final volume of the Diary, particularly the latter half, written as she was writing *Between the Acts*, is markedly different from the previous volumes. The images that filter into it are of suspension, arrest, images of death, freezing and horror. Isolated moments now begin to come accompanied not by a sense of truth or release, but by feelings of suspension and entrapment: 'These moments of despair – I mean glacial suspense – a painted fly in a glass case – . . .' (*D*, V, p. 260). There is a sense of a premature ending, and also a sense that there is no escape from a particular kind of imagery: the effort to side-step one kind of horror brings another into focus:

> the lyric mood of the winter – its intense spiritual exaltation – is over. The thaw has set in, & rain & wind, & the marsh is soggy, & patched with white, & two very small lambs were staggering in the east wind. One old ewe was being carted off; & shirking the horror I crept back by the hanger. Nor have I spent a virtuous evening, hacking at these phrases.
>
> (*D*, V, p. 261, 26 January 1940)

This particular passage is indicative of the kinds of confusion between unconscious anxieties, external disintegration and *writing* which was occurring for her at this time. Whereas previous volumes of the Diary had acted as a respite from or antidote to the writing process and had described almost exclusively Woolf's surface social and domestic life, or at least had described the conflicts between the surface life and writing, here, for the first time, Woolf seems unable to separate the strands of her life, which are becoming intertwined and entangled. The sense of dread accumulated rapidly, and in ways she was unable to control. In August 1939 she was reflecting, clear-headedly, as she was dressing, 'how interesting it would be to describe the approach of age, & the gradual coming of death' (*D*, V, p. 230). The following January, she found herself appalled by the spectacle of the old ewe being carted off and, remembering the hanger she had crept back by to avoid the horror, resolved in her Diary to persevere with her 'hacking' job: she was still struggling with the effort of writing the life of Roger Fry (*D*, V, p. 261).

The different kinds of writing she was engaged with were beginning to become confused, and it was as though her tricks, her mask, her strategy for keeping the 'writing "I"' separate, was becoming threatened. In addition, she recognised that the external integrity upon which she had always called to counter her sense of inner chaos and fragmentation began instead, with the onset of the Second World War, to *echo* that process of disintegration. Her house in London had been bombed, the sounds of guns were continually to be heard in the sky at Rodmell, and she and her Jewish husband had made a joint suicide pact, to gas themselves together in the garage, in case of invasion by the Germans. Thus, the stability of everyday life was threatened at the very core: the war, and the recent deaths of many of her friends, had effected the removal of her sense of an audience and thus her sense of herself as at once separate from and connected to an external reality. The image of the garage called up other images, and threatened to choke them: what she and Leonard dreaded at this time was the news that the French Government had left Paris: 'A kind of growl behind the cuckoo and t'other birds: a furnace behind the sky' (*D*, V, p. 293).

She responded to the sense of both internal and external disintegration by recreating this sense of history in crisis, in *Between the Acts*. The Diary entries for this period are increasingly spasmodic, fragmentary, cryptic; reading sometimes like clues or even cipher: 'I thought biography is like the rim of sea anemones left round the shore in Gosse's *Father & Son*: I thought Beresford, Ruth's father, has been killed by a bomb: . . . Gramaphone mended but bad; if I wait the thought may return; a lovely almost a red admiral & apple day; 24 vols of diary salved; [sic][24] a great mass for my memoirs' (*D*, V, p. 332), as though it were possible to break a debilitating silence only partially and intermittently and as though she were not sure which *kind* of living, which *kind* of writing, might be capable of effecting a change. In *Between the Acts*, language is similarly cryptic, similarly interspersed with silence, as though she wanted to show language in the process of breaking down, of being fundamentally irreparable: the broken gramophone is filtered directly into her writing: 'The gramophone gurgling *Unity – Dispersity*. It gurgled *Un . . . dis . . .*' (*BA*, p. 146).

The moment has come, for Woolf in this final stage of her writing and of her life, to be full of portentous implication but also full of danger. Her sense of the isolation of the moment has become intense, but she is also aware of its capacity for dislocation: 'weeded this morning. And was very happy – the moment can be that: only there's no support in the fabric – if you see what I mean, . . . – there's no healthy tissue round the moment' (*D*, V, p. 290). Her sense of herself is highlighted, here, by this record of one of the few – if not the only – instances in the Diary of her appeal to *herself* for understanding and the confirmation that she is still making sense. Moreover, concentration on the moment is accompanied by specific images which have obsessed her in the course of her writing, but where before these have represented, at least, the attempt to establish structure or the attempt to situate the moment in the context of a continuum, now the *same* images bring with them an immediate and unambiguous sense of disintegration. She is still, furthermore, alert to the sound of a woman's voice, but now the sound – of Elizabeth Bowen's stammer, for example – confirms her sense of *not* having isolated an aesthetic capable of centering the cross-currents of linear continuity and psychological excavation:

> the war – our waiting while the knives sharpen for the operation – has taken away the outer wall of security . . . We pour to the edge of a precipice . . . & then? I can't conceive that there will be a 27 June 1941 . . . And so, in this high wind, we reach the present moment; & I find it difficult to centre . . . E's stammer also had a disintegrating effect: like a moth buzzing round a flower – . . .   (*D*, V, p. 299)

Her own sense of disintegration seems everywhere to be echoed externally, and the familiar mechanisms and images which she habitually employed in order to try to centre herself (the moth; the flower) now seem empty and/or fragmented. Further, the attempt at repair seems doomed to failure. In the face of this, she adopts the only mechanism left to her: that of shutting down, effacing herself: 'Oh & I've mastered the iron curtain for my brain. Down I shut when I'm tied tight' (*D*, V, p. 330). The common, practical mechanisms for keeping the war at bay seem to echo her own private mechanisms, and the language of self-preservation becomes indistinguishable from her own: for the first time, 'facts' and her own psychological excavations share a common language: 'I must black out. I had so much to say . . .' (*ibid.*).

Writing autobiography

By this time she had already begun work on a new project, the writing of her memoirs which, significantly, represented a way of freeing herself from the constraints of her usual writing practice. The most notable aspect of the memoir is its preoccupation with the attempt to retrieve a sexual history which Woolf had nowhere else attempted to document. Though 'A Sketch of the Past' was begun entirely without strategy, she came to feel that the attempt to 'tell the truth about the body' – an attempt to which she had already referred, in *A Room of One's Own* – should constitute a vital aspect of autobiography by women. Writing to Ethel Smyth on 24 December 1940, she deflects her own attempt, declaring that Ethel should be the first to tell such truths. She had been thinking, she writes, that there has never been a woman's autobiography – at least, 'Nothing to compare with Rousseau'. She supposes 'chastisty and modesty' have been responsible: 'Now,' she urges Ethel, 'shouldn't you be the first to tell the truth about yourself? . . . I should like an analysis of your sex life' (*L*, VI, p. 453).

They entered into a brief correspondence on the subject, Ethel, apparently, writing to Virginia to chart her progress. By 12 January, Woolf was expressing interest in Ethel's reticence on the subject of masturbation, since 'as so much of life is sexual – or so they say – it rather limits autobiography if this is blacked out' (*L*, VI, pp. 459–60).

Whilst there is no evidence to suggest that 'A Sketch of the Past' was overtly designed as a 'woman's autobiography', it is clear from the writing, and from her Diary notes referring to the sense of release she derived from it, that she was writing spontaneously and without blacking anything out. Significantly, the process of free associative recollection calls up images, begins to tell a story, which Woolf had nowhere been able to tell: we are reading the narrative of these events as for the first time, but Woolf recalls them with facility, as though she has for a long time had access to them. Further, the imagery of 'A Sketch of the Past' recalls imagery which recurs again and again in the drafts of her fiction, but this time offering a context for significance, a 'history' which might be placed, within the history of Woolf's writing career, alongside the process of personal disintegration which was occurring for her at the time at which she wrote it. 'A Sketch of the Past' employs an impressionistic language of reflective notation interspersed with the language of fiction and to some extent acts as a catalyst, commenting on and taking imagery from both 'Virginia' and 'the writing "I"', and demonstrating the extent to which, at the end of her life, the writing 'I' began to become entangled with the remembering, subjective 'I' in a process of collusion which concluded in a complete breakdown of the distinctions between writing and remembering, between the ordering and the screening subject.

She embarked on 'A Sketch of the Past' 'without stopping to choose my way, in the sure and certain knowledge that it will find itself – or if not it will not matter – . . .' (*MB*, p. 74), and thus produced, with no preamble, her earliest memory:

> This was of red and purple flowers on a black ground – my mother's dress; . . . and I was on her lap. I therefore saw the flowers she was wearing very close; . . .   (*MB*, p. 74)

These early memories, then, are synaesthetic: they reactivate rhythms, sounds, colours, and a sense of complete integration, and she attempts, in describing them, to construct the sense of containment within a 'globed, compacted thing' which she has before tried to retrieve a sense of, in the face of feelings of disintegration. Her mother, here, is the originating source of the flower-image, and in another early memory there are flowers again: this time in contiguous relation to her, and evocative of the notion of containment. She remembers her mother appearing in the mornings on the balcony which ran between her parents' bedroom and the nursery: on the balcony there were 'passion flowers growing on the wall; they were great starry blossoms, with purple streaks, and large green buds, part empty, part full' (*MB*, p. 76).

The memories are predominantly visual: painting comes primarily to mind as a medium for depicting them; and a quality of transparency seems crucial. If she were a painter, Woolf reflects, she would make a picture that was 'globular; semi-transparent . . . of curved petals; of shells; . . . curved shapes, showing the light through, but not giving a clear outline. Everything would be large and dim; . . .' (*MB*, p. 76). This recurrent imagery of membranes, of semi-transparent shapes showing the light through, accords with the earlier sense (1923; *op. cit.*) of 'pushing through a screen; or as if something beat fiercely close to me' which she had connected with the sea and St. Ives. It is significant that such imagery echoes, also, the 'semi transparent envelope' which she began by wanting to conjure up as an image of subjectivity: the imagery of these first memories begins to make it clear that Woolf's imagery of subjectivity is connected, here, with the figments of her own subconscious. She remembers lying in bed at St. Ives and hearing the waves breaking behind a yellow blind, the sound of the acorn of the blind being drawn across the floor as the wind blew the blind out. She compares this memory to a feeling of 'lying in a grape and seeing through a film of semi-transparent yellow', and thinking, 'it is almost impossible that I should be here; . . . feeling the purest ecstacy I can conceive' (*MB*, pp. 75–6).

If she were ever to chart the 'semi mystic, very profound life of a woman,' she had noted prior to writing *The Waves*, then 'the fall of a flower might contain it': as though if she could only pick out of the container of these memories one of these early images of sensuality and integration, then she might, somehow, succeed in framing a life into which sexuality could be integrated or within which it might be defined. In the telling of such a story, 'time shall be utterly obliterated; the future shall somehow blossom out of the past' (*op. cit.*). Even before she began to sketch out these memories, she had sensed that there was an untold story, a hidden history – 'the past' – which might constitute a pool of imagery for a hitherto untold, at that stage, 'semi mystic, very profound,' not quite retrievable life of a woman.

That 'she' – the woman hovering behind the stories Woolf *did* succeed in telling – would need to originate in Virginia Woolf herself, becomes clear as the story she had never been able to tell – 'A Sketch of the Past' – unfolds. She considers the possibility that the techniques for the re-telling of this particular story are already integrated somehow with the process of recall, and in doing so wonders whether it might, in the future, be possible to invent a 'device' which, without having been able to name it, she is actually in the process of employing here. Sometimes, she notes, it is possible for her to 'go back to St. Ives . . . completely'; and she wonders whether, this being the case, things which have been intensely felt go on existing in the mind. If so, she reflects, perhaps, in time, 'some device will be invented by which we can tap them' (*MB*, pp. 77–8).

It seems obvious to a post-Freudian reader that what Woolf is actually talking about here is a process of tapping the unconscious mind for memories of events which the conscious mind has screened. For Woolf, though, the process is conceived as some more magical and more haphazard process of tapping a hidden history for events which have somehow remained suspended in an isolated historical moment, through not having been absorbed into the present narrative – that is, the mainstream of her life-story.

It is *possible* that she checked her theory against Freud's work. Certainly, she was reading *Group Psychology and the Analysis of the Ego* on 2 and 18 December 1939, and the note she made in her *Reading*

Notebooks relating to this suggests that she was making some – if only a cursory, impressionistic – attempt to relate the implications of Freudian theory to her own writing. The note reads, 'The point of view of any individual is bound to be not a birds eye view but an insects eye view, . . .'[25] recalling the snail tunnelling through the flower bed, in 'Kew Gardens'. She continued, again characteristically, '. . . the view of an insect too on a green glade, which oscillates violently with local gusts of wind' (pp. 155–16): the insect is here struggling to hold its own, in Woolf's mind, in the face of a 'different current'. The whole image is reminiscent of the moth fluttering around the flower, except that here the inanimate object has – as it were – changed places with the insect/subject.

She was still reading Freud in February 1940,[26] and possibly continued to do so intermittently throughout that year: this would explain the otherwise entirely cryptic Diary entry for 15 November 1940: 'I am a mental specialist now' (*D*, V, p. 339), and in addition the entry she made two days later, in which she analyses the importance of rhythm within the writing practice: this question of rhythm is, she notes, 'a curious trifle in mental history', but the observation that by reading her memoirs over she can break the obsessive rhythm set up in her head by *Pointz Hall* is, she reflects, 'rather profound' (*ibid.*).

Her expertise in the field of psychoanalysis cannot be assumed: certainly, her use of 'the herd instinct' in the writing of 'The Leaning Tower' suggests that her reading of Freud was impressionistic and her infiltration of his theories into her own work piecemeal at best.[27] What this reading does seem to have lent her, however, is a conviction in the importance of the 'alternative rhythm' of writing and the related absence of a structured procedure employed for the construction of 'A Sketch of the Past'.

The sketching out of these first few memories – the writing of the first few pages of 'A Sketch of the Past' – almost certainly preceded her reading of Freud, and it cannot therefore be assumed that she was here attempting to privilege in any way the events culled from her hidden history, nor was she setting up the incidents described there with any specific notion of their highlighting or acting as ciphers for her own consciousness – the version of her story which can be traced, for example, through to the penultimate volume of the Diary. The primary function of remembering, in this sketch, is to enable her to enact a re-integration of isolated events which she is suddenly equipped to perceive as having been screened off from her conscious thinking. She has simply, for the time being, 'gone back to the dawn of memory; and without being able to finish any sentence; without being sure in what order things came; without attempting to make a coherent story', just as she had had the Lonely Mind do, in the early drafts of *The Waves*.

Nevertheless, her conviction in the importance of past events is unambiguous, and it is clear that in the context of external disintegration and intermittent despair, she is suddenly aware of 'a long ribbon of scenes, emotions' to which she has, if not direct access, the means of 'listening in':

> I shall fit a plug into the wall; and listen in to the past. I shall turn up August 1890. I feel that strong emotion must leave its trace; and it is only a question of discovering how we can get ourselves again attached to it, so that we shall be able to live our lives through from the start.   (*MB*, p. 78)

The peculiarity of the early memories, she goes on to reflect, is that they seem very simple: the individual memories are inextricable from her sense of herself at the time. Remembering them, she noted, 'I am hardly aware of myself, but only of the sensation. I am only the container of the feeling of ecstacy, of . . . rapture' (*MB*, p. 78). Perhaps, she surmised, this is a peculiarity of all memories of early childhood; and it seems clear, indeed, that what she is beginning to reconstruct in 'A Sketch of the Past' is the close and sensual relationship with her mother which she had enjoyed as a very young child. The closeness of contact with the mother is suggested for the reader by Woolf's spontaneous technique of training our gaze outwards, from the red and purple flowers on a black background, to the fabric of a dress, to the mother's lap, to the information that a journey is taking place without, at any stage, giving the reader any points of reference or orientation. The technique echoes the condition of the child being described who, it is made clear, is unable to distinguish between the boundaries of her own subjectivity and the separate presence of her mother, and is 'hardly aware of myself, but only of the sensation'.

It is clear that what is being described at the beginning of the 'Sketch' is the young child's passage from a sphere of subjectivity which conceives the presence of the mother as an extension of its own presence, to the recognition of the mother's separateness and simultaneous acquisition of language, which will enable the child to articulate the boundaries of its subjectivity.[28] For Woolf, however, it soon becomes clear that her sense of what followed this 'symbiotic' phase of synaesthetic integrity is a phase not of articulacy but, on the contrary, of muteness. She sensed that the early lack of distinction between the self and external surroundings was probably common to all childhood memories, but was aware that, as soon as she began to remember later incidents, these came accompanied by a sense of fragmentation. She surmised that, 'Later we add to feelings much that makes them more complex; and therefore less strong; or if not less strong, less isolated, less complete,' (p. 78), and she supplies a memory which seems to accompany this feeling of fragmentation.

As a child of about six or seven, she recollects, she was in the habit of looking at her face in a small glass which hung on the wall of the hall at Talland House, the Stephen family's Summer house at St. Ives. She only did this, however, if she was alone, because of the feelings of shame and guilt attaching to it. She proceeds to try to analyse her reasons for this shame, and considers that she and her sister Vanessa were always regarded as tomboys, so that there might be some shame attached to the notion of vanity: it would have been against the 'tomboy code'. But since the feeling of shame seems to be more deeply rooted than this, she turns to history for an explanation, being 'almost inclined to drag in [her] grandfather – Sir James, who once smoked a cigar, liked it, and so threw away his cigar and never smoked another' (p. 78). In her mother's family, beauty was revered and enjoyed, so it seems to her probable that her puritanical streak is inherited from her father, who was 'spartan, ascetic, puritanical. He had I think no feeling for pictures; no ear for music; no sense of the sound of words' (p. 79). And yet, she goes on to claim, this did not prevent her from feeling 'ecstacies and raptures spontaneously and intensely and without any shame or . . . guilt, so long as they were disconnected with [her] own body . . .'. 'I thus detect', she went on, 'another element in [this sense of] shame . . . I must have been ashamed or afraid of my own body' (*ibid.*).

The notion that it might be possible to feel 'ecstacies and raptures spontaneously and intensely . . ., so long as they were disconnected with [the] body' is in itself intriguing and suggests that Woolf is here making a distinction between aesthetic and sexual experience: it is as though even feelings of rapture might more easily be reflected in objects than traced to an originating, subjective source. She has no difficulty, however, in connecting these feelings of shame and guilt to another memory: one which is contiguous with her recollection of the looking glass itself, since this memory, also, is of an event which took place in the hall in which the looking glass hung.

Recalling the glass, she uncovers the memory of being lifted by her step-brother, Gerald, on to a slab for standing dishes on, positioned in the hall, outside the dining room door. As she sat there, she remembers:

> . . . he began to explore my body. I can remember the feel of his hand going under my clothes; . . . I remember how I hoped that he would stop; how I

> stiffened and wriggled as his hand approached my private parts. But it did
> not stop . . . I remember resenting, disliking it – what is the word for so
> dumb and mixed a feeling? It must have been strong, since I still recall it.
> This seems to show that a feeling about certain parts of the body; how they
> must not be touched; . . . must be instinctive.   (*MB*, pp. 79–80)

This time, there is a distancing process involved in the re-telling. She is not, as she was with the early memories, able to conjure up precise sensations, and indeed finds here that she has no access to a language which might have enabled her to articulate the feelings which she is nevertheless able to recall quite clearly. The structure of her language here reflects that fragmentation: 'how they must not be touched . . . must be instinctive': the effect is of a gradual dissociation from herself, culminating in the deduction that a response of resistance 'must be instinctive': there is, oddly, nowhere any notion that what she is being introduced to is deviant behaviour.

The distancing process occurs again at the end of the passage, when the speaking subject translates herself into a persona, referring to herself in the third person and setting herself in an impossible, pre-historic time which defies retrieval into the present: her reaction, she surmises, 'proves that Virginia Stephen was not born on 25th January 1882, but was born many thousands of years ago; and had from the first to encounter instincts already acquired by thousands of ancestresses in the past' (*ibid.*). The feelings she is confronted with have now been displaced, having acquired a communal status, so that she effectively screens herself from the need to replace them within her present subjective conscious-ness: they belong to 'thousands of ancestresses in the past'.

This displacement of feeling from herself on to 'thousands of ancest-resses' has crucial connotations for Woolf's feminist writing, suggest-ing as it does, here, that when she speaks of thinking collectively – as in *A Room of One's Own*, for example when she says that a woman in writing is constrained to 'think back through her mothers' – we need to take her literally, and furthermore, to recognise the element of displace-ment in her thinking relating to such procedures. Here, attempting to analyse the 'looking glass shame', she is faced with the notion that language has deserted her and becomes, literally, speechless in the face of something which seems senseless but which is obviously bound up with its own inevitable logic, the processes of which she has not yet been able to fathom.

This notion of muteness, incapacity, and the inability to disentangle or interpret sensation, are important in relation to the link she tries to make between writing and gender in *A Room of One's Own*, where she surmises that on the whole the powerlessness of women can be attributed to their lack of education and the prohibition, in the past, of their entry into the universities. 'A Sketch of the Past' makes it clear that we need to read this thesis in the light of Woolf's own position, which filters into *A Room of One's Own* and is responsible for the unevenness of that text, but which – by its very nature – Woolf is not in a position to identify, still less to disentangle. Her writing about her own and other women's writing suggests that she had a strong, indeed guiding, sense of the connection between writing and sexuality, but what emerges quite strongly from the 'Sketch' is the sense that she lacked a way of articulating her *own* sexual narrative within the framework of the past.

What emerges next appears, at least initially, in the form of a technical problem, to do with constructing a narrative. Despite the decision to write, in the 'Sketch', without strategy or structure, to let one thing open out of another, she encounters a problem when she comes to try to analyse the reasons why some memories continue to have potency, whilst other incidents are passed over and forgotten. There is surely no reason, she reflects, why the fact that the first memories to come to mind should carry especial weight just because they were the first to surface. What about a whole plethora of other incidents, now forgotten, which must also have been exceptional?

In thinking along these lines, she reflects that she has always made a distinction between 'being' and 'non-being': charged, significant moments are always distinguishable from a continuum which seems to be made of 'a kind of nondescript cotton wool' (*MB*, pp. 81–2). She describes some 'moments of being', and almost immediately the question of shock surfaces again. She had been fighting on the lawn with Thoby, she remembers, when suddenly she stopped, fist raised, and asked herself, 'why hurt another person?' The feeling, as she recalls it, is one of 'hopeless sadness . . . as if I became aware of something terrible; and of my own powerlessness' (*MB*, pp. 82–3). They had been fighting in play: the episode was almost certainly a scene of sheer vitality rather than one implying any real physical ill will, yet this sudden display of physical energy is suddenly deeply troubling to her.

The memory is immediately followed by a second: they are precisely contiguous in Woolf's narrative:

> I was looking at the flower bed . . . 'That is whole,' I said. I was looking at a
> plant with a spread of leaves; and it seemed suddenly plain that the flower
> itself was a part of the earth; that a ring enclosed the flower; and that was
> the real flower; part earth; part flower. It was a thought I put away as being
> likely to be very useful to me later.   (*MB*, p. 82)

This memory is immediately followed by another, as though the three incidents – with the flower as centrepiece – constitute almost a single memory, or at least demonstrate aspects of a single, complex insight. In the third memory, friends of the Stephen family had been staying with them at St. Ives and had just departed: soon afterwards, the family received news of the suicide of their friend – a Mr Valpy. The next thing Woolf remembers is being in the garden at night, walking among the apple trees. It seemed, suddenly, as though the apple tree were somehow connected with Mr Valpy's suicide: 'I could not pass it,' she recalls. 'I seemed to be dragged down, hopelessly, into some pit of absolute despair from which I could not escape. My body seemed paralysed' (*MB*, pp. 82–3).

Recollecting these incidents, Woolf offers herself explanations for her reactions: the discovery that people hurt one another; that a man might take his own life, invokes horror, which renders her powerless, whereas 'in the case of the flower I had found a reason; and was thus able to deal with the sensation' (*MB* p. 83). But this is surely to pass too easily over the significance of her subject matter. In the case of the flower, what is being contemplated is its cohesion, its integrity, the sense that it is both vitally autonomous and entirely integrated within its surroundings: both bonded and earthed. If the small onlooker made comparisons – now being released into a narrative continuum – between an image of integrity and two contiguous images which triggered reactions of paralysis and shock, she is even by this stage already repeating a pattern which the sequence of events described in 'A Sketch of the Past' have begun to establish. At the centre of the 'Sketch' is the spectacle of the child coming face to face with an object expressive of integrity, but the overriding sense is that this experience is flanked by darker, more frightening experiences.

She attempts to distinguish between feelings of shock and feelings of integrity in terms of her writing practice. Such shocks as those caused by the experiences with Thoby and with Mr Valpy are followed by a desire to explain them, she notes, and she goes on to surmise that it is this desire to find an explanation for shock – to detect a pattern in moments of emotional chaos – which identifies her as a writer. Interestingly, it is the *style* of the pattern she perceives which she is anxious to analyse, rather than the psychological implications. A shock comes accompanied, she notes, by the recognition that she has had a blow, 'but it is not, as I thought as a child, simply a blow from an enemy hidden behind the cotton wool of life; it is or will become a revelation of some order; it is a token of some real thing behind appearances; and

I make it real by putting it into words' (*MB*, pp. 83–4). If there *is* an enemy 'behind the cotton wool' (which in the case of Gerald's interference, of course, there emphatically was), then writing will perform the function of screening out this presence and reinstating an order, an integrity.

From the realisation that it is the 'shock-receiving capacity' that makes her a writer, she goes on to expound her 'philosophy': 'that behind the cotton wool is hidden a pattern; that we – I mean all human beings – are connected with this; that the whole world is a work of art; that we are parts of the work of art . . . there is no Shakespeare, . . . no Beethoven; certainly and emphatically there is no God; we are the words; we are the music; we are the thing itself' (*MB*, p. 84). It is this, she reflects, that she perceives every time she has a shock.

There is no Shakespeare, no Beethoven, if the pattern which controls and makes sense of the 'non-being' that constitutes most of every day is as arbitrary as this, then there is, perhaps, no 'Virginia Woolf'. Moreover, though the sense of vague, cocooned wholeness which accompanies her contemplation of the flower is reminiscent in this context of satisfaction, it is significant that when she comes to translate this image into *writing*, the three images become conflated and shock enters in to *disrupt* wholeness, in a process not unlike that of combustion, as in the incident in *Between the Acts*, for example, in which the small George is enraptured by the spectacle of a flower, similarly rooted in its place in the earth:

> The flower blazed between the angles of the roots. Membrane after membrane was torn. It blazed a soft yellow, a lambent light under a film of velvet; it filled the caverns of the eyes with light . . . And the tree was beyond the flower; the grass, the flower and the tree were entire. Down on his knees grubbing he held the flower complete. Then there was a roar and a hot breath and a stream of coarse grey hair rushed between him and the flower . . . he . . . saw coming towards him a terrible peaked eyeless monster . . .
> The old man had sprung upon him from his hiding-place behind the tree.   (*BA*, pp. 12–13)

The process of writing effects a conflation of imagery, showing that wholeness, tenuous as it is, is subject to disruption, interruption: the small boy's absorbed contemplation of a separateness possible even within an experience of integrity is shattered by another's interruption, just as, for Woolf, the contemplation of her own face in the glass is contiguous with another's interference. In the unconscious mind, moreover, the source of the interruption takes on nightmarish form: to the recollection of Gerald and the slab she adds a dream, which 'may refer to the incident of the looking glass':

> I dreamt that I was looking in a glass when a horrible face – the face of an animal – suddenly showed over my shoulder. I cannot be sure if this was a dream, or if it happened. Was I looking in the glass one day when something in the background moved, and seemed to me alive? I cannot be sure. But I have always remembered the other face in the glass, whether it was a dream or a fact, and that it frightened me   (*MB*, p. 80).

Writing, then, sets into play the interpretative function of the unconscious, juxtaposing memory and desire and here giving the lie to the 'philosophy' which offers one kind of experience as an explanation for another, thus attempting to seal meaning. The 'other face in the glass' infiltrates into the writing a deduction that Woolf herself manages to avoid making, at least overtly: that it always seems to be someone else's 'thing' that disturbs her sense of her own integrity, someone else's appalling, woolly 'reality' that becomes set against her own sense of being – like that 'straight, dark bar' that casts such a shadow, in the fiction described in *A Room of One's Own*. In the unconscious mind, and here, in the writing, the source of interruption takes on an appropriately monstrous form.

At the end of Virginia Woolf's life, the distinctions between types of writing began to break down and images of recollection filtered into her fiction, blurring the distinctions between 'Virginia' and 'the writing "I"'. She had sealed off, or so she thought, Roger Fry's life, but the synaesthetic history which she had been *un*able to trace on his behalf began to filter into her own memoirs, and the imagery of *Roger Fry*, *Between the Acts* and 'A Sketch of the Past' began to interweave, recalling, in addition, some of the 'unfinished' imagery from the copious drafts of *The Waves*. (It was during this time, coincidentally, that Woolf was taken to meet Freud, who ceremoniously presented her with a flower.)[29] The full power of this set of conjunctions, however, cannot be realised without attending to another aspect of the memories which began to surface in 'A Sketch of the Past'. Whilst the notion that a shock preceded explanation and thereby served a critical purpose is a restricting one, the distinction between shock and satisfaction *is* important, in that it draws attention to another factor in Woolf's hitherto hidden history: the anaesthetised sensations which for her typically attended instances of shock.

Woolf was thirteen the year her mother died, and she describes in the 'Sketch' the anaesthetising effects of her loss. She describes the room in which her mother lay, and in which the glass features, again, in a position of contiguity:

> I think candles were burning; and I think the sun was coming in. At any
> rate I remember the long looking-glass; . . . and the wash-stand; and the
> great bed on which my mother lay . . . I said to myself as I have done at
> moments of crises since 'I feel nothing whatever.'   (*MB*, pp. 106–7)

Again, she omits to reveal whether or not the looking-glass reflected back an image of her own face. There are candles burning: as in the passage describing George and the flower, in *Between the Acts*, ignition, crisis and a feeling of paralysis here co-exist. A diary entry recording an accident to her niece, Angelica, elsewhere bears out the revelation that she has often, since her mother's death, felt 'nothing whatever' in moments of crisis. She notes, on that occasion, 'a pane of glass shelters me'[30] suggesting that, as here, it was to become possible for her to use the glass as a *screen* for, rather than a reflection of, her feelings.

In the atmosphere surrounding this time, which was melodramatic, histrionic, 'unreal', any hallucination was possible. She thought she could see the figure of a man at her mother's side; sounds were hushed, light was subdued, the house was crowded with flowers. The burning candles, contiguous in this scene with the glass, can be seen to offer an alternative model for what is taking place here during the writing of 'A Sketch of the Past', and for the conflation of Woolf's various styles of identity. The glass, which does not reflect but rather seals and screens, is accompanied by a burning object, and the two images become conflated in the section of the memoir immediately following the passage in which Woolf recounts her visit to her dead mother.

It is the expectation of Thoby's arrival home that breaks up the narrative of pent-up grief. Her most vital and least sentimental connection was with him: perhaps because of his great diffidence he and Virginia were 'naturally attracted to each other' (*MB*, p. 138) and he was always quietly receptive to her thoughts and feelings: he had 'an amused, surprised, questioning attitude' towards his younger sister that no one else seemed quite able to show. The prospect of his return was clearly intoxicating: arriving at Paddington Station to meet him, she felt the atmosphere of everything around her flare up, become charged:

> It was sunset, and the great glass dome at the end of the station was blazing
> with light . . . I walked along the platform gazing with rapture at this
> magificent blaze of colour, and the train slowly steamed into the station . . .
> so vast and so fiery red. The contrast of that blaze of magnificent light with

the shrouded and curtained rooms at Hyde Park Gate was so intense. Also it was partly that my mother's death unveiled and intensified; made me suddenly develop perceptions, as if a burning glass had been laid over what was shaded and dormant. (*MB*, p. 108)[31]

This time, the glass acts as an object with the power to focus and magnify: the entire, dislocated sensibility of Virginia Woolf, the scattered, disparate parts; the divisions, within, the interruptions to, a stable sense of identity, are all focused and refracted by the image of the great, glass dome. It is, here, as if a burning glass had been laid over everything that had hitherto been kept in the dark, under the table; crouched, 'shaded and dormant'. The collision of grief and desire releases feelings of vitality and, at last, of expectation: 'coming events cast *light*'. But Woolf seizes, characteristically, on the aesthetic image; the aesthetic version of the story: it is as if the vehicle for all this were something being registered as something completely abstract: the glass dome is reminiscent of all those earlier membranes, those 'curved shapes showing the light through'.

She has one other, similar memory, in which this time 'the feeling of transparency' is conveyed 'in words' (*MB*, p. 108). She describes having gone with Vanessa to Kensington Gardens, where they lay in the grass behind the Flower Walk, Virginia reading *The Golden Treasury*. The feeling of transparency in words, evoked by a now forgotten poem, was such that they ceased to be words 'and [became] so intensified that one [seemed] to experience them': as though hitherto language had never been anything other than functional. Subsequently, this became a feeling she sometimes had when she was writing: 'the pen gets on the scent' (*ibid*.). But these moments were rare, occurring as isolated epiphanies within the narrative of Virginia Woolf's story, and failing to offer her anything in the form of an insight into the larger continuum.[32] 'Those two clear moments,' she wrote of the burning glass and *The Golden Treasury*, were 'almost the only clear moments in the muffled dulness that then closed over us' (*MB*, p. 109).

In the remainder of the 'Sketch', Woolf describes the 'outsider's feeling' which seemed to characterise her half-brothers' attempts to launch her into 'society': she and Vanessa felt exposed and estranged by such attempts, as though they 'had good seats at the show, but . . . were not allowed to take part in it' (*MB*, p. 153). The ensuing narrative reads as though she has abandoned the attempt to write subjectively, and the 'Sketch' ends – or is, rather, abandoned – in the midst of this dilemma:

> round the tea table, George and Gerald and Jack talked of the Post Office, the publishing office, and the Law Courts. And I, sitting by the table, was quite unable to make any connection. There were so many different worlds . . .   (*MB*, p. 158)

The 'Sketch' ends here, with a hopeless conjunction of worlds and languages and a whole conglomeration of perspectives, offering 'education' of a kind ('no sooner had I settled down to my Greek than I would be called off to hear George's case; then from that I would be told to come up to the study to read German; . . .') but in a life composed entirely of cotton wool. At this point the 'Sketch' has circled back to the preoccupations of Woolf's early fiction – *The Voyage Out* and *Night and Day* – having given glimpses of the way in which the vitality of Virginia Woolf could suddenly flare into being, but having given also a quite graphic description of the narrative within which such moments were restrained and withheld.

A 'Sketch of the Past' re-traces early 'moments of being' in the life of Virginia Woolf, and happens, in the process of effecting their retrieval, upon a design of a kind: the burning glass is a figure which demonstrated that the mirror of Virginia Woolf's imagination, which might have framed and reflected her creative potential, functions most prevalently as a glass which the rays of memory and desire are trained *through*: the source of her deepest feelings and most significant insights is in a curious way not her own psyche, but some imagined reserve just outside or beyond her, as it were, just over her shoulder. She seems to identify herself as a vessel for feelings which she is nevertheless unable to contain: it is as though it is someone else, or even something else, who/which is responsible for originating them, and she herself functions as a membrane, or semi-transparent envelope, through which desire is trained like a ray of light, but focused elsewhere than in her: she is a leaf, showing the light through, but she looks for the source of light to a mark on the wall.

This being so, she looked to others to be the source of sexual expression, expecting to find it in them, rather than in herself. 'Why isn't there something I can lay hands on and say "This is it?"' (*op. cit.*) she asked herself, at moments of high excitement threaded through with numbness. She found nothing in herself, but could take comfort in imagining the moon over Persia, as a kind of burning glass over Vita (here, both the source and the object of the feeling are displaced), who would soon be arriving there.

In 'A Sketch of the Past' the construction of Woolf's own story is shown for the first time, and the difficulty of integrating creative imagery within the narrative of history definitively demonstrated. For the reader there is thus, now, a 'pattern behind the cotton wool', but for Woolf herself writing the 'Sketch' at the end of her life, there was no such possibility of integration. She had hit on an effective method, by employing the 'dodge' of beginning with reflections and writing without stopping to find her way, but having no design for the book she was unable to resolve the deeply lodged paradoxes and crises it produced. She could not, of course, subject herself to analysis; nor was this 'writing as an art', so she is left, as the 'Sketch' peters out, with a series of charged fragments, just as she had predicted as the fate of the modern novelist.

'A Sketch of the Past' is a perfect demonstration of the problem she had identified in the work of Dorothy Richardson. It vividly exemplifies Woolf's early thesis that 'the still hidden facts of our still unknown psychology' constitute a hindrance to the development of women's creativity. But what the 'Sketch' makes clear is that it was not 'facts' that were lacking, but rather access to a new method of interpreting history; a new writing style. She had sensed this throughout her writing practice and went on experimenting with style and form up to and during the writing of *Between the Acts*, but this final novel, which borrowed imagery from the 'facts' of 'A Sketch of the Past' and is designed as compactly as a Chinese box, acted as a burning glass for the unbridled feelings which the writing of the 'Sketch' had begun to stir, causing a sudden ignition of uncontrollable feelings, a conflagration of all the incompatible 'I's. It was a process of combustion from which Woolf, unlike the invented child George, was unable to seek refuge: her friends were mostly dead, her sister was in mourning following the death of her elder son, and her husband was himself potentially in danger. It was left to Virginia herself to find a way of extinguishing this intolerable confusion of feelings. She went to the water, to try to put them out.

In her fiction, she had been consistently attempting to construct a self based on surer foundations and now, in *Between the Acts*, she was focusing again on the notion of history as a scene of origination. She exposes it as a sham, but she also thinks back as far as prehistoric times, just as in 'A Sketch of the Past' there was a sense in which she was attempting to retrieve a 'pre-historic' Virginia Stephen. In *Between the*

Acts something was happening to set up a fuse between two kinds of writing – autobiography and fiction – and two aspects of herself: 'the writing "I"' and Virginia. She was beginning to bring together, finally, the 'dark places' and the light of day; the alternative imagery of house and water. Isa is her first fully realised character who functions both on the surface and introspectively and who is struggling to bring both aspects of herself together; sexuality is for the first time, in *Between the Acts* uncompromisingly explicit, through into the published draft. The backdrop of England at war, the interruptions of the aeroplanes overhead, focus such shocks as the small boy's in the flower bed, rendering the 'cotton wool' of Miss La Trobe's enacted history tedious and absurd.

Was *Between the Acts* beginning, uncontrollably, to become autobiography? The Diary entries relating to the writing of it produced images of arrest, screening, decay, and phantasmagoria. The 'little pitter patter of ideas' she collected there were her 'whiff of shot in the cause of freedom' (*D*, V, p. 235), her defence against the war, and a challenge to the suicide pact. She must have imagined the two petrified bodies, and perhaps remembered her mother and the hallucinated other who, in Virginia's imagination, had accompanied her in death[33] '– so I tell myself,' she noted, 'thus bolstering up a figment – a phantom: recovering that sense of something pressing from outside which consolidates the mist, the non-existent' (*D*, V, p. 235) – the 'cotton wool'.

Paradoxically, the anonymity she was experiencing as the result of her lost audience[34] was coinciding with the bringing of *herself* into play, in her fiction: with 'A Sketch of the Past', such images as suggest her own desire, her own distress, come to take on discernible significance. At the close of *Between the Acts*, a story is about to be told which will presumably draw together all the disparate narratives: the history of Pointz Hall; the sexual history of the Olivers; the history of England; the history of the world since pre-historic times; the relationship between others' stories (La Manresa's; Haines the farmer's) and one's own. Virginia Woolf could not tell it.

Instead, she committed suicide. In her suicide notes, she resorted, as at the end of 'A Sketch of the Past', to a language of non-being, a narrative which recounted rather than evoked the importance of her relationships with her sister and husband. She urged them to go on: to wrap their grief in cotton wool. She wrote of hearing voices again, and of going so far over the edge into madness that she feared she would never come back. To Leonard she wrote,

> I don't think two people could have been happier till this terrible disease
> came. I can't fight any longer. I know that I am spoiling your life, that
> without me you could work. And you will I know . . . Everything has gone
> from me but the certainty of your goodness. I can't go on spoiling your life
> any longer.

To Vanessa,

> You can't think how I loved your letter. But I feel that I have gone too far
> this time to come back again. I am certain now that I am going mad again. It
> is just as it was the first time, I am always hearing voices, and I know I
> shan't get over it now. All I want to say is that Leonard has been so
> astonishingly good, every day, always; . . . We have been perfectly happy
> until the last few weeks, when this horror began. Will you assure him of
> this? I feel he has so much to do that he will go on, better without me, and
> you will help him.[35]

In the final analysis, the 'cotton wool', the screening devices, prevail.

But the plot, despite insistent attempts, proved irretrievable. She had no
choice about the way she wrote, but that is not to suggest that she
worked complacently within her limitations. She put herself at risk
with every novel, working consistently at the attempt to align her
'choruses' with a plot which would yield interest and vitality. That she
could not achieve exactly this had to do with the powerful relationship
between writing and a search to retrieve her own gender identity. 'She
is a theorist of fiction', Elizabeth Hardwick has suggested,[36] and many
readers have agreed with this, although a close analysis of her working
methods suggests that a 'theory' was precisely what she lacked, though
she went on seeking one. '(Perhaps,)' Hardwick adds in parenthesis,
'(there is something feminist in this, a way of testing and confronting
the very structure of the novel itself.)' Certainly, for her, the issues of
writing and gender were at all times inextricably and delicately linked.

Her desire in writing was certainly to devise new forms, new designs,
new structures for her own narrative: 'to use writing as an art, not as a
method of self-expression', but the source of her artistic endeavour was
always located within herself. 'Her own hurt feelings'[37] both initiated
and shaped her writing. In her resistance to closure or conclusion, she
remained always faithful to the task of transposing into works of art the
complexities of her most deeply rooted experiences of loss and
desire, attempting at all times to net the very thing which continued to
prove most elusive: her confused and complicated sense of her own
womanhood.

Part II

Virginia Woolf's Later Novels

Here came in the great space of life into
which no one had ever penetrated.
(*VO*, p. 217)

1

The Mirror Cracked
(*To the Lighthouse*)

Did Nature supplement what man advanced? Did she complete what he began? With equal complacence she saw his misery, condoned his meanness, and acquiesced in his torture. That dream, then, of . . . finding in solitude on the beach an answer, was but a reflection in a mirror, and the mirror itself was but the surface glassiness which forms in quiescence when the nobler powers sleep beneath? Impatient, despairing yet loth to go (for beauty offers her lures, has her consolations), to pace the beach was impossible; contemplation was unendurable; the mirror was broken.   (*TL*, p. 153)

In *To the Lighthouse*, Virginia Woolf created a potent atmosphere in which to explore Lily Briscoe's potential as an artist, and in which to demonstrate the highly complex, highly individual conditions attendant on the artistic process, and its grounding in sexuality. She approached the writing of this novel with a specific idea: to immortalise, and so to exorcise, the characters of her own parents, who had continued throughout her adult life to haunt her. She later noted of her achievement in *To the Lighthouse*, 'I suppose that I did for myself what psychoanalysts do for their patients. I expressed some very long felt and deeply felt emotion. And in expressing it I explained it and then laid it to rest' (*MB*, p. 94).

What developed from this initial plan can be read as a successful depiction of the oblique relationship between Mrs Ramsay – the archetypal mother figure, based on Julia Stephen – and Lily Briscoe, the artist and representative of a succeeding generation of women. Implicated within this relationship are their respective relationships with an archetypal, demanding patriarch, the 'Old Man' Mr Ramsay, based on Sir Leslie Stephen.[1]

The Diary entries relating to the composition of *To the Lighthouse* show Virginia Woolf making up phrases and calling up recollections as well as sketching out a design for the book. It was to be shaped as 'two blocks joined by a corridor',[2] though she afterwards recalled that

'Blowing bubbles out of a pipe gives the feeling of the rapid crowd of ideas and scenes which blew out of my mind, so that my lips seemed syllabling of their own accord as I worked' (*MB*, p. 94). The novel was constructed out of a process of recollection, transposed immediately into figures of the imagination, constituting a high point in her departure from the early 'novel of facts', *Night and Day*, and setting a stylistic precedent for *The Waves*.

Writing to Roger Fry shortly after completing it, however, Woolf defended its central figure against charges of symbolic significance, protesting that she 'meant *nothing* by The Lighthouse. One has to have a central line down the middle of the book to hold the design together.' She saw, she conceded, that all sorts of feelings would accrue to this, but 'refused to think them out, and trusted that people would make it the deposit for their own emotions.' She was unable to manage 'Symbolism', she added, except 'in this vague, generalised way . . . directly I'm told what a thing means, it becomes hateful to me' (*L*, III, p. 385).

Stylistic questions, then, took precedence, and Woolf was here using her own process of recollection as a source of creativity, but not dramatising it directly. As a result the reader is left to find his or her own way around the structures of the novel as it moves back and forth through, and circles round, the central theme of the composition of Lily's painting, and her simultaneous process of recollection. The narrative seems to float freely from one character to another: it sometimes seems to be 'attaching meanings to words of a symbolical kind',[3] but nowhere offers an unambiguous point of reference. The narrative weaves and repairs and knits and unpicks memory and desire in rather the same way as Mrs Ramsay turns to the knitting of her stocking: as one way of marking the progress of the narrative through time.

As she often did in the face of subject matter based closely on lived events, she felt baffled by the notion that she could draw so closely from life without creating a 'sham'. Reacting to Vanessa's admiring comment on the closeness of Mrs Ramsay to the character of their mother, she claimed that it was a 'psychological mystery' to her that she had managed to evoke so closely the character of her model, except that, 'dying at that moment, I suppose she cut a great figure on one's mind when it was just awake' – she seems to some extent, in this novel, to have drawn on the enquiring, impressionable child's mind that she was later to explore more fully in 'A Sketch of the Past' – 'Only then,' she added, 'one would have suspected that one had made up a sham – an ideal' (*L*, III, p. 383). The attempt to really excavate a character or situation and show something 'whole', in all its facets, perhaps seemed a little like showing off: as when, during the writing of *Mrs Dalloway* she had resolved to expose the entire social system and 'show it at its worst', but added, ' – but here I may be posing.'

For if she paid homage, in *To the Lighthouse*, to Julia Stephen's great beauty and her widely acknowledged gift for encouraging and nurturing the vitality of others, she also exposed the workings of a 'system' which had its insidious aspects. In this novel, she looks closely at the institution of marriage, considers the dynamics which Mr and Mrs Ramsay's marriage seems to run on, and to some extent exposes as a sham their respective roles and functions by identifying the potential for regeneration and renewal elsewhere than within the confines of this often constraining, often disingenuous institution.

To find a language for reinterpretation is one of the novel's endeavours, and Mrs Ramsay's 'strange severity' demonstrates the difficulties and dangers of beginning to do so. Her severity is inseparable from her beauty, and even this, it is suggested, somehow emanates from her desire to uphold the values of the aristocracy and of patriarchal Victorianism, preserving for herself a position of power which is based on, rather than in any way challenging, her deference to her husband. Mrs Ramsay's model, Julia Stephen, was active in the Anti-Suffrage Movement, a group of women who firmly believed that their power was derived from their position of command within the household, and that without their compliance with a structure that put them in a subordinate role vis-a-vis their husbands, their own 'superior' power, as matriarchs, would cease to hold sway. Mrs Ramsay was 'formidable to behold', and it was only in silence that her daughters could 'sport with infidel ideas which they had brewed for themselves of a life different from hers; in Paris, perhaps; a wilder life; not always taking care of some man or other . . .' (p. 9).

Lily Briscoe represents an alternative to all this. She may well have been modelled on Vanessa, who even while the Stephen sisters' father was still alive had escaped from the household to attend classes at the Slade, and had thence become progressively 'wilder'. But there is a problem about comparing Lily and Mrs Ramsay in terms of their respective styles of creativity, as critics have traditionally tended to do.[4]

While critics for a long time saw Mrs Ramsay's style of 'artistry' – the arranging of marriages, the getting and rearing of children – as being in some sense superior to Lily's, recent revolutions in feminist thinking have meant that the traditional relationship between Lily and Mrs Ramsay can be seen to be reversed, since, as one critic puts it, Lily's avoidance of heterosexuality as Mrs Ramsay perceives it, and her refusal to marry (not that she gets the chance) 'are not a failure to be womanly, for being womanly no longer means being defined by one's relations to men or one's reproductive system.'[5]

There is still a problem, though, since Mrs Ramsay's chastity is seen to be 'revised' by Lily into a position which cannot be regenerated, so that the stagnation which Woolf perceives as being implicit in the Ramsay marriage, and in Mrs Ramsay's point of view, can only be repeated by Lily, even within her revisionary perspective. What is unique in *To the Lighthouse*, however, is the *way* in which Woolf re-rehearses the same set of problems from within a very different perspective, the way in which Lily 're-drafts' the story Mrs Ramsay tells, in the first 'block' of the novel, and the way in which time itself, and the process of recollection, contribute to Lily's being able to tell, in the second 'block', another story.

Mrs Ramsay is first seen, in *To the Lighthouse*, not as a subject in her own right but as a loved object, even by her small son, who 'endowed the picture of a refrigerator as his mother spoke with heavenly bliss. It was fringed with joy' (*TL*, p. 5) because it signifies her nearness, even if the image he has chosen is not entirely insignificant. Her role as matriarch and as harmonising principle is always at once acknowledged and potentially usurped – for James, as for her daughters. When Mrs Ramsay's own view of the world is given, it appears in the terms of ambiguity and contradiction: 'Strifes, divisions, difference of opinion, prejudices twisted into the very fibre of being, oh that they should begin so early, Mrs Ramsay deplored . . . The real differences, she thought, standing by the drawing room window, are enough, quite enough' (p. 11). The harmonising principle might, then, merely be a way of sealing over, or veiling, the fundamental disparities which she is the first to recognise.

The veiling process almost becomes her hallmark: a feature, almost, of her physical beauty, as the formulation of her by Charles Tansley suggests. For him, she has 'stars in her eyes and veils in her hair, with cyclamen and wild violets', but this is nonsense: she is 'fifty at least', with eight children. Despite the ridiculousness of all this, however, it constitutes a fantasy which prevails, and in which the onlooker plays a vital part: 'Stepping through fields of flowers and taking to her breast buds that had broken and lambs that had fallen; with the stars in her eyes and the wind in her hair – he took her bag' (pp. 17–18).

It is as though with each conception of Mrs Ramsay two alternative versions emerge: she belongs both in reality, and in the observer's 'fiction'. The style of the narrative encourages this duplicity and seems to slide in and out of her and the other characters' consciousnesses; between their images of Mrs Ramsay and their images of themselves. There seems to be, as John Mepham has noted, no narrative authority from which this weaving and circling emanates, so that meanings are infiltrated within the text which seem not to have their source in the fictional subjects themselves.[6]

As a result, the characters can sometimes seem as though they are not quite within the control of the narrator, but nor are they quite in control of themselves. There is, however, a reason for this, which has to do with a kind of obsessive displacement activity, practised most deftly by that expert in the art of deflection, Mrs Ramsay. Her husband was a failure, he said. 'Well, look then, feel then', she implies, as she flashes her knitting needles. She succeeds in holding him off by directing his attention towards the house, vibrant with young life; the garden full of flowers – anything but herself. And 'so boasting of her capacity to surround and protect, there was scarcely a shell of herself left for her to know herself by; all was so lavished and spent' (p. 45).

At times, the narrative seems to 'know' more about Mrs Ramsay's frame of mind than she herself is capable of putting into words. As she reads to James the story of 'The Fisherman's Wife' – that belligerent and outspoken matriarch – she undergoes, by contrast, 'some disagreeable sensation. Not that . . . she knew precisely where it came from; nor did she let herself put into words her dissatisfaction when she realized . . . how it came from this: she did not like, even for a second, to feel finer than her husband' (p. 46). As Mepham has noted, it is essentially Sartrean 'Bad Faith' which is at the source of Mrs Ramsay's strange elusiveness, so that she is always deflecting attention from one character to another, one agony to another, one story to another, so that in the end 'one petal closed in another, and the whole fabric fell in exhaustion upon itself.' At the dinner party, the climax of her 'story', she has a sense of being 'past everything, through everything, out of everything, . . . It's all come to an end, she thought, . . .' (p. 96).

Her tendency to edit or censor her knowledge to some extent echoes the author's, for there is a sense in which the dinner party is for Mrs Ramsay a 'fictitious' structure – a diagram of how she would like things to be – which acts as a figurative representation of her knowledge, offering a point of view without giving it, as it were, in full. *To the Lighthouse* is, similarly, a selective representation of Woolf's memories of her parents, though, as in Mrs Ramsay's depiction of events, the warp as well as the weave of the fabric shows through. In this novel the narrative voice both tells and remains aloof from the telling, so that in another of the lines running through the centre of *To the Lighthouse* – the 'corridor' which connects parts one and two – there is no speaking subject at all, simply an empty, haunted house: the disembodied repository of feeling which represents the history of the Ramsay family, the subject collapsed in on itself; the withered flower, the 'ghosts' set up in the present by the resonances of the past. Only art, of course, can achieve this, and it is in this, indirect sense – not through her chastity, her maternity or her beauty – that Mrs Ramsay, no less a figment of the artistic imagination than the Fisherman's Wife, practises her artistry within the text of Woolf's novel.

In a contiguous relation to Mrs Ramsay, Woolf positions Lily Briscoe, who grapples with her own problem in a style which runs counter to Mrs Ramsay's, for Lily's problem is that she must *release* rather than veil meaning, in order to maintain the subjective integrity essential to the making of a work of art. Lily's painting is a representation of the story we are being told, with Mrs Ramsay as yet another centrepiece: Lily is painting Mrs Ramsay in her setting, in Modernist form, in what she envisages as a reinterpretation of the image of Madonna and Child. Where Mrs Ramsay constantly grapples with her surface projection of herself, which must hold its own against the current of more subversive, less comfortable feelings, Lily's project is to get beneath the surface in order to present, in her painting, things as they really are, in a perspective suggestive of psychological authenticity. If Mrs Ramsay's story is reliant on her disingenuousness, the picture Lily paints must tell another story. If for Mrs Ramsay, 'beneath it is all dark, it is all spreading, it is unfathomably deep; but now and again we rise to the surface and that is what you see us by' (p. 73), for Lily the surface implies exposure, vulnerability, superficiality. Whenever she exchanged the fluidity of life for the concentration of painting, she experienced 'a few moments of nakedness when she seemed like an unborn soul, a soul reft of body, hesitating on some windy pinnacle and exposed without protection to all the blasts of doubt' (p. 180). The tension between darkness and light, the surface and the depths, drags at both Lily and Mrs Ramsay: both characters need to mediate between levels of experience and there are two separate stories which present two different ways of negotiating between the demands of the self and the demands of the world. At the centre of the narrative, and providing another space, in which the reader is invited to make the transition between stories, Woolf gives us, highly significantly, the passage of time itself.

The 'Time Passes' section follows directly on from the dinner party, which features Augustus Carmichael and Mr Ramsay chanting poetry, and from its aftermath, which finds Mr and Mrs Ramsay alone together reading, he from Scott, she from Shakespeare's Sonnets. As the dinner party draws to a close, Mrs Ramsay's mind is already beginning to wander:

> The sudden bursts of laughter and then one voice (Minta's) speaking alone, reminded her of men and boys crying out the Latin words of a service in some Roman Catholic cathedral. (*TL*, p. 127)

As she collects herself again, she hears her husband speaking and realises that he is repeating something: 'she knew it was poetry from the rhythm and the ring of exaltation and melancholy in his voice' (*ibid.*). The spoken word has the effect of at once engaging and dislocating her: the chant is striking in that it seems to suggest an organic, regenerative quality, and yet has no discernible source:

> The words (. . .) sounded as if they were floating like flowers on water out there, cut off from them all, as if no one had said them, but they had come into existence of themselves.
>
> And all the lives we ever lived and all the lives to be
> Are full of trees and changing leaves. (*ibid.*)

The rhythms and cadences of poetry seem to offer her the illusion of something shaped: a structure for experience which comes fully formed. Later, as she waits for her husband to emerge from Scott's narrative, she reads, 'Nor praise the deep vermilion in the rose', and feels as though she is 'ascending . . . to the top, on to the summit':

And . . . there it was, suddenly entire shaped in her hands, beautiful and
reasonable, clear and complete, the essence sucked out of life and held
rounded here – the sonnet.
    But she was becoming conscious of her husband looking at her.
                                                        (*TL*, p. 139)

The Sonnet seems to encompass or encapsulate life, and yet it is perhaps
more true to say that it displaces or even replaces 'the essence sucked
out of life'. By the time Mrs Ramsay has finished reading, she has re-
instated herself in her position as object and taken up her knitting again:
the two strategies to which she always resorts in an attempt to put two
and two together. Conscious that she is being looked at, she attempts
somehow to gain control over events, assemble the fragments of a
narrative that might make a reasonable story: something to tell him, to
keep him at bay: 'She remembered dressing, and seeing the moon;
Andrew holding his plate too high at dinner; . . . Charles Tansley
waking them with his books falling – . . . Which should she tell him
about?'

  'They're engaged,' she said, beginning to knit, 'Paul and Minta.'
  'So I guessed,' he said. There was nothing very much to be said about it.
  Her mind was still going up and down, up and down, . . . So they sat
  silent.   (*TL*, p. 14)

She goes on manoeuvring them in this way, until the unspoken
agreement between them that it would, after all, be wet tomorrow
(hence no going to the lighthouse) constitutes the realisation that 'she
had triumphed again' (p. 142) not, of course, by being right, but by
tempering their connection in such a way as to resist his outbursts and
to control the way in which she is reflected in his gaze: '(She knew that
he was thinking, "You are more beautiful than ever.")'
    Like the lighthouse beam, she sends out silent signals to steer him
safely away from her; and there is an element of this disingenuousness
which is mutual. He pays attention to her to deflect his own desires, not
in response to hers. As they sit together, reading, he wishes she would
tell him she loved him: 'for he was roused, what with Minta and his
book . . .' (p. 142).
    In the 'Time Passes' section, the far-reaching effects of this style of
communication are examined, in a long series of elegiac meditations
such as would doubtless have soothed Mrs Ramsay, punctuated with
cryptic moments of a 'factual' nature of which Mr Ramsay would no
doubt have approved. The juxtaposition of this intermittent and
brusque reportage with the elegiac prose comes, each time, with a
shock: the staging of events marks time with a relentless and a

disinterested ruthlessness which jars, after the effects, in the first 'block' of the novel, of all Mrs Ramsay's screening devices. Clearly, there are two different ways of telling a story running concurrently, here, and the effect of their combined impact will eventually issue in a fundamentally new and different vision.

At first, time passes in a 'profusion of darkness' (p. 143) which penetrates the house after everyone has left for the Winter. But 'behind' that darkness, even though the house is uninhabited, a narrative voice chants a meditation attributable to a narrative point of view which has been implicit in the previous, long section of the novel. In 'Time Passes', the guiding moral and spiritual perspectives of the Ramsay household are first explored, then put to question. There is such a thing as 'divine goodness', which now '[parts] the curtain' and reveals a series of separate images: 'the hare erect; the wave falling; the boat rocking': these treasures 'should be ours always', but alas, 'divine goodness' is not pleased by what he sees:

> he covers his treasures in a drench of hail, and so breaks them, so confuses them that it seems impossible that their calm should ever return or that we should ever compose from their fragments a perfect whole or read in the littered pieces the clear words of truth. (*TL*, p. 146)

There is, then, 'buried treasure', but the discovery of it is subject to sudden and arbitrary disappointment: images are subject to fragmentation; illusions are easily and suddenly shattered. 'No going to the Lighthouse, James' (p. 18), the despicable Charles Tansley had pronounced, shattering all the child's hopes and dreams. His father, too, had promised rain: it seemed as though all expectation might be subject to disappointment; as though there might be no way of actually gauging or assessing the potential which appearances seemed at once to promise and to withhold. Mrs Ramsay herself spread veils, drew down shutters, over what was actually the case, composing for herself an image of wholeness and integrity only in solitude. The landscape, in 'Time Passes', echoes this fragmentation, this sense in which the subject is constantly under threat of disappointment, and now that Mrs Ramsay is dead, there is not even the promise of comfort in a substitute for the real thing: 'no image with a semblance of serving and divine promptitude comes readily to hand bringing the night to order and making the world reflect the compass of the soul' (p. 146). The world does not, simply, reflect meaning.

The entire basis of Mrs Ramsay's illusion of harmony, with its tacit assumption that the subject has control over what she or he reflects, is challenged here. The hovering divinity she resorts to when off her guard – 'I am guarding you – I am your support' (p. 19); 'We are in the hands of the Lord' (p. 74) – is here inaccessible; the sense in which the self is somehow contained or circumscribed in the imagery of nature which suffuses the Sonnets, is here put to question. There is no mirror to be held up to Nature; no implicit meaning, to be excavated like buried treasure.

The whole of the 'Time Passes' section happens in a kind of dreamtime, while the characters are absent – either asleep or dead – and in this section, the house functions as a metaphor for the landscape of the unconscious which, by accumulating images, observations and reflections like flotsam and jetsam, seems to reach provisional conclusions, to construct provisional perspectives. Filtered through the anonymous narrative are instances of the struggles of a series of minds. In many minds, it seems impossible to resist the 'strange intimation' that 'good triumphs, happiness prevails' (pp. 150–1). Yet the continuum of human events persists in disproving this: '[Prue Ramsay died that summer in some illness connected with childbirth, which was indeed a tragedy, people said. They said nobody deserved happiness more]' (p. 151). As the section continues, the First World War breaks out, killing many of England's youth, among them Andrew Ramsay, and making, again, 'something out of harmony with this jocundity, this serenity' (p. 152). It is difficult, in the face of these ruthless, external interruptions, to go on marvelling at 'how beauty outside mirrored beauty within' (*ibid.*): as the interruptions persist, the language of the predominant narrative voice begins to seem nonsensical. If Nature cannot *mirror* men, then perhaps there is a sense in which, at one level, the human mind engineers or composes the shapes and lines of the landscape and seascape in which it seeks to see itself reflected as a subject: 'Did Nature supplement what man advanced? Did she complete what he began?' (p. 153). If with equal complacence 'she' witnessed 'his' misery, 'condoned his meanness, and acquiesced in his torture', then perhaps the dream – that dream of seeing oneself reflected in Nature, 'finding in solitude on the beach an answer', – is itself only a reflection, and the mirror only 'the surface glassiness which forms in quiescence when the nobler powers sleep beneath' (*ibid.*). Perhaps the very desire to seek in the rhythms and imagery of nature an image of harmony was itself only an illusion, or possibly even a way of screening off the desire for something else: something different from all this, which could only be achieved with much greater difficulty and under much greater duress; something 'nobler', accessible only when the more superficial desire – to see oneself reflected favourably in others – could eventually be conquered or broken.

Eventually, this is the possibility that breaks through into the narrative:

> Impatient, despairing, yet loth to go (for beauty offers her lures, has her consolations), to pace the beach was impossible; contemplation was unendurable; the mirror was broken. (*TL*, p. 153)

Under pressure of *this*, enquiring gaze, 'Mother Nature' (the illusory house full of treasures; Mrs Ramsay herself, even, perhaps) cannot be sustained as a unifying image, guiding principle, or centrepiece, and it is at this moment in the text that *To the Lighthouse* swings on its axis, turns its other face, and prepares for the final section, which will present and explore the reverse side of the Ramsay marriage and all its well-worn and woolly minded values, allowing Lily Briscoe, the artist, to pierce the veil of Mrs Ramsay's romantic illusions and to make sense of all the connecting threads which together compose, not something round or hard, like a diamond in the sand – a 'treasure' – but the possibility of unpicking loose ends, and of making sense of all that lies within the interstices of daily life; all that is implied by ragged, makeshift structures of most human relationships.

The process of painting points up for Lily Briscoe, in section three, some problematic break in the continuity of her thinking about Mrs Ramsay. There was:

> something she remembered in the relations of those lines cutting across, slicing down, and in the mass of the hedge . . ., which had stayed in her mind; which had tied a knot in her mind so that at odds and ends of time, as she walked along the Brompton Road, as she brushed her hair, she found herself painting that picture, passing her eye over it, and untying the knot in her imagination. (*TL*, p. 178)

The relations of lines, the mass of the hedge, seem somehow to relate to some forgotten insight relating to Mrs Ramsay. As Lily squeezes her tubes, attacking the problem of the hedge, she suddenly sees her, quite clearly in her mind's eye, 'stepping with her usual quickness across fields among whose folds, purplish and soft, among whose flowers, hyacinths or lilies, she vanished' (p. 206). This, Lily surmises, is merely some trick of the painter's eye. She imagines her courtship with Mr

Ramsay: an 'old fashioned scene' featuring Mr Ramsay in peg-top trousers, in which Mrs Ramsay steps out of a boat onto the shore, and agrees to marry him. In imagining all this, she is not inventing; 'only trying to smooth out something she had been given years ago folded up; something she had seen' (pp. 225–6).

What is significant here is Lily's emerging *method*, rather than the details of the story: she is beginning, here, to tell a whole new story, composed of history, the imagination and some barely recoverable memory, the telling of which will enable her to put into a new perspective the whole notion of romantic love as an uninterrupted, impermeable continuum. At the same time, she is beginning to 'smooth out' something to which, during Mrs Ramsay's lifetime, she has been denied access; something 'folded up'. The function of the story, then, is that it will enable Lily, if she can find a way of telling it, to begin to untie the 'knot' of confused emotions to which she has all along been subject.

Once she begins to disentangle buried memory and desire, it becomes all at once possible for her to begin to tell another story: a story which for once allows her to explore the significance of Mrs Ramsay's 'fiction' of the importance of marriage, this time uninterrupted by the distorting medium of Mrs Ramsay's own perspective on the shape of things which, like the mass of the hedge, had always obstructed her. And, once she begins to hit on a medium for deconstructing one version of love and marriage – the traditional one, which seems to be seeped in historical assumptions and implications – she has the germs of a technique for deconstructing another, and for bringing this knowledge about the events of the past to bear on the present.

As Lily squeezes her tubes of green paint, she reflects on the more violent, more contemporary imagery of the Rayleys' marriage – that 'descendent' of Mrs Ramsay's great idea. The Rayley marriage is of course, to some extent, a fabrication of Mrs Ramsay's: a result of the match-making impulse which had enabled her to displace her own feelings of fragmentation onto dreams of 'wholeness' or harmony on behalf of others. The Rayleys' marriage is more revealing than the Ramsays' of disruption: Lily conjures up the figure of Minta, 'wreathed, tinted, garish on the stairs about three o'clock in the morning.' Paul, in Lily's story, hears the noise and, thinking he has burglars (doesn't he know his wife has been out?), appears, in his pyjamas, carrying a poker. Minta, 'eating a sandwich, standing half-way up by a window' on a carpet with a hole in it, irritatingly continues to eat her sandwich as he speaks. He is 'withered, drawn'; she 'flamboyant, careless'. For, reflects

Lily, 'things had worked loose after the first year or so; the marriage had turned out rather badly' (p. 196).

The passage functions as an ironic parody of the notion of the Rayley marriage as an 'inheritance' from Mrs Ramsay: Minta now eats a sandwich instead of the *boeuf en daube*, she is 'wreathed, tinted, garish' in place of her golden-reddish glow; she stands, irritatingly, half-way up by a window as though to taunt Mrs Ramsay, who had posed for Lily seated at a window. Untying the knot in her mind, Lily perceives the significance of the fact that the Rayleys' marriage had worked loose by imagining the story of that process, thereby challenging on her own terms the wisdom of Mrs Ramsay's principle, that her bevy of young women should marry, and that the institution of marriage would out-live generations and effect the continuity of the living after her own death (' "the Rayleys" – she [had] tried the new name over; . . . it was all one stream, . . . and Paul and Minta would carry it on when she was dead' (p. 131).

In the terms of the narrative order, it is the death of Mrs Ramsay which makes possible the telling of Lily's story of the Rayleys, which enables her to begin to untie the knot in her imagination and, by 'summing up' the Rayleys, assert her own creative triumph over that of Mrs Ramsay (pp. 198–9). In the final section of *To the Lighthouse*, time has usurped Mrs Ramsay's presence, rendering absurd her old fashion-ed principles and beliefs, and bequeathing Lily a new place in the scheme of things from which she can see Mrs Ramsay's anachronistic, and disingenuous, values in perspective. However, turning her atten-tion again to the scene depicted in her painting, Lily is again struck by the force of Mrs Ramsay's presence: by her tactile rather than her tac-tical qualities. The process of retelling augments rather than diminishes feelings of lack and loss:

> To want and not to have, sent all up her body a hardness, a hollowness, a strain. And then to want and not to have – to want and want – how that wrung her heart, and wrung it again and again! Oh Mrs Ramsay! she called out silently, . . .   (*TL*, p. 203)

The repetitive nature of desire, the pain of the terrible inertia imposed by loss, and the seeming impossibility of ever being able to move these feelings forward into anything new, seem to impede even the possibil-ity of quite putting these feelings into words. Silently, Lily appeals to this new, composite Mrs Ramsay, reconstructed out of memory, in-vention and desire, who seems to be the object of the entire weight and breadth of Lily's capacity for desiring. In the face of all this, the only way of moving forward seems to necessitate the transference of such feelings from one impossible object to another. The pain of Mrs Ramsay's loss calls up the memory of the unforgettable dinner party, which had seemed to encapsulate Mrs Ramsay's vision of the order of things, but this time, Lily's memory homes in on some newly identifiable sexual focus. 'What was this mania of hers for marriage? Lily wondered, stepping to and fro from her easel':

> (Suddenly, as suddenly as a star slides in the sky, a reddish light seemed to burn in her mind, covering Paul Rayley, issuing from him. It rose like a fire sent up in token of some celebration by savages on a distant beach. . . . The whole sea for miles round ran red and gold. Some winy smell mixed with it and intoxicated her, for she felt again her own headlong desire to throw herself off the cliff and be drowned looking for a pearl brooch on a beach. And the roar and the crackle repelled her with fear and disgust, as if while she saw its splendour and power she saw too how it fed on the treasure of the house, . . .   (*TL*, p. 199)

This is the dinner party, raised, as it were, from the dead and transmuted into the art of Lily's fiction; transposed, moreover, into a language in which art is capable of releasing and inscribing desire. In the process, the 'indeterminancy of attribution' which allows the narrator, throughout the text of *To the Lighthouse*, to float freely in and out of the characters' minds and sometimes even to make seemingly unattributable statements, effects here the transmutation of the Rayleys' sexuality, which had cast a 'golden-reddish glow' over the dinner party, into Lily's consciousness. Recalling the dinner party, Lily is overcome by a winy smell reminiscent of the *boeuf en daube*. A reddish light burns in her mind, recalling Minta's bewitching sensuality. The reddish light now 'rose like a fire sent up in token of some celebration by savages on a distant beach', giving this new – as it were, revised – version of the dinner party a primitive quality, and re-situating it on the beach where the 'engagement' between Paul and Minta had taken place. The sea which 'for miles round ran red and gold' is suffused with the imagery of Minta, and Lily experiences a sudden desire to throw herself headlong into it from the cliff which had earlier signalled her feelings of abandonment and exposure.

Before, the cliff had symbolised Lily's exclusion from the entire scenario of romantic and sexual love: she had offered to go with Paul to look for the brooch which Minta had lost on the beach and he had laughed, as if he had said, 'Throw yourself over the cliff if you like, I don't care' (p. 118). In that moment she had felt all the violence and ambivalence of desire: 'He had turned on her cheek the heat of love, its horror, its cruelty, its unscrupulosity. It scorched her, and Lily, looking at Minta being charming to Mr Ramsay at the other end of the table, had flinched for her exposed to those fangs, and was thankful' (*ibid.*). Now, having to some extent unravelled the 'knot' of subdued desire, she can see the extent to which the violence of desire is integral to its power, and to its capacity to be 'glorious, inspiring, tenacious', so that 'one only had to say "in love" and . . . up rose Paul's fire again. And it sank and she said to herself, laughing, 'The Rayleys' . . .' (p. 200).

For she has now devised a language in which she can keep the more dangerous aspects of her feelings in perspective without their being completely stifled. Looking again at her fear of being rejected, un-qualified, exempt, she can reinstate the powerful and potent imagery of desire and can see, in addition, that her response to Paul's offhandedness was perhaps excessive. And yet it was this that had enabled her to identify the fictitious nature of Mrs Ramsay's injunction to 'Marry, marry!'. Over the intervening years, she has reflected on this sham, this made-up story of married life and avoided falling into the same traps herself, although, she now sees, only just. Evading marriage, she has nurtured a friendship with the gentlemanly William Bankes, who always left her plenty of time to 'wash her hands' when they visited Hampton Court together, and with whom 'many things were left unsaid' (pp. 200–1). This was, of course, true of the Ramsay marriage, too, and Lily, musing on her own relationship with William Bankes, now reflects that perhaps there had been imperfections even within the marriage between Mr and Mrs Ramsay: her beauty had perhaps not after all been an unequivocal symbol of complete harmony but had masked irregularities, flaws: 'She was astonishingly beautiful, William said. But beauty was not everything. Beauty had this penalty – it came too readily, came too completely. It stilled life – froze it. One forgot the little agitations . . .' (pp. 201–2).

Her connection with William Bankes enables insights which allow her to untie some fundamental knots – Mrs Ramsay's myth of perfect harmony, for example – so that she can now discern, through the veil of Mrs Ramsay's beauty, something of the more ambivalent, less perfectly synchronised, nature of male and female sexual love. And yet, the acquisition of this knowledge and, as it were, the end of innocence – not being able to believe in Mrs Ramsay's stories any more – comes accompanied by all the overwhelming experiences of emptiness and loss: 'For how could one express in words these emotions of the body? express that emptiness there?' (pp. 202–3). Moreover, this new perspective enables her, also, to consider the implications of the imperfections of her own relationship, with William Bankes, for if the 'beauty' of chastity stilled life, it ultimately froze it, and there is, after all, an anaesthetised quality about her relationship with William Bankes.

The effects of thinking about the Rayleys and about her discreet and partial feelings for William Bankes call up in her an overwhelming desire for connection which only Mrs Ramsay had ever really recognised. She appeals silently to Mr Carmichael, asleep in his deck-chair: she must make contact with someone: '"What does it mean? How do you explain it all?" she wanted to say' (p. 203). He is inscrutable, but with his 'poetry and his puzzles' he seems to sail serenely through the world as though – it suddenly occurs to her – 'he had only to put down his hand where he lay on the lawn to fish up anything he wanted' (pp. 203–4).

He was inscrutable, he was selfish – in some respects like Mr Ramsay, though Lily does not consciously make this connection – but there is, perhaps, some connection to be made. The narrative takes over from Lily in order to suggest connections she herself is unable to make, and, having given the merest hint of some connection to be made between the garden and the sea ('the whole wave and whisper of the garden became like curves and arabesques flourishing round a centre of complete emptiness'), takes over from Lily, consumed with inarticulate grief, and makes it again, more overtly: for a moment it seems as though if only Mr Carmichael would get up from the lawn and demand an explanation as to 'why [life] was so short, why . . . so inexplicable' then perhaps Mrs Ramsay might be raised from the dead:

> then, beauty would roll itself up; the space would fill; those empty
> flourishes would form into shape; if they shouted loud enough Mrs Ramsay
> would return. 'Mrs Ramsay!' she said aloud, . . .
>
> [Macalister's boy took one of the fish and cut a square out of its side to bait
> his hook with. The mutilated body (it was still alive) was thrown back into
> the sea.]
>
> 'Mrs Ramsay!' Lily cried, 'Mrs Ramsay!' But nothing happened . . .
> Anyhow the old man had not heard her.'   (*TL*, p. 205)

Again, the narrative hints at a connection not fully available to Lily herself: perhaps Mr Carmichael, the old man on the lawn, might at some level prove to be interchangeable as the agent of desire and grief with the other Old Man, with whom Virginia Woolf began in the first stages of sketching out her ideas for *To the Lighthouse*: the patriarchal presence at the basis of the entire assemblage of stories both contained in and implied by the idea for the novel and dramatised in the main, authorial narrative in the figure of Mr Ramsay. Looking out to sea, Lily vaguely discerns the ability of the memory to promote connections and confuse signifiers, so that meaning can become entangled, and mysteriously capable of some obscure, cross-referencing process. For, as sometimes happened in fine weather, 'the cliffs looked as if they were conscious of the ships, and the ships looked as if they were conscious of the cliffs, as they signalled to each other some secret message of their own.' At the centre of this network, the unifying image becomes a ghostly presence: 'the Lighthouse looked this morning in the haze an enormous distance away' (p. 207).

The cliffs looked as if they were conscious of the ships, and the ships looked as if they were conscious of the cliffs: by a circuitous, tortuous route Lily is forging, though not quite acknowledging, a connection between the imagery of Mr Ramsay, in his boat out at sea, and Paul Rayley. She calls up again the possibility of reconciling emotions which had hitherto seemed separate: pleasure and pain, grief and a desire for repair, the desire for disintegration and the desire to shape up; having released this possibility of putting two and two together by comparing Mrs Ramsay's marriage with the 'looser' marriage of the Rayleys. Perhaps, it now seems, Lily is not wholly without access to Mrs Ramsay's secret, after all. In which case she might after all be able to begin to speak Mrs Ramsay's language:

> 'Where are they now?' Lily thought, looking out to sea . . .   (*TL*, p. 207)

This time she is looking, not for Paul and Minta, but for Mr Ramsay and his children. Mrs Ramsay had interrupted the story of the Fisherman and his Wife to frame her question as to Paul and Minta's whereabouts; Lily now interrupts her own story with this sudden, unarticulated insight into the possibility of thinking, now, not simply about Mrs Ramsay but about 'The Ramsays'. By doing so, she is able, finally, to bring Mr Ramsay into the picture:

> Where was he, that very old man who had gone past her silently, holding a
> brown paper parcel under his arm?   (*TL*, p. 207)

Perhaps his silence, like hers, actually veils an intolerable burden of grief, and a desperate desire for communication. In that case, she and Mr Ramsay might after all have something in common; might, in this sense at least, be 'well matched'. She moves gradually towards him in her reflections, not as before with Paul Rayley, rashly and impulsively and silently, but by re-telling quietly to herself the story of their strained relationship, recalling its imperfections, and seeing that something of value had, after all, emerged from it which might be significant for them both. At the close of *To the Lighthouse*, the narrative endorses this connection:

> 'Bring those parcels,' he said, . . . He rose and stood in the bow of the boat, very straight and tall, . . . sprang, lightly like a young man, holding his parcel, on to the rock.
>   'He must have reached it,' said Lily Briscoe aloud, feeling suddenly tired out. For the Lighthouse had become almost invisible . . . Ah, but she was relieved. Whatever she had wanted to give him, when he left her that morning, she had given him at last.   (*TL*, p. 236)

Unlike Mrs Ramsay, Lily will not be broken by this giving. Because of the nature and the history of her final dialogue with Mr Ramsay, because of the re-telling involved in the process of drafting her own desire, and her own position, into shape, she can, now, complete her own creative endeavour, and move some way towards resolving her feelings of loss and grief.

In doing so, she finds a way of exploding the myth of the Victorian matriarch – the Angel of the House, or chaste Madonna – and does, eventually, move some way towards the possibility of a life 'more infidel' than Mrs Ramsay's. Even Lily Briscoe, with her puckered face, her little Chinese eyes, her earnestness and her chastity, seems to know more about sexuality than Mrs Ramsay, with all her patriarchal disingenuousness and her 'beauty' and her veiling techniques, had seemed able to bequeath.

At the close of *To the Lighthouse*, it is an understanding of the paradoxes and complexities of vitality – and thence, desire – which surfaces, and which begins to establish its own 'beauty', but it does so by presenting a new analysis of Mrs Ramsay as the 'model' of female creativity, since 'beauty' with Mrs Ramsay as its model cannot alone characterise pleasure or desire. For Lily, telling a different story, desire and longing have to be acknowledged as being synonymous, and pleasure calls up loss, elicits grieving. There is such a thing as female creativity, but it is hard-won; the patriarchal hearth is possibly the last place on earth suggestive of harmony. There is a far more complex mapping out of female desire than can be suggested by the route that simply leads to the source of one's own reflection. Like a boat picking its way carefully among the rocks, the artist must make her own way, on her own terms, to the shore, not simply be content to hover around the most obvious source of light. Landing on a rock (being king of the castle) is one thing; creating a new space in which it might be possible to live with vitality and speak out with candour, is quite another.

2

Floundering
(*A Room of One's Own*)

> '"Flounder, flounder, in the sea,
> Come, I pray thee, here to me;
> For my wife, good Ilsabil,
> Wills not as I'd have her will."
>
> "Well, what does she want then?" said the
> Flounder."' And where were they now? Mrs
> Ramsay wondered, reading and thinking,
> quite easily, both at the same time;
> for the story of the Fisherman and his
> Wife was like the bass gently accompanying a
> tune, which now and then ran up unexpectedly
> into the melody.   (*TL*, p. 66)

As she mimics the Flounder's voice, Mrs Ramsay, reading this traditional story about a tyrannical wife to her son, frames her own question, about the whereabouts of Paul and Minta. The story of the Rayleys absorbs her: it is a story she has invented to encapsulate her ideal of marital harmony, despite the misgivings which occasionally filter through to interrupt the continuity of her reflections: 'Was she wrong in this, she asked herself, . . . wondering if she had indeed put any pressure upon Minta, . . . to make up her mind. She was uneasy . . . Marriage needed – oh all sorts of qualities . . . one – she need not name it – *that* was essential; the thing she had with her husband. Had they that?' (p. 70). Such reservations are interspersed with the material she actually speaks aloud – from the story of The Fisherman's Wife – so that this traditional story of marital disharmony seems on occasion to have some ominous bearing on the story of the Rayleys.

A similar dialogue occurs in *A Room of One's Own*, where again, some 'match-making' impulse brings about an interruption to the main story. This time, the story is a discursive one, about the connections between women and fiction – which might mean 'women and what they are like' (there's a joke in there somewhere); or it might mean women and the fiction that is written about them; or it might imply an inextricable mixture of the three (p. 5). One thing is clear: this story can have no conclusion, and Woolf's forays in the British Museum, where she goes in search of supportive material for her lecture on the subject ('Condition in the Middle Ages of, / Habits in the Fiji Islands of, / Worshipped as goddesses by, / Weaker in the moral sense than, . . .' (p. 30)) only serve to prove her point.

The examination of the relationship between women and fiction is bound to be inconclusive because 'when a subject is highly controversial – and any question about sex is that – one cannot hope to tell the truth' (p. 6). Therefore, she will illustrate her own opinions on the subject by the ingenious means of recounting the story of all the impediments and interruptions she encounters in the course of trying to tell it, since 'fiction is here likely to contain more truth than fact' (*ibid.*).

In the course of her story, she recounts the well known incidents of dinner in a women's college, being chased off the grass by a patriarchal beadle, being barred from using the University Library; and she invents a series of characters: Mary Seton, the penniless female student of Fernham, the women's college whose paucity reflects women's historical lack of financial sources; Mary Carmichael, the hapless novelist and depictor of the lot of women who will one day speak out about themselves, but not yet, because she is as yet still 'encumbered with that self-consciousness in the presence of "sin" which is the legacy of our sexual barbarity' (p. 88). Her discoveries in the course of telling this story alert her to the presence of a male elitism, a conspiracy to ensure that women are not only prohibited from utilising resources, but censored so that they are unable to voice their protests, since 'Women have served all these centuries as looking-glasses possessing the magic and delicious power of reflecting the figure of man at twice its natural size' (p. 37), and it is in the interests of men to make sure things remain that way.

Though it may have no conclusion, then, the story does at least have a feminist moral – one that, like the story of The Fisherman's Wife, endorses the power of protest. Using her thesis on women, exemplified by the case of Mary Seton, to endorse her thesis on fiction, illustrated by that of Mary Carmichael, she argues that education for women and a state payment (or a private income? – this is never made clear) of £500 together with a room of one's own, would constitute the sure foundation for all the freedom of speech and movement that a woman needs. It might even enable her to write better fiction, she muses, putting *Life's Adventure*, by Mary Carmichael, tactfully back on the shelf.

Having hit upon this Great Idea, the narrator prepares to put aside her lecture and resume the routines of ordinary life, in which 'nobody cared a straw – . . . – for the future of fiction, the death of poetry or the development by the average woman of a prose style completely expressive of her mind' (p. 94). At this moment, however, an incident occurs which carries tremendous weight in the overall context of Virginia Woolf's writing practice:

> there was a complete lull and suspension of traffic. Nothing came down the street; nobody passed. A single leaf detached itself from the plane tree at the end of the street, and in that pause and suspension fell. Somehow it was like a signal falling, a signal pointing to a force in things which one had overlooked. (*ROO*, p. 95)

The fall of the leaf seems to symbolise a new order of things, but not only that: it seems suggestive of an entirely new mood. A feeling of peace and containment prevails; the pause feels pregnant, and suggestive of both continuity and change; reminiscent, perhaps, of the 'semi mystic, very profound' life of a woman which, Woolf had promised herself, might all be told on one occasion, symbolised, perhaps, by the fall of a flower. The signal, moreover, here seems to point to something concrete: the flow of people up and down the street, a force like an invisible river, which 'took people and eddied them along'. At this moment, it brings together two people: a girl in patent leather boots and a young man in a maroon overcoat (very much the 'modern couple'), together with a convenient symbol of movement and connection, a taxi-cab, into which the couple get and are 'swept on by the current elsewhere'.

The distinguishing feature of this invisible 'current', which seems to be signalled by the falling leaf, is that it is a unifying current – a much less fragmentary and troubling image than that of the two warring currents with which Woolf would have to deal in writing the drafts of *The Waves*, in which 'she' is eventually subsumed into the voice of the male narrator. Here in *A Room of One's Own*, the couple seem to meet as equals, they come from different directions, and they move off together in a third. What was striking and strange about this image, the narrator notes, was not the sight itself, but rather the 'rhythmical order with which [her] imagination had invested it: the sight of two people coming together seemed 'to ease the mind of some strain', as though the effort the narrator has been making to think of the female sex as distinct from the male is an effort, which somehow 'interferes with the unity of the mind' (p. 95).

It is as though the entire project of attempting to identify patriarchal oppression through special pleading by accumulating psychological and material obstructions to clear thinking becomes at this point something of a red herring: the mind of the observer having been, it now seems, distracted, reclaims a feeling of unity from watching a man and a woman come together: the sense of the inevitability of this union and the satisfaction the sight offers echoes the business of Mrs Ramsay's 'match-making', and her sense of the 'rightness' of the union between Paul and Minta:

> it is natural for the sexes to cooperate. One has a profound, if irrational, instinct in favour of the theory that the union of man and woman makes for the greatest satisfaction, the most complete happiness.   (*ROO*, p. 96)

Perhaps Mrs Ramsay was right, after all.

Woolf attempts to redeem her theory from this interruption by weaving the image back into her main theme. The image prompts a new question: perhaps there are two sexes in the mind, as well as – and corresponding to – the two sexes in the body (p. 96). If so, this would serve to prove her contention that a writer cannot write effectively in the face of gender discrimination, by endorsing the theory that a writer must needs have an androgynous mind: a mind capable of employing both male and female perspectives, which would save the woman writer from running the risk of writing against the grain of the male sex, and stridently and reductively in favour of her own.

The theme of androgyny, then, strikes something of a false note, in *A Room of One's Own*, in the sense that it smacks of an attempt on Woolf's part to re-establish a theory she has inadvertently demolished, and it is the origin of the image suggestive of androgyny in a moment of distraction, rather than its philosophical or theoretical implications, which seems significant to the overall perspective, and 'rhythms', of Woolf's writing practice. The power of the idea of androgyny to dislocate or interrupt narrative *seems* to endorse, rather than refute, the project of *A Room of One's Own*, and yet it simply triggers further instances and examples of dislocation. Clearly, the narrator notes, the mind has no absolute integrity, but rather the power constantly to attach itself here, find a mirror for its reflections there, and one can identify oneself with or distinguish oneself from others more or less at random. This is also historically true, so that 'It can think back through its fathers or . . . mothers, as I have said that a woman writing thinks back through her mothers. Again if one is a woman one is often surprised by a sudden splitting off of consciousness, say in walking down Whitehall, when from being the natural inheritor of that civilisation, she becomes, on the contrary, outside of it, alien and critical' (p. 96). As Mary Jacobus has noted, Woolf appears, here, to be writing about sexual difference.[1]

'Difference', as described by Jacobus in relation to *A Room of One's Own*, is a style of feminism which, as Woolf herself did, eschews strident polemicism in favour of a more subtly subversive position, and is distinguishable from Derridian *différance* in that it takes no account of Derrida's theories of time and deferral: for Jacobus, '*difference*, in fact, becomes a traversal of the boundaries inscribed in Virginia Woolf's terms, but a traversal that exposes these very boundaries for what they are' (Jacobus, pp. 12–13). In Jacobus' theory, simultaneity is a key factor, and a woman seeking to expose the more insidious aspects of patriarchy would *simultaneously* seek to identify an unwritten refutation: 'Though necessarily working within "male" discourse, women's writing (in this scheme) would work ceaselessly to write what cannot be written' (*ibid.*). But the problem, as Woolf discovers when she considers the case of 'Mary Carmichael', is that this awareness cannot seem to change the nature of what women actually say, actually write. The only solution to this problem seems reminiscent of Mrs Ramsay's strategy, since it smacks of disingenuousness. In the end, it seems, one can only go on telling stories. As she resolves to make full use of 'all the liberties and licences of a novelist', the narrator begins to tell her story, and as hard fact dissolves into fluid fiction, so the authorial 'I' becomes 'only a convenient term for somebody who has no real being'.

What *is* left in a state of suspension or deferral, in this account, is that symbolic moment in which the leaf detaches itself from the tree and is left suspended, in a state of pause. It is as though no thesis or treatise can actually contain the actual elements of writing practice; there is no way of tracking that 'conclusion' back into a story *about* writing; there is no prior established sign-system that can actually contain the female 'I' in the image of the fall of a flower, or a leaf in the process of detaching itself from a tree.

It is at this point, however, that the thesis, and the style, of *A Room of One's Own* does begin to filter, at some level, into the business of writing as a process: the process Virginia Woolf sat down to daily, the process she lived and breathed, and through which she expressed and defined herself; the creative process which had to remain separate in her mind from the business of 'writing about' such issues as women's oppression; women's education,[2] but it does so by way of presenting new problems, rather than by offering conclusions or solutions.

The plural 'I' touched on in *A Room of One's Own* was constantly experienced by Woolf as a constraint on creativity. As John Mepham has shown, her subtle endeavour to reveal the multiplicity of the writing subject, and the duplicity inherent in the process of subversion involved in writing/'difference', was actually at odds with another quest: the search for some unified centre, some nexus of truth which she would have liked 'to lay hands on and say, "This is it"'; some cohesive subjective identity which would act as a catalyst, in the business of writing and thinking.[3] She sought this all her life, possibly in an unconscious bid to compensate for the absence of a Victorian notion of belief which it was, in part, the business of her writing to subvert.[4]

The danger of identifying a cohesive project for *A Room of One's Own* – a strategic subversion capable of exploiting its own contradictions as an integral part of the subversive process – is that this implies a prior authorial control over her subject matter which both the construction and the genesis of the text belie. She wrote it in response to an invitation to speak on the subject of 'Women and Fiction' at Newnham College, and allowed her mind to range freely over the subject in the initial stages of composition, just as she did when beginning a new novel. 'My mind is woolgathering away about Women & Fiction,' she noted in her Diary (*D*, III, p. 175).

The actual text of the finished work echoes – and parodies – this associative process, in marked contrast to the genesis of *Three Guineas*, to which the very first reference calls up, immediately, a problem of conflicting styles. (The idea for *Three Guineas* interrupted the writing of *The Waves* because it made her 'too much excited', and 'the didactive demonstrative style conflict[ed] with the dramatic') (*D*, IV, p. 6).

She composed *A Room of One's Own*, then, with 'the writing "I"', and encountered in the process a problem she faced with each of her novels. This time, she dramatised it in the persona of Mary Carmichael, the novelist, whom, she prophesied, would ultimately be impeded in her endeavour to tell the truth about women's lives because she would 'still be encumbered with that self-consciousness in the presence of "sin" which is the legacy of our sexual barbarity' (*ROO*, p. 88). Sin is not a theme which is developed at any length in *A Room of One's Own*, though it is given full rein in the later text, 'Professions for Women' (1931), possibly because of the particular context in which it was written and delivered.[5] 'Sin', it transpires from this later piece, amounts when committed by female writers simply to the capacity to think about sexuality, but even that imprecise definition gives an insufficient impression of the full extent of the vacuousness of the term, since the activity is only definable in terms of its failure to achieve expression. 'Sin', in fact, implies the full range of imaginative ground a woman writer is necessarily precluded from covering, given the tenacity of the censorship imposed on women by social and political convention.

In 'Professions for Women', Woolf personifies the censor in the figure of the Angel of the House, thereby drawing attention to the extent to which Victorian women tended to collaborate in strategies to preserve their 'chastity'. As in *A Room of One's Own*, she also invents an additional character: that of the woman writer who is recounting the central story. The Angel in the House, the writer/speaker tells us, used to 'come between me and my paper' (*DoM*, p. 150). She would hover at her shoulder, making encouraging noises about the proper way to review a novel by a 'famous man' ('Be sympathetic; be tender; flatter; deceive') (*ibid.*), her directive quality as a prompt being all the more ironic in the light of the writer's observation that she 'never had a mind or a wish of her own' ('If there was chicken, she took the leg; if there was a draught she sat in it') (*ibid.*).

Under the influence of the Angel, it becomes impossible for the writer to express 'what [she thinks] to be the truth about human relations, morality, sex' (p. 151), not only because chastity is essentially disingenuous, but because Angels 'must charm, must conciliate, they must – to put it bluntly – tell lies if they are to succeed' (*ibid.*). Denying all knowledge of sexuality is the most destructive kind of lie, because it trains women to silence,[6] and in a state of 'chaste' paralysis the only alternative to silence is Bad Faith, a strategy which effectively silences dialogue within a relationship, relegating husband and wife – as in *To the Lighthouse* – into positions of respective tyranny: his overt, hers none the less forceful for being essentially undermining. Eventually, under this regime, it comes to seem as though there is simply no story to tell. ('They both felt uncomfortable, as if they did not know whether to go on or go back. She had been reading fairy tales to James, she said. No, they would not share that; they could not say that') (*TL*, p. 79). This kind of self-censorship, which necessarily silences the other as

well as the self, is ultimately exhausting: 'and [as] she turned to the
Fairy Tale again, Mrs Ramsay felt not only exhausted in body (. . .) but
there also tinged her physical fatigue some other faintly disagreeable
sensation with another origin: . . . she . . . could not bear not being
entirely sure, when she spoke to him, of the truth of what she said' (TL,
p. 46).

The dangerous implications of this censoring process begin to
become apparent during Mrs Ramsay's solitary communications with
herself, during which the reader is given to realise the full extent to
which she can only function on the surface of herself: 'Beneath it is all
dark, it is all spreading, it is unfathomably deep; but now and again we
rise to the surface and that is what you see us by' (TL, p. 73). The
character of Mrs Ramsay is in fact positioned somewhere between that
of the stereotypical Victorian matriarch and that of Lily Briscoe, who
cannot go on indefinitely playing the unwritten part of Angel. In the
text of *To the Lighthouse*, what began, historically, as strategic disingenuousness has gradually developed into something more dangerously resembling hysteria, which Woolf leaves largely, in that novel, in
a state of pregnant suspension: it is something which it will be left to
succeeding generations of 'daughters' to unravel. Lily can begin on it,
but it is a complicated process, this difficult art, which cannot yet be
fully assimilated into women's lives, of 'smooth[ing] out something she
had been given years ago folded up' (TL, p. 226).

This particular inheritance promises to be a long and painful process
since, as Woolf herself perceived, it would involve continually looking
backwards as well as forwards, and one aspect of looking backwards is
that key moments in the past seem veiled, shrouded, bearing the full
weight of their having been subject to a consistent and rigorous process
of censorship. In 'Professions for Women', Woolf was to go on to warn
the reader of this difficulty by inventing yet another novelist, the 'girl
novelist' (another version, perhaps, of 'Mary Carmichael'), whom she
likens (throwing her attention to gender to the wind) to a fisherman,
'lying sunk in dreams on the verge of a deep lake with a rod held out
over the water'. The fisherman is letting her imagination loose among
'every nook and cranny of the world that lies submerged in the depths
of our unconscious being', when suddenly, 'there was a smash. There
was an explosion. There was foam and confusion. The imagination had
dashed itself against something hard.' What had happened? She had
thought of something: 'something about the body, about the passions
which it was unfitting for her as a woman to say. Men, her reason told
her, would be shocked' (DoM, p. 152).

The phallic connotations of this hardly need pointing out. In the language of women's dreams, there *is* a story about passion, about sexuality, a story which could, presumably, be told with facility, but the fisherman's tale (here, the fisherman functions as her own 'Wife') forcibly reminds us of the legacy of Victorian patriarchy: that 'chastity' was not simply a linguistic euphemism for women's only right of access within patriarchy to a modicum of power, it also had to be taken literally.[7] Inherent in the conspiracy of female submission is, then, a practice of sexual censorship which ironically becomes interfused with a politics practised by women themselves – Mrs Ramsay's politics of sympathy, her 'knitting' – so that their practice of subduing the male sex begins insidiously to work against them. The sustaining image of the Rayleys takes on a double edge in the light of all this. The main problem with the manipulative and disingenuous style of 'chastity' practised by Mrs Ramsay is that it so closely resembles – and thereby implicitly encourages – other repressive practices, but also that it uses the female body as the focus of all these subversive practises. In the final analysis, then, women are rendered inert, inarticulate and frigid, like Mrs Dalloway, who has managed to preserve her 'virginity' even through the experience of childbirth. If the Rayleys' marriage has 'worked loose' and cannot encapsulate this nexus of social and linguistic systems, perhaps this has something to do with Minta's sexual integrity, her slightly sluttish nonchalance, and her related disregard for the conventions of polite time-keeping (she is 'wreathed, tinted, garish . . . at three o' clock in the morning') (*TL*, 196).

If the image of the 'modern couple' in the taxi in *A Room of One's Own* occupies the same function and status within the text as that of the Rayleys, in *To the Lighthouse*, then the concept of androgyny takes on a dubious value as a means of interrogation, and may even turn out to be yet another of Virginia Woolf's distancing techniques. The 'splitting off of consciousness' which suggests an androgynous possibility becomes important because it seems to suggest something more cohesive, more fully functioning, than women's silence, but the sight of the couple in the taxi, signalled not by some new cohesion but rather by something first dislocated, then suspended, seems to suggest something *beyond* the possibility of androgyny: the possibility of inventing – or even of being – a much more fully operative, 'whole' woman, who might function with facility within a dialogue, within a sexual relationship: someone who might actually be able to take up, and maintain, a position *vis-à-vis* the outside world. This remains, though, a vision which is simply glimpsed, glanced at, and as soon disappears. It is a vision and a possibility which will need to be held – like Mrs Ramsay's bevy of daughters' dreams of a more 'infidel' life – in suspension; it must happen in its own time.

Referring, in 'Professions for Women', to the two 'genuine' experiences of her own, the 'key adventures of [her] professional life' (*DoM*, p. 153), the narrator of the piece asserts her conviction that the first adventure – the killing of the Angel – has been successfully accomplished (it is a version of this 'adventure' that Lily Briscoe slowly and painstakingly undergoes in order to complete her painting, in *To the Lighthouse*). But, she admits, 'the second, telling the truth about my own experiences as a body, I do not think I solved. I doubt that any woman has solved it yet. The obstacles against her are still immensely powerful – and yet they are very difficult to define' (*ibid.*). The very syntax of the sentence, which effects the separation of the subject from her own body, serves to exemplify this assertion.[8] Though the project outlined in *A Room of One's Own* does indeed announce the beginnings of a strategic, feminist intervention, to be achieved in writing, a comparison of the text with other 'fictions' by Virginia Woolf – 'Professions for Women'; *To the Lighthouse* – reveals the extreme delicacy, subtlety and elusiveness of this vision. There is still a great deal to be undergone before Virginia Woolf can begin to construct within *herself* – even within the relatively safe confines of the imagination – the relevant, and effective, means of transport.

3

Writing About Love (*Orlando*)

> She was married, true; but if one's husband was always sailing round Cape Horn, was it marriage? If one liked other people, was it marriage? And finally, if one still wished, more than anything in the world, to write poetry, was it marriage? (*O*, pp. 186–7)

In *To the Lighthouse* Virginia Woolf cracked the code of Mrs Ramsay's veiled surface; dramatised her ability to maintain the illusion of harmony in place of loss, and showed Lily undoing, or piercing the veil of, that drama, by substituting for Mrs Ramsay's 'harmonizing principle' another story. Lily's painting functions in the novel as a new attempt to fill in the gaps in Mrs Ramsay's story, and represents for Lily a triumph not only over Mrs Ramsay but over her own experience, with William Bankes, of disingenuous love.

Given the nature, and complexity, of *To the Lighthouse*'s message, it was inevitable that one aspect of Lily's self discovery should have been left unresolved. How, given the vagaries of female sexuality, might it have been possible; how – in another story – might it be possible; for Lily to resolve her discovery of desire – its roots in the unconscious and its connections with the artistic process – with her desire for human continuity? The germ of such a story, as the ending of *To the Lighthouse* makes clear, is in her tenuous relationship, not with William Bankes, but finally with Mr Ramsay who, displaying his parcel of grief, suddenly manifests his need for condolence: for sympathy, that is, but this time without selfishness: for a connection forged on the basis of a shared emotion which is now, in both Mr Ramsay and Lily, tied up, smoothed over. Intimacy, Lily discovers in this novel, might after all be based on the mutual recognition of shared experience which can no longer, or not yet, be enacted; on a sharing of *unconscious* desires and recollections.

In *To the Lighthouse*, this relationship cannot be pursued, partly because the design of the novel cannot fully contain it, and partly because the needs of Mr Ramsay and Lily are not synchronised in time: Mr Ramsay is old enough to be Lily's father. Perhaps, in order to fully explore the notion of intimacy, it might be necessary to write a story in which human time were wholly usurped, in which roles were reversed, man and nature seemed almost interchangeable, and all the rules of individual and historical development in time were broken. If playfulness of this kind were to turn out to be just another distancing technique, so much the worse. Virginia Woolf went on to follow *To the Lighthouse* with just such a novel, in *Orlando*.

One of the most important elements of the new novel was ascertained at the outset. Woolf recorded in her Diary her first few, cursory thoughts, noting that she seemed to have shelved the idea of her earlier thoughts 'of a flower whose petals fall; of all time telescoped into one lucid channel through wh. my heroine was to pass at will' (*D*, III, 131). The genesis of *Orlando* came out of a conversation with Faith Henderson during which Woolf, 'valiantly beating the waters of conversation', began to sketch out 'the possibilities which an unattractive woman, penniless, alone, might yet bring into being' (*ibid.*). The initial idea was to turn this into a 'Defoe narrative', and out of this she conceived a fantasy, to be entitled 'The Jessamy Brides', centred around two women, 'poor, solitary at the top of a house', from which they can 'see anything'. Significantly, these two are conceived as looking outwards onto the world, rather than inwards into the leaves of a plant, as 'she' was originally to have been able to do.

From the outset, *Orlando* was conceived as something of a jaunt: 'No attempt is to be made to realise the character. Sapphism is to be suggested. Satire is to be the main note – satire & wildness . . . My own lyric vein is to be satirised. Everything mocked . . . For the truth is I feel the need of an escapade after these serious poetic experimental books whose form is always so closely considered. I want to kick up my heels and be off' (*ibid.*). It *is* possible, then, to imagine a fully liberated, playful and vital female, but only in fiction. No matter: Woolf is a novelist, and she clearly feels, here, as though she has hit on a mood in which she can encapsulate some new note of recklessness. Having safely relegated the idea to the realms of 'escapade', she can begin to give the idea free rein.

The licence Woolf gave herself to parody her own lyricism was a crucial factor in the writing of *Orlando*, since it enabled her to write fluently and so to release, with tremendous vitality and verve, a whole influx of ideas and emotions which the tightly knit text of *To the Lighthouse* had initiated, but held in check. Again the new novel was to be about art and sexuality, continuity and design, and the connections between intimacy and the unconscious; but in addition, it parodied, and so illustrated in the most extravagant and dazzling of ways, the tendency of desire to masquerade. *Orlando* poses a number of deeply serious questions about the connections between writing and desire, but for both reader and writer it seems to happen upon such questions quite by chance, so demonstrating the curious limit to the writer's conscious control over her own creative processes.

Most obviously, the composition of *Orlando*, and the spirit in which it was written, enabled Woolf to write about eroticism; about pleasure and desire. It is as though the erotic element which Lily Briscoe had gradually and painstakingly teased out of her narrative could now be released, in *Orlando*, into a novel of its own. The sexuality of both man and woman is dramatised from the point of view of the central subject; Orlando changes sex in the middle of the narrative, to make this possible. The inheritance of sexual freedom is traced not only from one generation to the next, but from the Elizabethan period to the present day. Purity, Chastity and Modesty – the Victorian trappings of a culture which kept women in subservience and denied them sexual expression – are despatched with all the pomp and ceremony character-istic of the Victorian Age, and a prose which is playful, witty and sensual ensues.

Running through the jest which centres an entire novel around the notion of sexual freedom, however, there is also an implicit attempt to make a serious point about literary inheritance. *Orlando* is a mock biography and, at one level, the story of Virginia Woolf's affair with Vita Sackville-West.[1] But Orlando's source in Vita served a specific purpose within the novel. It has been suggested that Orlando's sex change represented for Woolf not only a way of writing about andro-gyny but also a way of documenting the appearance of the woman writer within the story of the literary tradition. But this is to ignore a central issue in the novel: the discussions about the real issue and status of Orlando's *writing*. Significantly, Orlando – as both male and female subject – spends a great deal of time in the novel trying to write an epic poem, 'The Oak Tree', and one of his/her predominant struggles during the course of the story is to liberate poetry (which arguably takes the strain which in Woolf's other novels has been carried by women) from ridiculous and decadent conventions.

Of course, writing is parodied in *Orlando*, along with everything else – inheritance, sexual politics and even the course of history itself – all of which Woolf exposes, in this novel, as being blindly followed and ludicrously misunderstood. Men, in particular, seem to take everything absurdly literally, and Orlando, the earnest male poet, is no exception:

> He was describing, . . . nature, and in order to match the shade of green precisely he looked (and here he showed more audacity than most) at the thing itself, which happened to be a laurel bush growing beneath the window. After that, of course, he could write no more. Green in nature is one thing, green in literature another.   (*O*, p. 11)

The patriarchal assumption that creativity is all a question of match-making prevails.

Compared with Lily Briscoe's attempts to grapple with the problems of the hedge, Orlando's diligent attempts seem farcical. He does no better, moreover, out of the other conventional route to fame, that of patronage. His meeting with the celebrated poet, Nick Greene, does nothing to ensure for him a foothold on the path to success, since the famous poet is far too bound up with his own public image to be of any particular help to the young Orlando.

He abandons the attempt, but takes up the pen again after his girlfriend, Sasha, with whom he is all-consumingly in love, has abandoned him. Her departure has a strange effect on him and a marked effect, too, on the narrative, which at this juncture suddenly takes on all the qualities of a fairy tale. Orlando lies as if in a trance for full seven days, and when he awakes, 'though he was perfectly rational and seemed graver and more sedate in his ways than before, he appeared to have an imperfect recollection of his past life' (p. 47). Loss affects the memory, affects the way we think back: in parody of this, Woolf has Orlando (who always does go to extremes) lose his memory altogether. Moreover, not only his memory but his creative powers are also affect-ed by the severity of his experience. His grief is repressed, masked (like that of many of the characters in Woolf's 'straight' novels), but visible to the reader through his listless desolation, which finally finds expres-sion when it is triggered (again, Woolf is here parodying a serious point) through a contiguous image: the sight of 'a Dutch snow scene by an unknown artist', which reduces him to tears (p. 51).

Significantly, the sudden articulation of his grief releases in *Orlando* the desire first to read, then to write, but again he is obstructed, not, this time, by the inability to match his prose to the real thing, but by the intervention of memory and desire. He has progressed significantly since his previous attempt, but is now baffled by the range of seemingly disconnected subject matter which his writing suddenly seems to release: sitting down to write triggers 'a thousand odd, disconnected fragments, now bright, now dim, hanging and bobbing and dipping and flaunting, . . .' (p. 55) which may, perhaps, anticipate the imagery of early passages from *The Waves*. What is being reactivated here is a parody of the kind of chaos that writing 'remembers': a flood of highly charged but seemingly insignificant images which, at first, seem to come in a rush of energy which frees them from their ordinary structures and codes of signification. Running in contiguous relation to this access of emotion, which affects the way things are seen and described, are the more plangent and seemingly more immediate questions relating to the current experience of loss: 'Where was she? and why had she left him? . . . Was she married?' (*ibid.*).

He tries to solve the problem by giving his full attention to the problem of love, which proves extremely time-consuming: 'It would be no exaggeration to say that he would go out after breakfast a man of thirty and come home to dinner a man of fifty-five at least' (p. 70); then he takes up again the problem of turning some of these thoughts into writing, but his inability to disentangle thoughts and images brings him back full circle to the problem of attempting to hold a mirror up to nature (after all, he is an Elizabethan):

> So then he tried saying the grass is green and the sky is blue and so to propitiate the austere spirit of poetry whom still, though at a great distance, he could not help reverencing. 'The sky is blue,' he said, 'the grass is green.' Looking up, he saw that, on the contrary, the sky is like veils which a thousand Madonnas have let fall from their hair; . . .   (*O*, pp. 71–2)

Finally, casting ambition to the wind, he gives up, reflecting that he would rather remain anonymous, amorphous, even rather primal, if by doing so he can somehow avoid taking responsibility for his own point of view, in a world seemingly composed largely of potentially hostile critics. Again, the language of *The Waves* is anticipated in parody: he lies, 'Sunk for a long time in profound thoughts as to the value of security, and the delight of having no name, but being like a wave which returns to the deep body of the sea; thinking how obscurity rids the mind of the irk of envy or spite . . .' (pp. 73–4).

This mood of his is auspicious, in the overall context of Woolf's writing practice. If *The Waves* can be glimpsed in embryo here, so, too, can *Between the Acts*, in which Woolf would go on to examine in detail the notion of literary origins. But in one sense, at least, *Orlando* sticks closely to the confines and constraints of literary biography in the old style: Woolf steers, in this novel, entirely free from any temptation to compose any radical framework for history or for her depiction of the unconscious, keeping, for the time being, her time span (here, of three hundred years) well within the boundaries of the traditional narrative. Rather than deviating from the frameworks of traditional story-telling structure or style, she instead offers a quite different method of examining Orlando's origins: Orlando becomes, at this juncture, a woman.

Orlando's sex change has received wide attention, most critics endorsing Winifred Holtby's early view that Woolf 'makes Orlando change from man to woman in order to pursue her own particular theory of the sexes' (Holtby, p. 178).[2] Woolf's 'theory of the sexes' is alluded to, of course, in *A Room of One's Own*, where she proposes to 'amateurishly sketch a plan of the soul' (pp. 96–7), based on the premise that there might be 'two sexes in the mind corresponding to the two sexes in the body' (p. 96). But the implications are complex, and the problem of depicting this theory in imagery, and in a narrative framework, which might be sustained for the duration of a story, is one which Woolf is no more able to solve than Orlando. The theory is straightforward, but the creative imagery which ensues suggests that what is actually at stake is the difficulty of sustaining a vision within the framework of which female potency might find a form in which it might be creatively re-appropriated within the patriarchal design: in *A Room of One's Own* Woolf envisages a man, a woman, and also an appropriate vehicle.

The main problem, as Orlando discovers, is that writing seems incapable of fully appropriating the other without cost to the stability of the self: as an activity, it releases powerful feelings of loss but with those feelings an accompanying sensation of lack, which feels debilitating rather than enabling, as the female Orlando is forced to realise when she tries to rehearse in writing her desolation at being abandoned by The Archduke Harry. There is something grandiose about such feelings, but the writing seems unable to reflect this, as the immortal (and unfinished) line, 'Life and a lover' (p. 130) denotes. It seems to sum up the feeling, but it 'did not scan and made no sense with what went before' (*ibid.*). Perhaps, then, the narrator suggests, this inability to give full expression to feelings of lack and loss might in some way be connected with the changes which have taken place in Orlando since her transformation into a woman: 'For example, . . . Orlando hid her manuscripts when interrupted. Next, . . . looked long and intently in the glass; and now, . . . one might notice her starting and suppressing a cry when the horses galloped faster than she liked' (p. 131).

The change of dress, it is hazarded, might well be a contributing factor to these changes in her character.[3] If women's clothes inhibit movement, perhaps they also function as impediments to self-expression. On the other hand, dress may simply be a disguise: the only concession to 'masculinity' and 'feminity' that in fact holds any sway. The image of a gendered person, which dress appears to serve to reflect, may in fact have nothing in common with the wearer's sexuality; 'sometimes it may be that underneath the sex is the very opposite of what it is above' (p. 133) The problem for the reader, in relation to all such asides within the narrative of *Orlando*, is that the narrator consistently plays tricks: no sooner has a hypothesis of this kind been set up, than its opposite is dramatised, for it is in fact not androgyny at all which occasions Orlando's completion of 'The Oak Tree'. It is love and marriage, just as Mrs Ramsay might have predicted: the poem can only be written when Orlando recognises that she wants to be married, just like everyone else, and that her creativity is actually bound up not just with definitions of the self, or of feminity in general, but with her dialogue and intimacy with the other – in this case, the ludicrously named and lavishly attired Marmaduke Bonthrop Shelmerdine.

Falling in love is, of course, also subject to parody, but there is, as always, a serious point at the back of Woolf's depiction of Orlando's route to full-blown, disorientating and creatively productive desire. Pulling out her blood-stained, travel-strained manuscript again after a hundred years or so, Orlando recalls her youth as a gloomy boy, reflecting that, after all, very little has really changed: 'The house and garden are precisely as they were,' she reflects (p. 167). 'Not a chair has been moved, not a trinket sold. There are the same walks, the same lawns, the same . . . pool, which, I dare say, has the same carp in it.' The reflection evolves into a parody of a statement about history (and anticipates the imagery of a similar scene in *Between the Acts*),[4] but almost immediately 'history' is interrupted by the arrival of her butler and her housekeeper. Writing poetry was impossible with these two in the room, but no sooner has this thought taken shape than 'to her astonishment and alarm, the pen began to curve and caracole with the smoothest possible fluency' (p. 167).

She is suddenly inspired to compose some truly romantic poetry, being much influenced by rhyme and metre and, as ever, becoming lost for words when she is lost for a rhyme. What she writes here – practically the reader's only glimpse at the text of 'The Oak Tree' – is important, since it influences the ensuing narrative. The verse, needless to say, is pure doggerel, but she nevertheless has something significant to say. The lyric runs,

> I am myself a vile link
> > Amid life's weary chain,
> But I have spoken hallow's words,
> > Oh, do not say in vain!
> Will the young maiden, when her tears,
> > Alone in moonlight shine,
> Tears for the absent and the loved,
> > Murmur –
> >   (*O*, p. 168)

'I am thine' is, presumably, the rest of the couplet, but the reader is not given this: perhaps it is too intimate, or perhaps she hides it from the view of the butler and housekeeper, Bartholomew and Basket, who are continuing to grunt and groan about the room. She pauses here to dip her ink, and continues, uninterrupted, to write about time:

> She was so changed, the soft carnation cloud
> Once mantling o'er her cheek like that which eve
> Hangs o'er the sky, glowing with roseate hue,
> Had faded into paleness, broken by
> Bright burning blushes, torches of the tomb,
> >   (*O*, p. 168)

But here she spills her ink: 'She was all of a quiver, all of a stew . . . What had happened to her?' (*ibid.*). What is happening is that she is responding, on a deeper level than she is aware of, to what she has just written, the gist of which is disturbing, despite the hackneyed style. Despite her consistent and flamboyant transcendence over the constraints of history, history is finally here catching up with her. She is ageing, along with the century. She is mortal. She is alone.

At this point, it is as though what she has written begins to filter back through to its originating source. Her entire body becomes highly tuned, at first indiscriminately: she is conscious of 'an extraordinary tingling and vibration all over her, as if she were made of a thousand wires upon which some breeze or errant fingers were playing scales. Now her toes tingled; now her marrow. She had the queerest sensations about the thigh bones' (p. 168). But soon, (in parody of a Freudian symptom) the sensation becomes focused, and its location enables her to identify the cause of her distress: the 'quivering' feeling comes to rest in the second finger of her left hand which, by contrast with the housekeeper's 'thick ring of rather jaundiced yellow' (p. 169), is noticeably bare.

From this moment on, everywhere she goes, she notices wedding rings. The tingling persists, preventing her from writing, and enabling the narrator to arrive at a piece of wisdom to do with the writing process: '– that we write, not with the fingers, but with the whole person' (p. 171). As ever, though, an insight which would, in any other novel by Virginia Woolf, have been excavated, or perhaps simply, here, a colophon which might elsewhere have been traced to its medieval source, is passed over, enabling Orlando to come to her revelatory conclusion: that though 'the seat of her trouble seemed to be her left hand', she was in fact becoming 'poisoned through and through': there was nothing for it, therefore, but to 'yield completely and submissively to the spirit of the age, and take a husband' (p. 171).

That this impulse goes markedly against her independent nature stays her temporarily from doing so. In the face of her feelings of lack and loss, she is drawn to thoughts of death, romantically styling herself 'nature's bride' and 'giving herself in rapture to the cold embraces of the grass as she lay' on the moor (p. 175). But because this is *Orlando*, the spirit of the age triumphs in the end. Just as she is falling asleep, having flung herself romantically to the ground, she hears the unmistakable sound of horses' hooves approaching. The hooves were coming nearer and nearer:

> She sat upright. Towering dark against the yellow-slashed sky of dawn, with the plovers rising and falling about him, she saw a man on horseback.
>
> 'Madame,' the man cried, leaping to the ground, 'you're hurt!'
>
> 'I'm dead sir!' she replied.
>
> A few minutes later they became engaged. (O, p. 176)

The marriage is a 'modern' one: Orlando and Shel discover in each other both manly and womanly qualities, and neither has the least desire to curb the other's freedom: 'they would talk; and then, when her feet were fairly covered with spotted autumn leaves, Orlando would rise and stroll away into the heart of the woods in solitude, leaving Bonthrop sitting there . . . making models of Cape Horn. 'Bonthrop,' she would say, 'I'm off' (p. 182), and off she would go. (Vita Sackville-West's marriage to Harold Nicolson was obviously a model for Woolf here.)[5] It should be said, of course, that a few hours of solitude were always enough: presently a jay would shriek, 'Shelmerdine'; the echo – 'Orlando' – would reverberate, and they would passionately re-unite.

Soon, however, the consistent stength of the liaison is such that something curious begins to happen: the wind gets up; she appeals to him by his full name and he replies – 'Orlando!':

> and the words went dashing and circling . . . like wild hawks together among the belfries higher and higher, faster and faster they circled, till they crashed and fell in a shower of fragments to the ground; and she went in.   (O, p. 185)

This is as momentous and as unexpected as anything that has happened so far to turn the tide of the narrative and, for the reader, perhaps more difficult to decipher than anything that has preceded it. There is some mysterious process afoot, which seems to demand the presence of Orlando behind the scenes. It is not at all clear, until the reader turns the page and comes upon an entirely new chapter of Orlando's life, exactly what it is that is taking place, but at the beginning of Chapter Six all begins to be revealed: it is time for Orlando, having organised all the other conditions of her life to most fruitful advantage, to retreat and finish writing 'The Oak Tree'. The arousal of her passion has mobilised her creative resources (again, Woolf is here dramatising in parody a serious point), and she must finish her poem.

But not – as always in *Orlando*, whose narrator is meticulous – without, first, a diversion: if she is so anxious to take up her pen again, what is the status of her marriage? She had yielded to the enticement to become a wife, given herself in marriage in a spirit of proper submission: what, then, is she doing brandishing this powerful instrument of her independence and individuality? Significantly, it is not *just* the writing that prompts this question; there are, to put it discreetly, other areas of dissatisfaction: her husband seemed to spend most of his time sailing round Cape Horn (a bit like Mr Ramsay in his boat): was it, then, marriage? She liked other people (as, it is hinted in *To the Lighthouse*, did Minta Rayley): then was it marriage? And finally, she 'wished, more than anything in the whole world, to write poetry': what, then, is the status of this marriage? (pp. 186–7).

Again, a digression which in other novels by Virginia Woolf would have been developed and explored is here broken through by Orlando's capacity to triumph over introspection: it is, after all, a potentially dangerous set of questions. The narrator wisely declines to allow Orlando to dwell on them and, in the style of 'in one bound Jack was free', the narrative takes over and spares her the necessity of worrying about her marital problems by immersing her in her writing (it may be noted in passing, here, that this was of course Virginia Woolf's own solution): ' "Hang it all!" she cried, with a touch of her old spirit, "Here goes!" And she plunged her pen neck deep in the ink' (p. 187).

A power resembling the Angel of the House appears at one point, to question a risqué use of imagery ('the snaky flower – a thought strong from a lady's pen, perhaps, . . .' (p. 187)), but she makes a quick mental check on Orlando's credentials and decides to let it pass: 'You have a husband at the Cape, you say? Ah, well, that'll do' (*ibid.*). Husbands can come in useful, particularly as foils to androgynous tendencies. The interruption draws Orlando's attention to the suspicion that if the contents of her creative mind were held up for examination, there might indeed be much that might not escape the censor. However, she has managed, 'by putting on a ring and finding a man on the moor, by loving nature and being no satirist, cynic or psychologist' (p. 188) to pass herself off as a good Victorian, and so, effectively masquerading chastity, she encounters no further interruptions from the Angel to the writing of 'The Oak Tree'.

'The Oak Tree' is a success, receiving accolades and a speech from Nick Greene, though Orlando cares only for the oak tree itself and has attempted in her poetry to celebrate its organic nature, rather than (in the Nick Greene mode) her own ego. Eventually she decides to bury the manuscript, as a tribute, 'a return to the land of what the land has given me' (p. 229), but the words sound very silly, since the writing of poetry is essentially 'a secret transaction' (*ibid.*). The echo of the writer's voice in the public sphere is therefore insignificant to Orlando, and if the narrative can devise a language which offers the reader the *illusion* that he or she is a party to the secret – and this illusionist capacity is fundamental to the parody of *Orlando* – it cannot make a consistent narrative of such moments: it cannot turn Orlando's moments of being – ' "Ecstacy!" she cried, "ecstacy!" And then the wind sank, the waters grew calm; and she was the waves rippling peacefully in the moonlight' – into a consistently amusing narrative such as the one that tells the story of *Orlando*.

While Orlando is completing 'The Oak Tree', turning aside from the surface life in order to give her full attention to her work of art, the narrative is, somewhat embarrassingly, left idle:

> It was now November. After November, comes December. Then January, February, March and April. After April comes May. June, July, August follow. Next is September. Then October, and so, behold, here we are back at November again, with a whole year accomplished.
> This method of writing biography, though it has its merits, is a little bare, . . .   (*O*, pp. 188–9)

The problem is that the subject of the biography is having very little visual impact at the moment: she is simply sitting in a chair, writing her poem. There is, to all intents and purposes, surely no 'Life' to be written if the sum total of the subject's activities amounts to 'sitting in a chair and thinking' (*ibid.*).

Perhaps for this reason, we are given no more of the content of 'The Oak Tree', only the news of its completion and of its success; and the narrative is able to bound back into action only when Orlando has put her writing behind her and proceeds to produce a son, mourn the absence of her husband at Cape Horn and observe, by looking about her in the streets, that the times are again in the process of changing. The process of having produced her poem has put her in touch again with the raw edge of her creativity, and the novel's grande finale is the news of Shelmerdine's return. Since it is by now 1928, he returns in an aeroplane, to an Orlando 'trembling in the moonlight': 'Her pearls' (like Vita's?) 'burnt like a phosphorescent flare in the darkness' (p. 232).

As 'Shel' arrives, a wild goose flies cryptically overhead and the stroke of midnight sounds: it is (pedantically) 'the twelfth stroke of midnight, Thursday, the eleventh of October, Nineteen Hundred and Twenty-Eight' (the publication date of *Orlando*). And that is the end of the story. As one critic has observed, the moment is quite empty.[6] The entire story, it now seems, has been an illusion: a literary mirage.

4

No Quite Solid Table
(*The Waves*)

There is *something* there (. . .) but I can't get at it, squarely; . . . I am in an odd
state; feel a cleavage; here's my interesting thing; & there's no quite solid
table on which to put it.   (*D*, III, p. 264)

In *Orlando*, Virginia Woolf had invented a character capable of
transcending history, a character who could articulate desire, loss, and
aspiration; a character who was capable – as both man and woman – of
both falling in love and creating a work of art. She framed the story of
Orlando in a narrative capable of encompassing all these aspects of her
character's personality, but without ever 'digging' into any of these
issues: she slid across the surface of them in a witty parody of the
agonies and the ecstacies of love and creativity, and the novel's
conclusion is – as it were – a puff of smoke, in which the whole of the
novel goes up, and as swiftly disappears. We are asked, as readers, to
take for granted the narrator's authority but never guaranteed that we
can trust it. Orlando's memory is far from reliable, and warns us not to
expect him/her to reflect too deeply on such recollections as do emerge.
The narrator, as is revealed when Orlando finally sits down to complete
her poem, cannot be expected to linger for a moment, let alone to
include a retrospective dimension of any depth: this is not a novel
which furthers the development of Woolf's 'tunnelling process'.

  Orlando is about history, but history set firmly within its traditional
frameworks and constraints, and the question of Orlando's origins
is presented as all part of the running jest. The notion of the individual unconscious is parodied rather than seriously explored, though
Orlando is clearly drawing on its reserves. 'A voice answering a voice'
(p. 229) is Orlando's definition of the creative process, but *Orlando* is
presented in such a way that there is no real opportunity to dwell
on the implications of this definition: *Orlando* is about the surface
life; history, if not gender, is what you see us by; 'life' is visible,

and linear. If it leaves a lot to be desired, it does at least make a good story.

In *Orlando*, Woolf indulged herself by exposing, rather than calling to question, this set of assumptions, and there is a sense in which the writing, in its spontaneity, seems to be indulging her: Vita Sackville-West brought out the playfulness in Virginia, and both *Orlando* and *A Room of One's Own* bear the marks of this dizzy weightlessness. The holograph draft of *Orlando* bears, by contrast, a note on the intended text which suggests that, despite her initial, sudden desire to write something playful and fluent in the style of Defoe, she had originally intended something in a rather more serious vein. The note reads:

A Biography
This is to tell a person's life from the
year 1500 to 1928.
Changing its sex,
taking different aspects of the character in
different centuries. The theory being that
character goes on underground before we
are born; and leaves something afterwards
also.[1]

Though *Orlando* does, in a lighthearted way, trace a character as he/she evolves through several centuries, the idea that 'character goes on underground' was not something Woolf chose to explore with any degree of seriousness in *Orlando*. She opted, instead, for a cohesive and shapely narrative, and noted, on completing the first draft, 'a serene, accomplished feeling, to write, even provisionally, The End.'[2] She was well aware of the cost to her original plan of this rare, luxurious feeling, recording even as she noted her satisfaction with the completed novel that she would nevertheless want to go on to develop her 'tunnelling' process, on completing it. She noted in her Diary that in avoiding her usual tendency to 'explore', she had managed, in *Orlando*, to 'keep the realities at bay': *Orlando* was, she judged, 'a very quick brilliant book', which 'taught [her] continuity & narrative', but, she added, 'I purposely avoided of course any other difficulty.' As a result, she had failed to make the kinds of connection she had managed to forge in *To the Lighthouse*: 'I never got down to my depths & made shapes square up, as I did in The Lighthouse' (*D*, III, p. 203).

The impulse, now that *Orlando* was finished, was of course to go on, but she realised that, in one sense at least, this would mean backtracking her steps in order to retrieve and re-shape 'the depths'. There was always, for Woolf, a thread connecting one novel to the next, and she had already, on finishing *To the Lighthouse*, 'toyed vaguely with some thoughts of a flower whose petals fall; of time all telescoped into one lucid channel'[3] by the time she hit upon the original idea for *Orlando*, but what emerged was an idea on a much grander and more flamboyant scale. Following on from the idea to lighten the tone and write a 'Defoe narrative', she conceived of an idea 'to sketch here, like a grand historical picture, the outlines of all my friends':[4] again, the idea was abandoned in favour of a 'grand, historical' portrait of a colourfully androgynous creature, to be modelled on Vita.[5] By the time she came to write *The Waves* both the idea of the flower in a state of pregnant suspension, about to fall, and the idea for a *collective* sketch – a 'historical' sketch of a group of friends – were beginning to re-emerge as themes.

The idea to sketch a kind of group portrait seems to have formed the basis of Woolf's subsequent work, *The Waves*, and with the idea to extend outwards to cover more than one individual went the attempt to sketch out something that might be more profoundly suggestive of 'character' and its origins; and the method of providing rough outlines or sketches, brief snatches of dialogue recording impressions and recollections, seemed to predominate throughout the drafting of this new project.

From the outset, *The Waves* seemed to present Woolf with par-ticularly gruelling problems of composition. She felt, almost straight away, that the work was somehow cleaving or splitting her: it seemed to have profound and contradictory roots in her, but she could not identify quite *what* it was that she seemed to be working towards:

> There is *something* there (. . .) but I can't get at it, squarely; nothing like the speed & certainty of The Lighthouse: Orlando mere childs play. Is there some falsity, of method, somewhere? Something tricky? – so that the interesting things aren't firmly based? I am in an odd state; feel a cleavage; here's my interesting thing; & there's no quite solid table on which to put it . . . (*D*, III, p. 264)

She was convinced that she was 'right to seek for a station whence [she could] set [her] people against time & the sea', but experienced difficulty in 'digging oneself in there, with conviction' (*ibid.*).

It seemed difficult to retrieve access to the level of engagement with which she had written *To the Lighthouse*, and thence to 'feel out' her subject matter, since an engagement with 'the depths' of her creative resources would entangle her again in all the imagery of time and the sea which for her was connected so closely with feelings of loss and confusion. But it was that very quality of loss – and obscurity – which seems nevertheless to have haunted her throughout the writing of *The Waves*, and to which she clearly wanted, there, to give expression. She was writing this time, she resolved, about the present and about the lives of her friends, not about death or grieving, but an analysis of developing human vitality, and its inter-connectedness, brought back into play some 'thing' for which there seemed to be no ready description. Interestingly, the 'thing' seems intact, if indescribable; what is lacking – or at least, intangible – is the object by comparison with which it would gain definition. (This fumbling gesture towards a description of subjectivity is reminiscent of Lily Briscoe's attempt to follow Andrew Ramsay's advice and think of Mr Ramsay's work on 'subject and object and the nature of reality' in the form of a kitchen table when there's nobody there (p. 28): the image of a scrubbed kitchen table becomes for her the 'symbol of her profound respect for Mr Ramsay's mind.' (p. 30).) For a woman describing the 'nature of reality' in terms of the relationship between subject and object, it seems much more difficult to find a suitable object to take as a starting point: Lily's is borrowed, provisional, rather than entirely integral to her purposes.

If the initial germ of an idea (conceived, now, as many as two years ago) for a book which would chart the 'semi mystic, very profound life of a woman' gradually evaporated as *The Waves* developed through successive drafts, perhaps this had to do with Virginia Woolf's deeply rooted intuition, at some level, that by comparison with the solidity of more or less any random object suggestive of maleness (the old philosophers' stand-by, the table, would do as well as any), the quality of femininity had recourse in language only to such abstract descriptions as time, space, lack, split ('I . . . feel a cleavage; here's my interesting thing; & there's no quite solid table on which to put it . . .'). Certainly Woolf worked, in composing *The Waves*, with random images, spinning out from them networks of evocative phrases, and writing spontaneously and to some extent automatically as never before. She produced a work, the composition of which spanned three copious, sprawling drafts, which offers a network of raw edges and unresolved connections.

The published text of *The Waves* is summed up, insofar as this is possible, by the character of Bernard, the male story-teller who never finishes a story. At the close of the novel, this self-appointed spokesman takes the reader to a restaurant and summarises, over dinner, the main stages of the narrative, thereby offering some explanation as to what the novel has, to all intents and purposes, been 'about'. He has been engaged, along with the other 'characters' ('parts', might be a more appropriate description) in an attempt to describe his life: to capture in words the complex network of sensations and reactions that seem to constitute the aspect of individual human character which 'goes on underground'. On occasion, he notes, it seems possible to hold the illusion that life is cohesive, intact, circumscribed:

> The illusion is upon me that something adheres for a moment, has roundness, weight, depth, is completed. This, for the moment, seems to be my life. If it were possible, I would hand it to you entire . . .   (*W*, p. 204)

The description, however, like the imagined, equally romanticised gesture of giving one's life to another as a gesture of love and/or respect (as Mrs Ramsay appears to have given hers, in the name of Mr Ramsay's wellbeing; as Orlando gives herself submissively to Marmaduke Bonthrop Shelmerdine) is merely an illusion. A life can never be represented in its entirety, as even the narrator of *Orlando* realised, but only in a series of attempts at depicting cohesion, and by employing a series of random, arbitrary frameworks. In order to make you understand, Bernard tells the reader, it would be necessary to tell a story, and the problem with a story is that it can never be definitive: 'there are so many, and so many – stories of childhood, stories of school, love, marriage, death and so on; and none of them are true' (p. 204). As an alternative, Bernard ruminates, he would like to think in terms of making a new narrative, one that might be spun out of fragments of description in the interstices of the main narrative or story-line: a new kind of story, written in a new form, descriptive of the moments between the key 'acts' – school; marriage; death – of life: 'I begin to seek some design in accordance with those moments of humiliation and triumph that come now and then . . .' (*ibid.*).

The problem with which Woolf began – that there is *something* there, but something so intangible that to substantiate it would be to misrepresent it – is thus handed back to the reader, at the close of *The Waves*, to think back on. We will have been reading about the development – through stray threads of broken narrative and discontinuous trails of imagery issuing from six respective unconscious minds – of six separate and individual, though connected, lives, and observing the ways in which various different motifs are formed, 'held' and then seen to evaporate. Now, at the close of the novel, we sit face to face with Bernard as he attempts to explain that the seemingly random, 'undesigned' imagery of the unconscious is, to a large extent, what the novel 'means'. As a character himself – he is no omnipotent analyst, merely, himself, one of the band of friends – he is unable to form a pattern on which the meaning of the novel might be seen to hinge; the sense is that there is meaning; there is a 'story' of human development, in all its complexity, but he is not equipped to tell it.

There is an odd sense, running through *The Waves*, in which Woolf might almost be amassing raw material for an analyst she cannot invent. The six characters are described in the early drafts as being seated together round the schoolroom table, but they might just as well, in terms of the lines they speak, be pooling the resources created by accumulating material from an analyst's couch. There is an important sense in which Woolf is back-tracking into the reserves of individual memory and attempting to depict the significance of remembered imagery, but by using such lines as the basis of a story about group dynamics, rather than by analysing the individual stories, she cannot get beyond the point at which each individual character embarks on a process of re-telling. She is unpicking the fabric of a life, in much the same way as an analyst works, but she lacks the materials with which to re-compose the self on the basis of the raw material she has accumulated. Significantly, if she had been reading Freud's works as they appeared (The Hogarth Press had by this stage for several years been publishing *The International Psycho-Analytical Library*)[6] she nowhere indicates this. The only references to the reading of Freud occur later, during the drafting of *Between the Acts* – though this cannot indicate definitively that she had *not* been influenced, directly or indirectly, by a partially digested sense of what Freud was doing.[7] (We do know that on the day *The Waves* was published the Woolfs were planning to remove to Rodmell, the ceiling of Virginia's study in Tavistock Square having collapsed, in the process ruining 'all Freud's works' (*L*, IV, p. 387).)

If neither Virginia Woolf nor the fictitious story-teller, Bernard, is able to reassemble such fragments into a 'better' story, this leaves the six speakers, Bernard included, in a state of exposed fragmentation. As always in Woolf's work, the reaction to feeling exposed and wounded is to form a seal or shell; to create a sense of great divide between the 'inner' and the 'outer'. In the fictitious world of *The Waves*, Bernard tells us, 'Outside the undifferentiated forces roar; inside we are very private, . . .' (p. 219). There is a sense that the only reality is the interiorised one: it is 'in this little room, that we make whatever day of the week it may be': even time itself becomes personalised, secret. And so, 'A shell forms upon the soft soul, nacreous, shiny, upon which sensations tap their beaks in vain' (*W*, p. 219), and one gets on with the business of convincing the world that one knows about the business of grown-up living; that one is authentic: 'One fills up the little compartments of one's engagement book . . .' (*ibid.*).

But as Bernard's summing-up – his story – illustrates, this method of pasting over the cracks cannot take account of a troubling stream of fragmented and disorganised sensations which essentially constitute the vitality of the human subject. It is 'a mistake, this extreme precision, this orderly and military progress; a convenience, a lie': this business of resolving not to stop short, but to proceed. If one does stop short, something else is revealed: 'There is always deep below' this military progress, this military sentence, 'a rushing stream of broken dreams, nursery rhymes, street cries, half-finished sentences . . .' (*ibid.*). There is a story, Bernard seems to be saying, that we are still crying out for a chance to tell; there are things we should still like to remember, and to go on trying to understand. But the difficulty is in finding a 'design' for such things which would make their existence compatible with our progress through, our presence in the outside world. It is impossible, he seems to want to say, to make the expression of our desires compatible with the execution of our responsibilities.

The Waves, so it seems, has been (we are asked as readers, significantly, to make sense of it in retrospect) about the difficulty of finding a shape or framework for desire, without resorting to the putting on of a carapace of social convention, obligation and constraint. If the shell could be in some way transparent – more like a membrane than a screen – then perhaps a narrative position, if not a narrative design, might be achieved. But the shell may need to be too sturdy for this, since *The Waves* is also about the extent to which the 'spirit of the age' makes demands which go against the grain of the deeper rhythms and structures of the self, composing one kind of history at the expense of another, more deeply rooted kind, which seems invisible except through the sudden, visionary glimpses prompted by recollection, desire or the endeavour to create.

The Waves can be seen, then, very much as a supplement to *Orlando* – the 'straight' text to *Orlando*'s fall-guy counterpart. This novel, too, begins with the notion of character, 'which goes on underground before we are born; and leaves something afterwards also' (see above, p. 104), though it can no more resolve such an idea in serious prose than could the slapstick narrative of *Orlando*. Somewhere woven into the interstices of both novels, as in *To the Lighthouse*, is the germ of another story: the story of the vital relationship between individual identity, desire, and the passage of time.

Given Bernard's difficulty, and the constraints on Virginia Woolf's as well as Bernard's vision, *The Waves* raises the problematic question for the reader of not only how to read the text but *what*, precisely, to focus on as the only recuperable 'story'. Woolf herself consistently hoped that it would not be read as a novel: at some moments it seemed to be emerging in the form of something more closely resembling an elegy.[8] But an elegy to whom? 'The six'? Percival? Percival seems to be depicted as an outsider whose distinguishing feature is that he seems to have no 'inner' life, so that he hardly deserves the chorus of mourning that is directed towards him as a kind of heroic scapegoat. It is as though grieving, like desire, and like the subject, must have an object if it is to take on the nature of reality, and Percival, 'flung from his horse' like a character who would be more at home in *Orlando* seems rather a compromising choice.

For some readers, the power of *The Waves* is in its capacity to create an atmosphere of sensuousness, but this by no means works for everyone. Wilfrid Mellers, the music critic, reviewed it on publication and described an imagery 'pinned to her prose like so many dead butterflies';[9] Muriel Bradbrook referred, in her review, to 'the futile counterpointing of *The Waves*.'[10] Elizabeth Hardwick has more recently admitted that she 'cannot think of anything to say about it except that it is wonderful.'[11] The impression of a kind of circular absorption, the feeling, as a reader, of disorientation, seems to strike admiring and unsympathetic readers alike, and to reduce the reader to a childlike state of wonder or petulance, as though we can either be rocked and soothed by it, or completely left out. What seems to be at stake in attempting to get to grips with this particular attempt of Virginia Woolf's to describe 'the nature of reality' is the relationship between ourselves as reading subjects and the object of our study. *The Waves* seems to want to make an intrusion into our own unconscious, and if it cannot do that, it tends to leave us cold.

One way of reading *The Waves*, in the face of this, might be to reflect on the patterning of the unconscious as exemplified by the six speaking parts, and perhaps to discern, in the process, the germs of the story Bernard's friends had not been able to tell. It is clear, for example, that Woolf is here concerned at some level with a notion of pre-history, and in particular to show that there is a subversive, primal level of existence which not only precedes but goes on accompanying the self throughout and between the key 'acts' of birth, childhood, sexuality and the absorption of the self within social structures, and social 'sentences'. As in *Orlando*, the notion that there might be one omnipotent 'biographer', or analyst, able to capture and describe an entire, cohesive life, is put to question, but in *The Waves* this is because not only the 'biographer' but also the subject of the 'biography' – the Life – lacks access to a language which would be capable of reinscribing – or 'revising' – subjective recollections and impressions. If the analyst and the biographer both, in their different senses, 're-write' history, so, too, does the novelist, but the novelist's story would always be different from that of the analyst or the biographer. The novelist, in his/her own way, can always not only re-tell but *invent* another story.

Throughout the composition of *The Waves*, Virginia Woolf strove to find metaphors, or to forge a symbolic language, for what she wanted to say, and as the drafts developed she worked increasingly with the idea of juxtaposing landscape and seascape. Throughout the text of the published novel the six speakers articulate their respective desires to reclaim lost origins, to be released into obscurely pleasing landscapes and seascapes which have been almost but not quite obliterated by the demands of life outside the shell. They are plaintively nostalgic for the idea of origination, as Bernard tells us: 'It was different once, . . . Once we could break the current as we chose' (p. 185). By contrast, the sentence of adulthood seems riddled with clutter, and utterly constraining: 'How many telephone calls, how many postcards, are now needed to cut this hole through which we come together . . . I am wedged into my place in the puzzle' (*ibid.*). It is striking that when an escape route is perceived, it is in the form of a mental projection: 'it is only my body,' Bernard protests, 'that is fixed irrevocably': the imagination has powers which can overreach the limitations of human subjectivity, but when Bernard does imagine a form of potency, he does so in the form of an identification with a potent object. The landscape – Woolf's literary metaphor, and object rather than subject – seems to be the originating force, and source of fertility, and the subject can only imagine the realisation of his own potential by imagining an elaborate form of dialogue, or communication, with the 'shining ploughland': 'I throw my mind out in the air as a man throws seeds in great fan-lights, falling through the purple sunset, falling on the pressed and shining ploughland which is bare' (*ibid.*). There is impotence, and displacement, in this: Bernard 'throws' not his seed, but his mind: 'as a man throws . . .' – the man is not Bernard, the subject can only be inhabited through a process of projection, and in the medium of the imagination; the body remains 'wedged' into its 'place in the puzzle'.

In childhood, everything is fluid, sensuous; even the passage of time does not denote constraint: the child Bernard describes a fluidity which gives the landscape a watery quality:

> We shall sink through the green air of the leaves, Susan. We sink as we run. The waves close over us, the beech leaves meet above our heads.   (*W*, p. 13)

Equally, however, the characters are soon shown needing to *resist*, or let go of, such moments, such flights, both of the imagination and of spoken language:

> 'Now you trail away,' said Susan, 'making phrases. Now you mount like an air-ball's string, higher and higher through the layers, out of reach . . . You have escaped me. Here is the garden . . . Here is Rhoda on the path . . .'
>
> (*W*, p. 14)

Loss, particularly, can focus a desperate desire *not* to succumb to rhythms of, nor become grounded in, a form of susceptibility from which one might never be released. It is always necessary to deflect the gaze from spectacles of absence or loss, to fix upon some other body, some other object; to objectify the world in order to make one's identification with it manageable. Rhoda, attempting to come to terms with Percival's loss, is shown training her mind; turning it, in her mind's eye, into plaster (or marble) casts:

> the square stood upon the oblong. 'The house which contains all,' I said, lurching against people's shoulders in an omnibus after Percival died; . . . . Walking on the embankment, I prayed that I might thunder for ever on the verge of the world where there is no vegetation, but here and there a marble pillar.   (*W*, p. 176)

The harshness of grief evokes the need to identify some equally harsh, objective world which will satisfactorily mirror the subject, and the characters in *The Waves* consistently seek to exchange self-knowledge for a newly constructed world of objects, which will reflect the subject back intact. As a backdrop to all this, the language of *The Waves* moves consistently towards a language of origination, in which the subject is pure, primal, elemental, but this, too, must be rendered objective, as though it would be too painful, because too reminiscent, a world for the subject to continue to inhabit, except by remaining in the realm of the imagination.

The imagery of the waves gathers momentum as the narrative advances on its course, representing, increasingly, an alternative to the material imagery of everyday life – the 'puzzle' – whereas when the characters were children and the narrative was 'younger' the two styles of imagery tended to be more interchangeable. If the achievement of this novel is explicable in terms of Woolf's endeavour to show the characters' increasingly *conscious* preoccupation with, but sense of increasing separation from, origins, the holograph drafts are little short of revelatory. In the original drafts, waves and mothers are indistinguishable, and the characters are shown actually being born out of the waves themselves:

> Many mothers, & before them many mothers, & again many mothers, have groaned, & fallen back, while the child crowed. Like one wave, & then succeeding another. Wave after wave, endlessly sinking & falling as far as the eye can stretch. And all these waves have been the prostrate forms of mothers, in their flowing nightgowns, with the tumbled sheets about them holding up, with a groan, as they sink back into the sea, innumerable children.   (*W*, Holo. Draft I, p. 7)[12]

The extraordinary starkness of this image is unusual in Woolf's work, and it is about the closest she ever gets to describing unbridled physicality, despite the 'flowing nightgowns' (in which Victorian mothers did deliver their infants). In addition to this revealing exposure of her intention to find a way of describing, even in metaphor, the actual, organic process of childbirth itself, the holograph draft of *The Waves* also encompasses Woolf's early experiments with the origins of narrative and narrator who, in the early drafts, was not Bernard at all, but a separate, unspecific entity labelled 'the lonely mind'. Originally, this figure carried the main weight of narrative responsibility, and it was in this figure that the subjective and material fragments of *The Waves* were to have been collected together, providing, as it were, a reef between land and sea; the paraphernalia of the social world and the residual imagery of the unconscious.

In these initial stages of drafting the novel Woolf had already moved on from her early plans for a central 'she': the lonely mind was to be either male or female, its gender immaterial, or at least, unspecified – 'mans or womans, it does not matter which' – though its primary function was always clear: 'I am telling myself the story of the world from the beginning' (Holo. Draft I, p. 9). The essential *anonymity* of man and woman when seen in the context of his or her ungendered origins is the most likely reason why Woolf eventually deleted the lonely mind from the finished text, though his/her initial reflections on loss and the definition of the self throw light on the finished novel and supplement our understanding of the way the text evolved into its finished state. The lonely mind reflects, as Bernard seems unable to do, on the notion that the 'perfect vessel' of symbiotic cohesion which is broken by the temporal continuum of human life is, though perhaps retrievable through moments of recollection, nevertheless extremely fragile, and that it is only by recovering from the experience of loss to which it is haphazardly subject that any sense of equilibrium can be regained:

> The perfect vessel? But it was not by any means made of durable stuff. For it was only when the thing had happened . . . and the violence of the shock was over that one could understand, or really; live; . . . Then in that darkness, which had no limit, . . . whose shores were invisible, whatever had just happened, expanded; and something dropped away. Then without a companion, one loved; spoke with no one to hear; & carried on an intercourse with people who were not there more completely than [when] one's chair was drawn close to theirs.   (*W*, Holo. Draft I, p. 9)

This passage, which appears towards the very beginning of the first drafts of *The Waves*, sums up more coherently and succinctly than Bernard ever does a thesis: that it is through the process of coming to terms with the loss of innocence that the subject moves towards the possibility of being fully in touch with and at one with the self. The final, published text of *The Waves* might be seen as a dramatisation – a play for six voices – of this passage from innocence to experience, except that there are certain features of this thesis which remain unresolved.

Firstly, it is apparent from this exposition by the lonely mind that the notion of shock is an important and significant one within the narrative. It is, then, no accident that when Susan sees Jinny kissing Louis her reaction of faltering desolation draws her back into the language of light and shade, the predominant imagery of seascape, which denotes and circumscribes the idea of childhood innocence. But predominant within this childhood mental and imaginary arena is a keynote of distress. In the aftermath of what she has seen, 'she is blind after the light and trips and flings herself down on the roots under the trees, . . . The branches heave up and down. There is agitation and trouble here . . . There is anguish here' (p. 11). Rhoda, struggling miserably with her arithmetic, experiences a similar state, which renders her almost senseless. The figures on the blackboard mean nothing. The black bars on the clock face are 'green oases. The long hand has marched ahead to find water' (*W*, p. 17). The agonies of education into the world of adult knowledge arouse, yet again, the desire for a return to a symbiotic fluidity, and the obliterating imagery of the sea.

Each of the six is haunted by the memory of childhood humiliation or shock. Bernard (like Virginia Woolf) cannot forget an incident described cryptically as 'death among the apple trees' (p. 20); Louis goes on remembering the appalling humiliation of being the only child around the Christmas tree for whom there seems to be no present (p. 28). An outsider, he watches the others 'brush the surface of the world' (p. 9), while he feels abandoned, rooted to the spot and already, like the adult Bernard, can only experience physicality through projection: 'My hair is made of leaves . . . My body is a stalk' (p. 9). The emissions from such a body take on a surreal quality: 'A drop oozes from the hole at the mouth and slowly, thickly, grows larger and larger' (*ibid.*).

The development from innocence to experience is punctuated, (punctured, even) by distress, grief and the fragmentation effected by shock, and the speakers' characteristic recourse to a language of the symbolic usually comes about as a response to emotional pain. Is Virginia Woolf telling us, then, that normal childhood development hinges on the experience of grief, that the normal process of separation is accompanied – even characterised – by pain and distress; or is she writing, precisely, about the origins of *grieving*?

Bernard remembers, as he sums up, that 'We suffered terribly as we became separate bodies' (p. 207): is Woolf presenting this suffering as an integral part of the normal process of a child's development, or is she, here, writing specifically about instances in which early development was *interrupted* and the course of individual history crossed? The histrionic despair which constitutes the only way in which she can achieve closure in this novel suggests – as do her deletion of vivid, vibrant and elucidatory material from her earlier drafts – that Woolf herself may not have known the answer to this question. What is clear is the extent to which her characters are struggling to make sense of a world which strikingly resembles the young Virginia's own as she herself depicted it, in retrospect, in 'A Sketch of the Past'. As in Woolf's own early experience, the early experience of being safely cocooned and responsive to pleasurably synaesthetic shimmering objects and glancing lights is starkly, sometimes even horrifically interrupted by the effects of sudden, arbitrary interventions which cut cruelly across the child's vista, rendering the child mute, incapacitated and insecure.

A striking feature of *The Waves* is its apparent lack of any overall authorial knowledge: its point of view shifts from one vision to another like the turning of a kaleidoscope, and even Percival, whose subjective vision we do not, as readers, see, is constructed when we see him by one or several of the other six characters. The 'Interludes' appear to be composed entirely in the abstract, as though the rhythms of sea and sky, dawn and dusk, can provide a backdrop for but do not have any real bearing on the development of the six lives depicted in the main text. Madeleine Moore has suggested that the lonely mind might be seen to exist, as it were in residue, in the finished text, in the form of the crouching woman who appears in some of the Interludes, half hidden beneath the waves,[13] as here:

> the sky cleared as if the white sediment there had sunk, or as if the arm of a woman couched beneath the horizon had raised a lamp and flat bars of white, green and yellow spread across the sky like the blades of a fan.
>
> (*W*, p. 5)

Moore points out that there are also, in the early drafts, hints of other hypothetical, shadowy figures suggestive of an overall authorial vision: in the first holograph draft there appears, for example, a 'hooded form', a figure 'bent over the table, in the room, where there was now a light' . . . 'Had there been an eye in [such a form], . . . it would have seen the spotted petals, the green plant' (*W*, Holo. Draft I, p. 151). But what of Woolf's qualifications, what of the reservations integral to her descriptions of such figures? That 'had there been', that 'as if' are all too familiar, and the function of the crouching woman, the hooded form, seems suggestive only of the possibility that there might, somewhere within the text, reside a potentially all-powerful, all-seeing figure but that in this instance, in this version – which is, of course, all the reader has to go on – she must remain discreet, hidden, even censored. The hooded form (which might even be suggestive of something slightly sinister, as though the form had something distinctive to hide) might have seen 'the spotted petals, the green plant', but this only makes any sense at all if we are in a position to trace such a figure back to her/its possible origins. The text of *The Waves* began with a flowerpot at its centre and was suggested by Virginia Woolf's vision of the possibility of a 'She' who might one day witness the fall of a flower, who might, by gazing at the central and organic motif of a plant, see 'anything' in its petals, but the reader of the published text of *The Waves* cannot be expected to guess all this. It is as though Virginia Woolf, as an integral part of her project to explore the organic origins of being in the world, needed to gradually delete from her text all traces of the origin of her story.

The sense of severance, dislocation and cleavage which is sustained throughout *The Waves* is followed right through to the final lament:

'Death is the enemy. It is death against whom I ride with my spear couched and my hair flying back . . . Against you I will fling myself, unvanquished and unyielding, O Death!' (p. 256). Even the final, tiny fragment of seascape contiguous with this protest, this desire to break the circle of mortality, is simply repetitive and suggestive of a continuing, possibly even insignificant rhythm in the order of things, rather than of any kind of interpretation ('The waves broke on the shore' (p. 256).) In the face of all this, then, the language of the symbolic appears rather to contradict or run counter to the only language available for normal social discourse or for the writing of stories, than to offer any kind of system of interpretation. Bernard may, then, be unable to finish his stories because he is unable to penetrate the language he needs to employ in order to 'go back to the beginning' and fully document his own or others' lives. The tragedy of *The Waves*, then, might be interpreted as the process of the characters' sense of *separation* from the experience which originated their stories, their respective experiences of being interrupted or blocked. Alternatively, Woolf may simply be representing the extent to which the transition from innocence to experience 'naturally' encompasses loss. The sense of incompatibility experienced by the six with the rhythms and lights and shades of the seascapes, their sense of distance from the perpetuity suggested by the natural rhythms of the sea itself, depicted as somehow the source of loss and grieving, might, then, be read as both the failure of, and 'the story of' *The Waves*.

But there may be another reason, to do with sexuality and with the presence and function of Percival, who in the published text of *The Waves* is clearly intended to be a focal point. For, as the spoken dialogue as well as the reflections of the six consistently show, sexuality is depicted in *The Waves* as an aspect of the conventional, even material life, and shown *outside* the contexts of organic development and symbiotic sensation. The reader's first glimpse of Percival, through Neville, reflects the extent to which he throws all the agonised and analytical efforts of the observer into confusion, eliciting a desire only to look like him, to be like him, to deny the agonies and complexities of subjectivity; to be, like him, a love object. He cannot read, but what, asks Neville, faced with the spectacle of Percival playing cricket, are words? 'Do I not know already how to rhyme, how to imitate Pope, Dryden, even Shakespeare? But I cannot stand all day in the sun with my eyes on the ball; I cannot feel the flight of the ball through my body and think only of the ball . . .' (p. 40). Percival does not read, does not think, does not reflect: he sees the world at first, rather than second hand; the world appears to come to him unmediated, direct: 'Not a thread, not a sheet of paper lies between him and the sun, between him and the rain, between him and the moon as he lies naked, tumbled, hot, on his bed' (*ibid*.). There is a paradoxical sense in which Percival, who will never acquire the linguistic and intellectual civilisation of the others, is nevertheless more integral than they will ever be. His sexuality, it is consistently hinted, is intact; that of the others is fragile, vulnerable, ambiguous, subject to interruption and paralysis; open to question.

Percival has somehow managed to avoid his own history: he has no recorded memory. He suddenly appears on the scene with no pre-amble, no introduction. He has avoided the necessity for origins. He is in every sense of the word truly anonymous, but all tremble at the very mention of his name. He is the object of desire: all the confusion and imprecision of eroticism is consistently brought into play whenever Percival is the object of anyone's gaze, because of his startling and literal capacity simply to be present, superseding all entanglements with the past, all necessity to negotiate with the future. Attempting to sum him up, Bernard can only gesture towards some possibility of creating a new structure, of reading between the lines: 'What is startling, what is unexpected, what we cannot account for, what turns symmetry to nonsense – that comes suddenly to my mind, thinking of him' (p. 208). 'No lullaby,' laments Bernard, on Percival's death, 'has ever occurred to me of laying him to rest' (*ibid*.).

There can be, in effect, no lullaby for, no elegy to Percival, whose end is as sudden and as arbitrary as his beginning; who seems to encapsulate the process through which, in *The Waves*, desire elicits and is bound up with grieving. For, (despite Jinny's somewhat manipulative shimmer-ings and shinnyings) there is no real erotic centre to the novel: the imagery of the unconscious exemplified by the group of six throws up some of the flotsam and jetsam of desire, and even seems at times to suggest that the novel is about the development, from six respective points of view, of sexual consciousness, but even had there been, as it were, an eye in the hooded figure – the authorial point of view which resides, under wraps, at the centre of the text – we would simply have been invited to see the odd spotted petal, catch the odd glimpse of the green plant. There *is*, somewhere in the vast, obscure origins of *The Waves*, a green plant – a central symbol of organic growth – but it will not flower. Nowhere in the published text is there anything approaching those early, spectacularly symbolic images of mothers, hurling newly born children from the waves. The sea, with its immense power to evoke for Virginia Woolf the connections between memory, loss and desire, is carefully framed in its discreetly evocative Interludes, and Woolf's 'vaguely' symbolic imagery fails to serve as a means by which she might originate a new language of desire.

The Waves comes cascading up to, then drags itself heavily away from, a story – that of the origin or history of sexuality – which neither Virginia Woolf nor her invented novelist, Bernard, could tell. This may well be the reason why the lonely mind, with its early speculations on androgyny, had to be gradually written out of the text, and why even the earlier idea, for a female consciousness plummeting through time like a falling petal, was so soon discarded. Gender and the unconscious are areas which, as Virginia Woolf knew only too well, are inextricably entangled, their imagery shared, their origins bound up together in space and time. But Woolf lacked a theory of sexuality, and in *The Waves* the true beginnings of a story she might one day tell, about female consciousness and differences of gender, was given only in fleeting glimpses, snatches and fragments, remaining, in the final analysis, untold.

It seems clear from the defiant ending of the novel, and from its determination to take a heroic stand against the premature death of its unambiguously mortal hero, Percival, that Woolf was determined somehow to find a way of telling this story. If its origins lay in a theory of the history of sexual difference, then she would construct that theory, research that history, re-tell that story. In *The Pargiters*, the 'essay-novel' which was to form the basis of her succeeding novel, *The Years*, she set out to do exactly that.

5

Reading Sexual Politics
(*The Years*)

The man in the loincloth gave three sharp taps with his mallet on the brick.
She was buried alive. The tomb was a brick mound. There was just room for
her to lie straight out. Straight out in a brick tomb, she said. And that's the
end, she yawned, shutting the book. (*Y*, pp. 104–5)

In *The Waves*, Virginia Woolf had experimented with an imagery of the
unconscious, beginning with a potent imagery of primeval mothers in
the act of childbirth, hurling newly born children from the waves, but
this imagery proved too strong for her. She could not sustain it, because
she was unable to establish a point of reference for this imagery of
sexuality. Her object of desire, Percival, is inarticulate; anonymous; he
lacks a history. As she developed the text of *The Waves*, she gradually
renounced the attempt to *originate* desire in this novel, leaving it to
Bernard, the male novelist, to sum up the histories of her six characters.
In conclusion, Bernard celebrates the immortality of the hero: the myth
of all-powerful, all-withstanding masculinity.

It was as though the spectacle of mothers in white nightgowns might
have recalled something prior to composition, something belonging in
the unwritten recesses of the mind of Virginia Woolf herself, which she
could not risk developing (perhaps the mothers in their nightgowns
were on some level as evocative an image of madness as of the process
of delivery). As an analysis of Woolf's writing practice increasingly
reveals, the attempt to *avoid* writing autobiography into *The Waves*
demanded tremendous restraint. It was almost as though she was
engaged in the highly complicated practice of developing a simultaneous, separate and contiguous imagery for her *own* sexual history – all
of which can then begin to surface with relative facility, in 'A Sketch of
the Past' – in the light of which her attempt to preserve her authorial
anonymity was an increasing source of strain.

In *The Pargiters*, her subsequent work, which came to be re-drafted as *The Years*, she set herself the more specific task of describing the history of female sexuality, an idea which emerged from an invitation to give a paper to the National Society for Women's Service,[1] and which was originally conceived as a sequel to *A Room of One's Own*, to be 'about the sexual life of women'.[2]

Significantly, when she broached the subject head-on in this way, one of the main things to emerge was the necessity for a new narrative style and a new authorial position *vis-à-vis* the text. This new rubric called up the need for her to establish, at the outset, a more 'traditional' authorial position of mastery over her subject matter. The genesis of the text in a public speech was enabling in this regard, and she noted, during the course of the writing, that she felt she was 'breaking the mould made by *The Waves*.'[3]

Paradoxically, she was able to establish a position of authority in relation to this new text by outlining, in the speech from which the idea for the novel sprang, the special nature of a novelist's close involvement with her material. She distinguished herself, in her speech, from Ethel Smyth, the speaker who preceded her and who was, she judged, 'of the race of pioneers, of pathmakers' (*P*, xxvii),[4] by explaining that for a woman novelist it was unnecessary to be a pioneer, since there are no material constraints: 'pens and paper are cheap . . . Pianos, models, studios, north lights, masters and mistresses (. . .) are not needed. One has only got to sit down and write' (xxviii). The raw material for a novel existed, she stressed, not in the paraphernalia but rather in the mind of the novelist herself. In *The Pargiters* she employs (as she was to employ again later, in 'Professions for Women')[5] the imagery of a novelist fishing into her unconscious to find a way of describing the experience of the professional woman writer, an experience contrasting markedly with those of women in other professions and, straight away, found herself identifying the one constraint with which the woman writer has to contend.

The fisherwoman she is describing to her audience is 'letting her imagination feed unfettered upon every crumb of her experience; . . .' when suddenly, her line slackens. 'Reason' hauls her onshore, and demands to know what the matter is:

And the imagination began pulling on its stockings and replied, rather tartly and disagreeably; its all your fault. You should have given me more experience to go on. I can't do the whole work for myself.

And I – the reason – had to reply: Many forms of experience are lacking to me because I am a woman. (*P*, p. xxxviii)

This is, of course, Virginia Woolf's own problem, transposed into a general problem for any woman writing and thereby providing her with a mechanism for both confronting and detaching herself from it. This – the lack of experience – is one problem, but there is another, she explains, which begins to present itself as soon as the fisherwoman/ novelist takes up her line again: 'Suddenly there is a violent jerk; she feels the line race through her fingers . . . "Good heavens she cries – how dare you interfere with me!" . . . And I – that is the reason – have to reply, . . .':

> 'My dear you were going altogether too far. Men would be shocked.' . . .
> You see I go on, trying to calm her, I cannot make use of what you tell me –
> about womens bodies for instance – their passions – and so on, because the
> conventions are still very strong. If I were to overcome the conventions I
> should need the courage of a hero, and I am not a hero.'
>
> (*P*, pp. xxxviii–xxxix)

> 'I doubt that a writer can be a hero,' she continues, 'I doubt that a hero can
> be a writer' (*ibid.*).

The problem of censorship is thus given the same treatment as the problem of having been sheltered from (sexual) experience. By identifying it, Woolf can take it as her subject matter and thereby impose control over it. (Significantly here, 'I' – the authorial persona – takes the part of Reason, and stands in a position of authority over the more feckless Imagination). In *The Pargiters*, the text which emerged out of this speech, Woolf proposed to maintain this degree of control by employing a new form, that of the 'essay–novel', in which she would intersperse short essays on the subjects of women's education and their (censored) sexuality with illustrative fictitious passages, thereby framing the fiction not simply, this time, with decorative Interludes, but with factual information. This method would also serve to 'hold' the fiction within conceptual limits and enable Woolf to comment on her own text, almost from the point of view of a disinterested outsider.

From the outset, she took as her theme in this work the question of the historical constraints on women's experience, and the prohibition of female sexuality. The secrecy and censorship which surround the Pargiter daughters' experience ensures that for them sexuality becomes tinged with mystery and confusion. But not only that: it is an aspect of their experience which has been repressed to such an extent that it is experienced as having no source, no origin, and because of this, no imaginable other. In the face of all this, the idea of sex can only be externalised; sexuality can only be modelled, never quite claimed as an experience of one's own: 'The [sexual] emotion was so generalized that the object of it [was] scarcely wanted' (*P*, p. 35).

Intrinsic to the sexuality of women in the repressive, class-ridden Victorian society of *The Pargiters*, then, was the prohibition of female sexual consciousness: the novel thus provided for Woolf an opportunity to dramatise, and thus historicise her own dilemma. She is painfully aware, in this novel, that sexual censorship not only limits the scope of lived experience, it also restricts development: the Pargiters' repressive (lack of) education 'was bound not merely to teach [them] a certain code of behaviour, but also to modify the passion itself' (p. 110).

Sexuality could not only not be described, it lacked a *source*, and this unequivocal fact was to present an ultimately insurmountable problem for the author of an essay–novel about the sexual life of women. Both the 'facts' and the 'fiction' of *The Pargiters* are revealing of the extent of Woolf's dilemma. She writes frankly of sexual ignorance and the ensuing confusion of identity and emotional distress as nowhere else in her work, but ultimately this ambitious and courageous project presented her with a major stylistic problem. The awkwardness Woolf certainly felt in relation to her subject matter is reflected in the clumsiness of the text. Milly and Delia standing at the window watching a baby as it is pushed past in its perambulator, for example, reflect the awkwardness of the author, who herself balked at the idea of the physicality of a mother's relationship with her children:

> Milly had felt a curious, though quite unanalysed, desire to look at the baby, to hold it, to feel its body, to press her lips to the nape of its neck; whereas Delia had felt, also without being fully conscious of it, a vague uneasiness, as if some emotion were expected of her which, for some reason, some vaguely discreditable reason, she did not feel; . . . she turned and came abruptly back into the room, to exclaim a moment later, 'O my God', as the thought struck her that she would never be allowed to go to Germany and study music. (*P*, p. 36)

If the idea of a career is in the process of being stifled, so, too (except of course in principle) is the alternative mode of motherhood. Woolf is clumsily gesturing, here, towards exposing the distressingly illogical Victorian idea that chastity enabled good mothering.

Woolf had anticipated the problem of finding the appropriate stylistic response to her subject matter in her speech to the National Society for Women's Service, when she had stressed that the professional writer could never be a hero: she parodies the problem in a mock-patronising little dialogue with the Imagination:

> I point out to her that the moment I become heroic, I become shrill and hard and positive – in short I become a preacher more like a critic – and that

I say, is extremely unpleasant for you, poor imagination. [The imagination]
becomes shrivelled and distorted, and you would not like to become
shrivelled and distorted would you? I say. It is your nature to understand
and to create. (*P*, p. xxxix)

It is interesting to speculate on Woolf's possible model, here: the
archetypal Victorian patriarch, giving a private lecture on the importance of duty to his recalcitrant and frustrated wife? As Woolf realised
only too well, and was beginning to expose here, in *The Pargiters*, the
imagination had somehow to find a way of functioning within the
bounds of patriarchal rule, which meant that, as she said in her Speech,
'The future of fiction depends very much upon what extent men can be
educated to stand free speech in women' (*ibid.*). But whether men
would ever tolerate being re-educated into a civilisation in which
'women too can be artists' lay, declared Woolf, in the laps of the Gods
. . . though she immediately changed her mind about this: 'no not upon
the laps of the Gods, but upon your laps, upon the laps of professional
women' (pp. xxxix–xl).

The potential civilisation and re-education of men was a project
Woolf was to outline in *Three Guineas*,[6] leaving, as it were, *The
Pargiters* and its successor *The Years*, to devote themselves totally to
the fictionalised problems of women's sexuality. Even in *The Years*,
though, the issue of whether an improvement in the education of men
would result in a society which valued women's creativity has almost
escaped notice. The issue of art in relation to women (which began by
being one of the central concerns of Woolf's speech) is given only
obliquely, through the character of Sara. But that elision – that the
issue of women's art (women's 'authorship') lies in the laps of the Gods
. . . no, not in the laps of the Gods, but upon the laps of professional
women – is central to the construction of *The Years*, and to the feminist
position – though an oscillating, precarious one – which frames Woolf's
text.

By the time Woolf comes to write the first paragraph of *The Years*
(written in conventional fictitious form), the public speaker has
absented herself, the heroic issue of women's suffrage has been
removed, and the narrative of fiction has been fully resumed. Yet also
by the first paragraph, the issue of narrative style is already being
obliquely raised. Woolf raised it specifically in her Diary, where she
noted that 'after abstaining from the novel of fact all these years' – since

1919, and *Night and Day* – she is finding herself 'infinitely delighted in facts for a change, . . . though I feel now & then the tug to vision, but resist it' (*D*, IV, p. 129).

As in *Mrs Dalloway*, her aim here is to present female sexuality in the context of 'the social system': 'I want to give the whole of present society,' she resolved, '– nothing less: facts, as well as the vision.' The blend of fact and fiction she sought by this stage was to be something along the lines of 'The Waves going on simultaneously with Night & Day' (*D*, IV, pp. 151–2). Gradually, the respective sections of *The Pargiters* – 'fact' and 'fiction' – merged into the text which would become *The Years*, and the style – a complete change from *The Waves* – reflects the integration of 'fractured' material.

The opening paragraph of the novel describes an ordered space: a city pavement, inhabited by diners-out; a moon so cohesive it seems polished like a coin; and one other important feature: 'a million little gaslights, . . . opened in their glass cages.' The gas lights are symmetrical, casting pools of light and thereby creating alternative stretches of darkness; they are mingled with the sun to reflect 'equally' in the placid waters of the Round Pond and the Serpentine: 'civilised' spaces, and the antithesis of the waves. The diners-out, who will presently be identified as the characters in the novel, survey the calm reflections of the mingled lights from their hansom cabs which both connect them to and separate them from the effects of the lights; at length, the perfectly symmetrical moon rises over the whole, cohesive picture.

The passage is significant in its emphasis on ordering properties, and for its oblique reflection of authorial control. For the spectacle of the street lamps and the procession of hansom cabs conjures a scene which seems to invite almost a direct challenge to Virginia Woolf's 1919 manifesto: 'Life is not a series of gig lamps symmetrically arranged; . . .'.[7] In the opening paragraph of *The Years* we are given both the gigs and the lamps and, by implication, the gig lamps: it is as though Woolf were going back on her own precedent and deciding here not only to revert in some ways to the writing of *Night and Day* but to 'precede' it, in terms of the position she is here taking up. One critic has compared the two novels by pointing up the extent to which Woolf celebrates, in *The Years*, the lives and work of 'less lovable sisters',[8] based on the puritanical life, perhaps, of her own Quaker aunt,[9] in contrast to the 'joyful eccentricities' of the aunts and mother depicted in *Night and Day*, but surely there are equally significant parts played in *The Years* by characters such as Eugenie, Mira, Rose and Sara, all of whom are flamboyant and colourful in their way, and each of whom respectively

represent the 'different kinds of love', the idea of which Woolf experimented with in *The Pargiters* and which constitutes àn important
aspect of the origins of this novel.

The central conflict of *The Years* – developing out of the initial
separation of the material into 'fact' and 'fiction' – is between 'being', of
the kind described by Mrs Hilbery in *Night and Day* (women in the
Victorian age just *'were'*, she claims),[10] and women's 'non-being' (in
the sense described in 'A Sketch of the Past') within a historical context
in which their sexuality and by implication their creativity – their
potential as 'artists' of their own destiny – has been to all intents and
purposes erased. In this sense, *The Years* functions as a kind of
companion volume to *Three Guineas*, where Woolf had urged women
to seek to exert political influence through the attempt to 'experiment
not with public means in public, but with private means in private.'[11]
She describes touchingly reactionary Suffragette-like practices: they
should hurl leaflets printed on their own private printing presses (these
were clearly to be women of means) down basement steps into the
servants' quarters, in a histrionic attempt to enlist in the cause of
educational opportunities for women not collective sympathy exactly,
but, more importantly, the support of individuals, since 'is there not
something in the conglomeration of people into societies that releases
what is most selfish and violent, least rational and humane in the
individuals themselves? . . . Inevitably,' she declares, 'we look upon
societies [all societies, now, not just the one to which and from within
which she is reacting] as conspiracies . . .' (*TG*, p. 121).

In response to this conviction, she argues in *Three Guineas*, the
daughters of educated men seeking better educational opportunities
and entry into the professions should capitalise on, rather than be
embarrassed or hampered by, their status as 'Outsiders', and a position
of eccentricity becomes increasingly germane to her theme: 'Outsiders'
may not be, she allows, 'a resonant name, but it has the advantage that
it squares with facts – the facts of history, of law, of biography; even, it
may be, with the still hidden facts of our still unknown psychology'
(*ibid*.).

Here, then, comes the 'ghost' of Dorothy Richardson again. Once
more, the 'dark places' become important; enlightenment (and its
exposure to potential censorship) is to be distrusted, and the whole
thrust of *Three Guineas* is towards turning women's position *outside*
the political structure to advantage, by idiosyncratic methods by which
individuality (the artist's prerogative) is to be encouraged and dramatised. The central tension which flaws Woolf's argument is between the

desire to refute the traditional ideal of the Angel of the House, and the desire to play on and exploit stances which flatter the male ego ('that restful sympathy which women know how to give'),[12] thereby retaining women's only traditional claim to a place in the scheme of things. Virginia Woolf's mother and aunts, for example, had tirelessly rehearsed the anti-Suffrage argument that within the household women exerted the only tangible modicum of power to which they had access, and that this should be retained, rather than abandoned, in the interests of women's power.[13] However, the personal dilemma which this latter argument tended to give rise to is poignantly dramatised by Virginia Woolf in her characterisation of Mrs Ramsay and, taken to extremes it simply becomes, as Mrs Ramsay amply demonstrates, another form of inertia.

An important aspect of all this, though – and one which *Three Guineas* fully rehearses – is the effect of Victorian patriarchal constraints on men. Woolf argues that the personal sacrifices made by professional men in the interests of maintaining their own egos and the status quo (and, she might have added, the British economy as it then was) would be entirely unacceptable to women, who must seek for the first time and as a first priority to define their own potency on their own terms. The problem with being a *man* in a man's world was the extent to which such a world appeared to devalue both the processes and the end results of creativity. One look at the stereotypical male is enough, she argued, to convince us that 'if people are highly successful in their professions they lose their senses. . . . What then remains', she despairingly asks, 'of a human being who has lost sight, and sound, and a sense of proportion? Only a cripple in a cave' (pp. 83–4). Whether or not she quite knew what she was talking about, she certainly had a strong instinct for the kinds of constraints she knew she wanted to avoid, and what characters such as Eugenie and Rose seem to know – even though Woolf herself seems unable, in *The Years*, to fully develop this point in her dialogue – is that influence is not necessarily exerted through self-denial. Thus, the manifesto of the Outsiders included this essential but politically unorthodox, Mrs Ramsayish clause: 'It will be one of our aims to increase private beauty' (*TG*, pp. 130–1).

In this context, *The Years*, Woolf's final attempt to describe a connection between female sexuality and politics, emerges not just as the story of the 'unloveable sisters' but as a rather more complex documentary of women's dialectical position: as Outsiders wishing at once to retain the special quality of their femininity and, at the same time, to subvert the system which cast them out. The problem, as

Woolf herself well knew, was that 'the system' worked to censor the expression of female sexuality more or less altogether, so that women's strength within the system was undermined by conventions that refused to recognise it even as it went on capitalising on it, and thereby, ultimately, eroding it. The female author who attempts to exclude herself from this network of problems in an attempt to impose control and order on it must surely, then, be viewed not as in the act of bringing the novel to a deliberate aesthetic collapse, as one feminist critic has gone as far as to argue,[14] but rather as using her theory of the 'Outsiders' to expose the subversive nature of the Victorian professional and domestic structures which form the centrepiece of the novel. As such, she may be seen to be not destroying but rather inverting the novel form.

It hardly seems surprising that to Virginia Woolf in the process of writing this novel it felt as though 'the horrible side of the universe, . . . had got the upper hand again.'[15] In a Diary entry which contrasts poignantly with the imagery of child-bearing mothers frolicking in the waves, she was to wonder, in retrospect, whether anyone had suffered quite so much in writing a book as she had, in the process of writing *The Years*. She remembered it as being 'like a long childbirth. Think of that summer,' she reflected, 'every morning a headache, & forcing myself into that room in my nightgown; & lying down after a page: & always with the certainty of failure . . .' (*D*, V, pp. 31–2).

What is striking about this description is the prevailing sense of paralysis or dysfunction. The 'certainty of failure' is sad, particularly given that the central thesis of *The Years* is strikingly, indeed uncharacteristically, clear. It is as though Woolf were unable to depict and describe a double bind without writing herself straight into the heart of it, and this process of identification with her material undoubtedly served, in this instance, to affect the novel's tone and mood. It seems almost as though *The Years* had demonstrated only too well Virginia Woolf's subtle thesis; as though she had described almost too successfully the constraints on creative expression, so that, writing it, she suffered 'catastrophic illness': had 'never been so near to the precipice of [her] own feeling since 1913' – the year in which she had first attempted suicide.

The Years demonstrates throughout, as it unfolds, the effects of Woolf's efforts to keep chaos in check. In the 1913 section of the novel, for example, she introduces the Pargiters' servant, Crosby, and her dog, Rover, almost as a stabilising force with which to keep some of the finer feelings which emerge during the course of that section under control. Crosby of course turns up again in *Three Guineas* in the context of Woolf's assault on infantile fixation in men and of her criticism of the convention of denying sensual responses by resorting to accepted conversational tactics:

> but we . . . become aware at once of some 'strong emotion' on your side 'arising from some motive below the level of conscious thought' by the ringing of an alarm bell within us; a confused and tumultuous clamour: You shall not, shall not, shall not . . . The physical symptoms are unmistakeable. . . . Intellectually, there is a strong desire to be silent; or to change the conversation; to drag in, for example, some old family servant, called Crosby; whose dog Rover had died . . . and so evade the issue . . .
> (*TG*, p. 179)

Mitchell Leaska has noted Crosby's appearance in the 1913 Section, and in answering the pertinent question, 'What . . . was it that prevented [Woolf] from completing the Essay–Novel as it was originally planned?',[16] he quotes Woolf's Diary reference to her 1913 collapse, arguing that it was her need to excise this experience from the text of *The Years* which caused not only the 'catastrophic illness' which she suffered again, in the course of writing the novel, but also the smoothing out of the project as it was originally conceived into conventional fictional form.

There is, moreover, more to say. If we read the Crosby section, as well as the autobiographical data to which its dating corresponds, the text of *The Years* shows the extent to which Woolf used Crosby as a means of controlling the mood of the story, and of focusing one of the central dichotomies of the book. Here, for example, is Crosby, having left Abercorn Terrace and the Pargiter family, setting out her things in her new room:

> It was small, but when she had unpacked her things it was comfortable enough. It had a look of Abercorn Terrace. Indeed for many years she had been hoarding odds and ends with a view to her retirement. . . . She ranged them askew on the mantelpiece, and when she had hung the portraits of the family – . . . it was quite like home.
> (*Y*, p. 168)

'It had a look of Abercorn Terrace . . . – it was quite like home.' Crosby's method of storing up the solid objects which had for her represented life with the Pargiters can be transposed from one locus to another and the scene of her past life recreated, in a Platonic mode in which a break in repetition can only be tolerated if the new is as like the old as possible. The old order is re-established, for Crosby, by the solid objects and habits of the Pargiters' family life; the new can only be tolerated as a version of the old.

This is the patriarchal system underlying the Pargiter daughters' existence, in which the difference between girls and women, for example, can only be tolerated if the transition is kept from view. Crosby, the female servant, is of course a product of the pre-war order: one textual significance of Woolf's dating of the Crosby section is that it sets her precisely on the eve of the First World War: her personal disruption and the precarious, faithful and somewhat naive re-establishment of an order which can now only exist in mementoes precedes a similar national disturbance, and a similar attitude on the part of many people to the objects of their desire (the Colonel's to his daughters, perhaps).

By contrast, the more intellectually orientated women in *The Years* are shown evolving a new, essentially Nietzschean order. In the section preceding Crosby's (the 1911 section) Eleanor goes to the country to visit her brother Morris and his wife, Celia. Upstairs in her room, Eleanor makes a contrasting transition from place to place:

> The maid had already unpacked her things . . . she slipped on her evening dress in front of the looking-glass. She twisted her thick hair, with the grey strand in it, rapidly into a coil; . . . and gave one glance at the woman who had been for fifty-five years so familiar that she no longer saw her – Eleanor Pargiter. That she was getting old was obvious; there were wrinkles . . . where the flesh used to be firm.
>
> And what was my good point? she asked herself . . . My eyes, yes, she thought. Somebody had once praised her eyes . . . But that's over, she thought, people praising my eyes, and finished her dressing. (*Y*, pp. 152–3)

The obvious differences between her material situation and Crosby's make one kind of comparison between the two worlds: Crosby's treasures are the Pargiters' cast-offs; Eleanor has a maid. This aspect of the novel is consistently weak, since Crosby has to carry the entire weight of working class life in her single personification, which is too passive to take the stress of Woolf's ideological point in relation to the whole, sprawling gamut of Pargiters and their class assumptions. But the other difference, represented here in the contrast between Crosby and Eleanor, concerns assumptions about change and identity. Where Crosby's world is based on Platonic archetypes, Eleanor's hovers on the edge of at least the possibility of Nietzschean disparity. Her assumption is that change is progressive and inevitable as well as irrevocable: the present cannot replace the past and the conditions of her everyday life do not perpetually call up, as they do for Crosby, the need for terms of comparison. Later, as Eleanor is falling asleep, this becomes even clearer, and in imagery more immediately characteristic of Virginia Woolf:

> Again the sense came to her of a ship padding softly through the waves; of a train swinging from side to side down a railway line. Things can't go on for ever, she thought. Things pass, things change, she thought, looking up at the ceiling. And where are we going? Where? Where? . . . The moths were dashing round the ceiling: . . .   (*Y*, p. 164)

Eleanor falls asleep with the words of the book she has been reading running in her head: it is an English translation of Dante: 'For by so many more there are who say "ours" / So much the more of good doth each possess' (*Y*, p. 163): 'the words did not give out their full meaning, but seemed to hold something furled up in the hard shell of the archaic Italian' (pp. 163–4). The suggestion of a Socialist principle, Eleanor's confusion, and the sound of the book being dropped to the floor, all seem to stir some rhythmical chant suggestive of change and transition ('And where are we going? Where? Where?') but the words seem to seek no source or origin: they simply seem to circle out into darkness and oblivion. At this point in the novel Woolf shows us Eleanor – whose life revolves around the structured and repetitious round of committee meetings, charity visits and social events that mark out her life – seeking oblivion, making an escape from the compromises of society; Eleanor – and this is most indicative of Woolf's intentions in this passage – in the presence of the moths, circling, as it were, between *The Waves* and *Between the Acts*, and harking back to a transitional moment in which Woolf had reflected on the possibility of writing a 'semi mystic, very profound life of a woman, which shall all be told on one occasion.'

In *The Waves*, only the signals of some obscure desire to articulate loss and longing survive as the residue of that attempt; in *The Years*, such passages as this one hint yet again at the necessity to *expurgate* such material, in deference to other, more forcibly established 'facts' of life. *The Years* does show Virginia Woolf 'breaking the mould made by The Waves' (*op. cit.*) by attempting, in the first instance, to marshall the material for a more structured work which would show up some of the central paradoxes and dichotomies of the system. But, as the passage about Eleanor shows, in the individual female mind the differences between the old order and any new one would be based on far more subtle and imponderable distinctions than that between 'fiction' and 'fact'. Further, how, from a woman's point of view, might it be possible to tell the difference?

The attempt to find a new 'mould' for her writing in *The Years* raised again for Woolf the question of the double standard of her role as narrator. In the earlier text, *The Pargiters*, she confronts the relationships between sexuality and social form, 'being' and 'non-being' and also, significantly, reading and writing, through the medium of the tortuous sexual consciousness of the bachelor-scholar, Edward Pargiter. In Chapter Three of *The Pargiters*, she gives a detailed examination of Edward's thought-processes on the subject of sex, which has been expurgated by the time it reaches its published form, in *The Years*.

The passage describes Edward Pargiter attempting to 'run through the Antigone' (p. 63) on the eve of his examination and finding, to his chagrin, that his concentration is ominously beginning to flag. He is all right until he begins to attempt to revise the sections describing the two women, Antigone and Isme, in conversation together, but at this point his imagination begins to get the better of him. Reading is for him a sensual experience: he sips a glass of wine and relaxes on his cushions as he reads, (capitalising, presumably, on the luxurious conditions to which students in men's colleges had – in Woolf's mind, certainly – become accustomed). But when he begins to run through the Antigone and Isme passages, this sensuousness begins to turn into something else:

> another sense began to assert itself – a sense that was quite familiar to
> Edward; that was sometimes a perfect plague; a sense that was almost
> entirely physical; that was worrying, bothering, because, almost instantly,
> Edward's mind came into conflict with it & said 'I will not let myself feel
> this – this is degrading – this is bestial – . . .'   (*P.* p. 67)

As male sexuality begins to assert itself, Virginia Woolf's prose begins to falter accordingly.

He forces himself to turn the pages and read – significantly – the Chorus, in which Antigone and Isme have no part. The problem is, though, that 'the thought of the two sisters, the one so fierce and daring, the other so simple, so charming, . . . coalesced to form an ideal of womanhood which moved Edward not to desire them, but to produce something, to be something' (*ibid.*). For 'if Isme was sympathetic, Antigone was tremendous, would bless & sanction & reward' (p. 68). The ideal of womanhood, then – chaste submission, combined with heroic omnipotence – is something he is moved not to engage with or even admire, but rather to appropriate to his own ends. From this, his thoughts move straight to Kitty Malone, the lover he appears to adore from afar, since 'he had passed by a natural transition from the abstract reverence for womanhood . . . to a thought that was less abstract, but

was still lustrous with something of the same wonder and awe' (*ibid.*).
Kitty may be made of flesh and blood, but she has here become a
mythical figure, endowed with the same qualities as Antigone and Isme
combined, and as unattainable as a character in a Greek drama. (Next,
he writes a poem 'in the Greek hand, very Greek', a marginal note
reveals). Can 'fluid fiction' really dissolve, as easily and effortlessly as
Edward would have it, into 'hard fact'?

Ironically enough, Kitty's function here seems to be to *allay* rather
than direct the sexual arousal which Woolf had attempted so fumbling-
ly to portray, though it is not clear that Woolf herself was alert to the
irony of this. Edward is reduced to standing at the open window, taking
deep breaths, until he can stand it no longer and stumbles back into his
room to write a poem addressed to Katharine Persephone Malone (her
middle name, as he has discovered quite by chance, is Persephone). The
poem expresses 'what was, after all, a very natural feeling' – that it was
'for her, now, more than for himself more than for his father, that he
desired success' (p. 69). If only he could live his life on her behalf.

In the Essay following, Woolf explains the way in which patriarchal
logic serves to turn male sexuality to male advantage, re-defining power
as the ability to conquer feeling (so she perceives, in *Three Guineas*, the
typical mode of the professional man). When, reading the *Antigone*,
Edward feels 'sensations with which he had long been familiar', he
simply proceeds to combat them, and as the process of suppressing all
this is disagreeable, this serves all the more effectively to generate self-
approval: 'He had conquered' (p. 81).

Thus the recognition of sexual inclination is 'conquered', in Woolf's
recitation, by its transposition into a paternal feeling in relation to a
notion of Ideal Womanhood, and Edward becomes the hero of his
own, entirely private, battle on two counts: not only because self
discipline (self-denial, rather) is in itself a manly virtue, but because the
Womanly Ideal he conjures up cannot fail to reflect on his good taste
and judgement, and so do him credit. In this way, another version of the
Platonic repetition which runs through *The Years* is here brought into
play: Kitty Malone becomes for Edward simply a version of an archetype supplied by the combined imagery of his learning and his imagination. In this case, however, a curious elision occurs in the course of the
transformation. In the process of his reading of the *Antigone* the two
female characters from Sophocles' drama, who have themselves contributed to Edward's notion of the female ideal, suddenly begin to tease
themselves into life, needing in their turn to be 'conquered' back into
their roles as archetypes. This is achieved by Edward's forcing a break

in the process of reading, which he does by casting around outside the framework of the text for some contrived distraction: '"I will not let myself feel this – . . . . I am not going to be beaten this time." And he looked instinctively at . . . the . . . photograph of a fine austere face (. . .) which stood on the mantelpiece. Old Bealby had conquered . . . had always taught them how to conquer. Exercise was one way. That was at the back of his passion for sports – partly' (p. 67).

It is thus, Woolf implies, that the public school system for boys nurtures the double standard which at once recognises and counters the sensation which she begins to characterise, from the woman's point of view, as 'different kinds of love', and has the heroic, apparently celibate male dismiss as 'a perfect plague'. Her own unease with what is being discussed comes across in her choice of vocabulary, the structural awkwardness of the prose and her apparent obliviousness to some of the central ironies; her innocence in the face of male education, and male sexuality, has its bearing on the composition of the text. But she very clearly here has something to say about 'the social system' that can breed a male race so responsive to its own efforts towards disingenuousness. The critique of Edward's 'heroism', which involves appropriating female silence in support of the suppression of inconvenient desire, draws attention to the extent of male Bad Faith. Edward, seen here in the process of subduing a force he fully understands the implications of, expects to appropriate a woman as his accomplice in this procedure, but knows (or at least, 'the system' 'knows') that women can only play such roles as long as they are kept in ignorance of the impulses on which their appropriation is based. Women, so the paradox runs, must remain chaste in order to be 'ideal women'.

Edward, so Woolf tries to suggest, is an impressive scholar – he understands things in theory – but the description of his scholarship makes poignantly clear just how little Woolf knew about the business of scholarship. Edward, she tells us, could not only read the *Antigone* without opening a dictionary, he also knew 'a mass of other facts – . . . who had used the word besides Sophocles, & where; & how Sophocles had used the same word with a different meaning elsewhere; & he knew exactly where the metre in the Choruses changed' (pp. 63–4): nothing very creative about this method of reading. Moreover, despite his impeccable scholarship (the limitations of which nevertheless serve to draw attention to Woolf's own limited access to the worlds of scholarship and education) there is a level beyond which Edward's intelligence cannot take him. In *The Years*, it is as though Edward's character shows all the marks of that dubious education exposed so graphically to the reader in *The Pargiters*. A wallflower at Delia's party, at the close of *The Years*, he is asked by North to explain the significance of the Greek Chorus:

> 'My dear boy,' [Eleanor] heard Edward say . . . , 'don't ask me. I was never a great hand at that. No, if I'd had my way' – he paused and passed his hand over his forehead – 'I should have been . . .' A burst of laughter drowned his words. She could not catch the end of his sentence. What had he said – what had he wished to be?   (*Y*, p. 325)

Where reading serves to screen or veil meaning, the process of reading becomes a restricted practice, and Edward, like Bernard (though Edward, significantly, has no thought of writing a novel; can only read, in the most conventional ways, selected texts) cannot finish his own story. By the same token, he can never completely extricate himself from the world of learning (presumably because he goes on resisting the temptation to fully understand what he knows and sees); he never marries; is never really convivial or socially integrated; he seems debarred from the world of social and personal intercourse on which, however unsatisfactorily, the world of *The Pargiters* is based.

In *The Years*, Woolf presents the reading process from the point of view of Sara, the slightly crazed character whose candidness is the result of her exploiting, rather than subduing, her creatively idiosyncratic vision. Sara, who is a partial invalid, is reading her cousin Edward Pargiter's gift to her of his own edition of the text of the *Antigone* (he has progressed thus far, since his appearance in *The Pargiters*). In the passage which describes Sara's reading, she lies in bed listening to the sounds of a party coming in through her bedroom window. It is a section of *The Years* in which the eccentric aspect of the novel is given free rein, and in which the writing shows again the attempt on Woolf's part to create a 'new mould':

> She opened the book at random; but her eye was caught by one of the couples . . . in the garden . . . What were they saying, she wondered? There was something gleaming in the grass, . . . the black-and-white figure stooped and picked it up.   (*Y*, p. 104)

As she watches the figure pick up the object, she imagines the dialogue between lovers: 'Behold, Miss Smith,' he says, 'what I have found on the grass – a fragment of my heart; of my broken heart, . . .'

(*ibid.*). She hums the words she has invented in time to the waltz music she can hear, then pauses, and glances at the fly-leaf of the book:

> 'Sara Pargiter from her Cousin Edward Pargiter.'
> '. . . for love,' she concluded, 'is best.'
> She turned to the title-page.
>   'The Antigone of Sophocles, done into English verse
> by Edward Pargiter,' she read . . .
> (ibid.)

Once more, she is distracted: the couple outside are by now moving up the staircase. She watches them, then turns to her book again:

> She skipped through the pages. At first she read a line or two at random; then, from the litter of broken words, scenes rose, quickly, inaccurately, as she skipped. The unburied body of a murdered man lay like a fallen tree-trunk, like a statue, with one foot stark in the air . . . Then a yellow cloud came whirling – who? She turned the pages quickly. Antigone? . . . the horsemen leapt down; she was seized; her wrists were bound with withies; and they bore her, thus bound – where?
>   There was a roar of laughter from the garden. . . . Where did they take her? (Y, p. 105)

Like Mrs Ramsay reading The Fisherman's Wife to her son, Sara's attention constantly wanders from the story to what is going on around her, so that what is happening in the here and now almost seems to take the form of a Chorus or audience, except that by comparison with what is happening in the story, external events take on an inconsequential or even faintly nonsensical air; the 'commentary' of the actual, living characters seems wide of the mark, as it does at the close of *The Years*, where nobody can quite find the appropriate thing to say at North's party.

Sara continues to read, at the same time continuing to observe the events taking place in the garden:

> The man's name was Creon. He buried her . . . [He] gave three sharp taps with his mallet on the brick. She was buried alive. The tomb was a brick mound. There was just room for her to lie straight out. Straight out in a brick tomb, she said. And that's the end, she yawned, shutting the book. (Y, pp. 104–5)

Once Antigone – the central focus of Sara's interest – is buried, the story is effectively over.

The difference between Edward's reading and Sara's is marked. Edward focuses initially on what each word signifies; on how and where Sophocles had used the same word elsewhere; on when the metre changes; then reads his own state of mind in the novel, so that the central female characters combine to endow the real woman in his life with the status of the reader's muse. Sara's reading process constitutes the antithesis of this approach. She skips pages; reads a line or two at random; turns her attention easily from the book to the scene outside her window and back again; and all the time maintains a relationship, as reader, with her text which ensures that the text, though a more gripping 'story' than what is actually happening, retains its status as fiction. The identification with Antigone is implied, but Sara is in no way swayed, as Edward is, into appropriating the world as though it were a fiction conducive to her methods of interpretation.

The relationship between Sara and the text of the *Antigone* is complex, partly because Sara is presented as an eccentric, slightly deformed character, and yet Woolf clearly intended her to play a central role: 'Sara is the real difficulty,' she recorded in her Diary, 'I cant [*sic*] get her into the main stream, yet she is essential' (*D*, IV, p. 281). Sara's closeness to the unconscious was intended to be instrumental in establishing a tone for *The Years* which would enable Woolf to avoid the note of propaganda which she kept coming up against and backing off from: 'I have a horror of the Aldous novel: that must be avoided. But ideas are sticky things: wont coalesce; hold up the creative, subconscious faculty: thats it I suppose' (*ibid.*).

One critic sees Antigone as a kind of simile for Sara, arguing that Sara's bedroom might be seen as a kind of burial chamber and that Sara's is 'the "divine voice" of the oracle, . . . She, the hunchback, says we are all cripples in a cave, . . .'[17] but Woolf's reference to 'cripples in a cave' is in *Three Guineas*, where she had outlined in detail her fears about society: 'if people are highly successful in their professions they lose their senses . . . What then remains. . . ? Only a cripple in a cave' (*op. cit.*). Of the entire population of characters in *The Years*, Sara is probably the only one who has *not* to some extent lost her senses to the cause of Society: it is Sara's crucial role precisely to remain *outside* the framework of society and its formalities and demands, and to act as outsider to and commentator on its constraints. Her inability to take society seriously, her difficulty with quite adducing significance to social actions and events, sometimes, makes society itself seem rather like an odd, formal dance, the 'black-and-white' participants conversing in a language which is not quite comprehensible, and 'the creative, subconscious faculty' is given an opportunity to show through the cracks almost solely through the personification of Sara and her 'readings' of the world.

There is an actual 'Chorus', in *The Years*: at the end of the novel, a group of children belonging to the caretaker begin to sing, but in a way that is neither portentous nor instructive: 'Their voices were so harsh; the accent was so hideous . . . There was something horrible in the noise they made. It was so shrill, so discordant, so meaningless' (p. 327). This – the 'commentary' of the younger generation and the promise of things to come – bears no resemblance whatever to a Greek Chorus, resembling rather, both in its impossible intonations and in the assembled company's reactions to it, the discordant shriek, heard earlier in the novel, of the sirens.[18] These are not sirens in the Greek mode, however: very far from it. They are simply the discordant, piercing warnings of further discord, disharmony, impending crisis. 'Where are we going? Where?' seems to be the predominant note around which *The Years* is constructed, and the mingling of generations and classes at the end of the novel seems to portend not harmony, but simply confusion, and a continuing *lack* of any hope for new modes of communication or means of exchange ('The children . . . began to make off. As they slipped past Martin, he slipped coins into their hands' (*ibid.*).

As in *Mrs Dalloway*, the early novel in which Woolf had also toyed with ideas for a possible Chorus, the desire 'to be; to exist; to sum it all up' also prevails, but here no one has the least idea how to do it, except by observing the conventions. Sara, like Clarissa Dalloway, can envisage the possibility of a phenomenological relationship with the world, but her description of it only serves to make this aspiration seem hopelessly reductive: 'she would let herself *be* thought . . . the whole of her must be laid out passively to take part in this universal process . . . living. She stretched herself out. Where did thought begin?' (pp. 102–3). Letting go seems, here, suggestive only of inertia; again, as in *The Waves*, there seems to be no origin; no way of originating a sense of self.

The difference between Sara and Clarissa is that Sara can never stop thinking, and the narrator is never fully absorbed in Sara's point of view: we are always aware, as readers, that Sara presents only one angle on the world, and a somewhat distorted one at that (though no more distorted than anyone else's for all that she may be more eccentric). In *Mrs Dalloway* social vacuousness and frigidity are countered by an alternative vision – of Clarissa scintillating in her mermaid green dress, Clarissa reflecting on the way things might have been – but in *The Years* there is no alternative, imagined framework: the gig lamps are symmetrically arranged; life is, and was ever, thus.

Woolf offers, in *The Years*, no artist's impression of a different kind of life, other than Sara's chaotic and spasmodic capacity to pick the whole fabric to pieces. If she can imagine the shattering of the glass, she has no way of envisaging how the world might be reflected differently: she is no Lily Briscoe. The vision of the future which Brown tries vainly to express, at the close of the novel, cannot be articulated because he has no language in which to express this vision, other than the terms in which the rest of the company seem intent on shouting him down. If Mrs Dalloway's vision of the future is lateral and imaginary, there seems to be no way forward for the characters in *The Years*, and yet no other way than forward into more of that which, paradoxically, can no longer ultimately be tolerated.

In this sense, at least, Woolf's earlier work may be seen to imply within its narrative frameworks a vision which she describes in *Three Guineas* as a society of Outsiders – with their focus on individuality, sensuality, and a refusal simply to absorb prior established values – in a way in which *The Years* cannot. What comes through in *The Years*, particularly in Woolf's characterisation of Sara, is the desire to be put in touch with something out of the present reach of the conscious mind: Sara hovers on the brink of some access to some profound and 'semi mystic' knowledge, or way of seeing, which may properly belong to, or at least originate with, women, but which is being edited out (within the 'story' of *The Years*, as well as in the process of composition) in the interests of the maintenance of the status quo and of an insidious process of sexual censorship. The almost unbearably arid quality of life in *The Years* predominates throughout the novel, and if Edward's fumbling attempts at learning seem to cry out for a contrasting female approach to the 'text' of life, Sara's reading – because she is uneducated and to all intents and purposes ostracised from most of life – cannot supply it.

There was, Woolf sensed, something about the world of the Ancient Greeks which she seems to want her characters to have access to in *The Years*: when she herself attempted to read the Greeks, she noted, she felt that they were 'more self-conscious than children, and yet, all those thousands of years ago, . . . know all that is to be known.' In an ancient Greek text, she felt, 'There is a sadness at the back of life which they do not attempt to mitigate. Entirely aware of their own standing in the shadow, and yet alive to every tremor and gleam of existence, there they endure', and it was to the Greeks that she turned, she wrote, 'when . . . sick of the vagueness, of the confusion, of the Christianity and its consolations, of our own age.'[19]

Ironically enough, the text in which she wrote this is entitled 'On Not Knowing Greek': she had a taste of what those texts evoked, through youthful discussions with Thoby and later in her lessons with Janet Case, but she was frustrated by her lack of detailed knowledge. What she sensed the possibility of there, however – some attention, in literature, to 'every tremor and gleam of existence', and some antithesis of the Platonic Christianity of her own age – is a mood, and a level of understanding, which she again and again finds ways of expressing in her fiction. Here in *The Years*, she goes some way towards depicting, through Sara, the difficulty of wanting to substitute one archetype for another, given that there can be no ultimate means of comparison, and of articulating the tension between Platonic ideals, which can so easily and objectively be expressed, and Nietszchean aspirations, which in Eleanor and Sara can only take the form of some barely articulable, essentially shadowy form of articulation. There is only so far that any of us can go, she seems to be saying, when hampered by lack of knowledge, frustrated in our desire for experience.

In a strange way the message of her earlier novel, *Mrs Dalloway*, the novel in which an archetype of womanhood *does* evolve and become dramatised, anticipates the message of *The Years*, prefigured in that initial speech from which the whole, ambitious project was to evolve. In that speech, the entire fictitious enterprise of *The Pargiters* and *The Years* is momentarily glimpsed, and then as soon elided ('The future of fiction depends very much upon what extent men can be educated to stand free speech in women. But whether . . . given a better environment . . . women too can be artists lies on the laps of the Gods, no not upon the laps of the Gods, but upon your laps, upon the laps of professional women' (*P*, pp. xxix–xl). It is women's knowledge, not oracles or the wishes of the Gods, which will ultimately effect changes in the lives of women, as Clarissa Dalloway, who muddled Armenians and Turks and has given up on the complicated and painful attempt to remain faithful to her own potential, illustrates, as it were, by default.

In that speech – which initiated *The Pargiters*, ultimately *The Years* and possibly also *Three Guineas*[20] – Virginia Woolf evoked, then dismissed, the Greek Gods in order to gesture towards an alternative possibility: an alternative way of conveying a message about the possibility of envisaging a new world, a world in which women might infiltrate something of their experience as Outsiders into the patriarchal structures which it might become newly feasible for them to inhabit as individuals in their own right. If *The Years* depicts a bleak world, a world of social and familial constraint, the censorship rather than the dissemination of meaning, in which inarticularcy prevails and creativity is discouraged, she does at least depict there, without self-deception or projection or fantasy, her vision of the infinitesimal, painful and painstaking beginnings of a challenge to the patriarchal world as she 'read' it: a world with both a history and a future of a kind, even if it was a future which could not easily be imagined; a world which seemed almost entirely resistant to, but which would surely be forced, at some stage or 'on one occasion', to accommodate change.

6

The Heart of Darkness
(*Between the Acts*)

> He felt that he had been in the middle of a jungle; in the heart of darkness;
> cutting his way towards the light; but provided only with broken sentences,
> single words, with which to break through the briar-bush of human bodies,
> human wills and voices, that bent over him, binding him, blinding
> him . . .   (*Y*, p. 313)

The Years closes on an unexciting family party, in which polite
conversation is attempted, questions posed but never really answered,
and it becomes more and more difficult to speak intelligibly above the
noise of the crowd. One of the characters, North, is being called upon
by the rest of the assembled group to make some kind of speech which
would sum up and mark the occasion, but the pressure on him to do so
simply focuses his feeling of being impeded or obstructed: he feels he is
'in the heart of darkness; cutting his way towards the light; but provided only with broken sentences, single words, with which to break
through the briar-bush of human bodies, human wills and voices, that
bent over him, binding him, blinding him' (*Y*, p. 313).

Virginia Woolf felt, after completing *The Years*, that she had failed to
achieve it in what she had intended for the book. Ultimately, the strictly
sequential story had constrained her, and she more or less agreed with
Stephen Spender, who wrote to say that though he liked *The Years*
better than her other books, the problem for him was that *all* the
characters seemed to look upon their experience as being in some way
invalid or unreal. 'Eleanor's experience was meant to be all right',
Woolf explained to him in reply, but the other characters were 'crippled
in one way or another – though I meant Maggie and Sara', she added, 'to
be outside that particular prison' (*L*, VI, p. 122). The form of the novel,
she explained, had also been a problem: 'I expect I muted the characters
down too much, in order to shorten and keep their faces towards
society; and altogether muffled the proportions: which should have
given a round, not a thin line' (*L*, VI, p. 116).

The invalidity of the characters' lives, Spender suggested, was probably an impression created by the lack of dramatised action: Woolf had not, for example, depicted the Front. She had not done so, she explained, because as a woman, fighting was not within the bounds of her experience, but also because, she explained, 'I think action generally unreal. Its the thing we do in the dark that is more real; the thing we do because peoples eyes are on us seems to me histrionic, small boyish. However I havent got this expressed,' she added, 'and I daresay difference of sex makes a different view' (*L*, VI, p. 122).

It seems from this as though there is a sense in which the point of *The Years* had been to dramatise the social constraints on 'the thing we do in the dark' in order to indicate its contrasting importance. But the finished text of *The Years* is so effective in its portrayal of the network of censorships operating in order to thwart the development of any significant inner life that this censored alternative becomes, in *The Years*, not only private, subjective, interiorised, but ultimately completely inaccessible – to both characters and, of course, the reader. Highly imaginative characters slide into madness; sexuality is taboo. There *is* some potential for change envisaged in *The Years*: the characters hover dangerously on the brink of the knowledge that the old order cannot continue indefinitely in the face of new social and political pressures, but there is also, just barely discernible in the published text, as well as in *The Pargiters*, some male intuition regarding the potentially dangerous influence of the female sex, which must at all costs be resisted. In the text of *The Pargiters*, we are explicitly shown Edward Pargiter's public school-boyish mechanisms for dealing with the power of women; in the published text of *The Years* North deals, a good deal more obscurely, with the imagery of falling petals, which suddenly materialise in his unconscious as he begins to fall asleep in the middle of the party: 'Through his half-open eyes he saw hands holding flowers . . . Then petals fell . . . There they lay, violet and yellow, . . . boats on a river. And he was floating, and drifting, . . . in a petal, down a river into silence, into solitude . . . (*Y*, p. 323).

It is as though Woolf must find for herself, here at the close of *The Years*, a way of re-invoking the imagery of unconscious femininity with which she had grappled earlier. Here, in a kind of reverie, North submits to an imagery of femininity which now takes on the form of a vessel or vehicle. Relinquishing all control, unable to make himself heard above the noise of the crowd, he submits, but Virginia Woolf cannot pursue this line of argument within the framework of *The Years*, since the balance of power in that novel is so firmly weighted towards patriarchal control. Each time she finds a language, in that novel, to subvert this structure of power relations, the narrative begins to slide into chaos, and such reveries are simply phased out. If a feminine point of view were to predominate, Woolf would perhaps be required to experiment with a much more chaotic, more disruptive narrative mode; to lift some of the veils over 'the thing we do in the dark', and to keep in mind the possibility that 'difference of sex makes a different view'. In *Between the Acts* she was to go on to do just that.

It seems clear from the early drafts of *Between the Acts* (originally to be entitled *Pointz Hall*)[1] that Woolf decided, at some level, to pick up again on an idea she had fleetingly had prior to writing *The Waves*: a 'play-poem idea: the idea of some continuous stream, not solely of human thought, but of the ship, the night etc. all flowing together' (*D*, III, p. 139): the germ of the idea is there at the close of *The Years*. The first Diary entry specifically relating to *Between the Acts* shows that she began to conceive it in the form of a scenario: 'Last night I began making up again: Summers night: a complete whole: that's my idea' (*D*, V, p. 133).

A fortnight later the idea had begun to develop, and she was now setting the scene at 'Poyntzet Hall', and planning to take in the whole of literature: 'why not Poyntzet Hall: a centre: all lit. discussed . . .' (*D*, V, p. 135). It is significant that she was also, at this time, writing her commissioned biography of Roger Fry, which necessitated an attention to factual detail which was driving her to distraction and in which there are strange, bland gaps, possibly occasioned by a certain amount of detail she would have needed to ignore in the interests of a number of individuals whose lives had converged with Fry's and who were still alive. Her 'nose rubbed in Roger' for hours at a stretch, she got into the habit of breaking off with a sense of great relief to write some fiction, into which she characteristically wanted to infuse everything: 'a complete whole' . . . '& anything that comes into my head; but "I" rejected: "We" substituted' (*D*, V, p. 135).

This shift from 'I' to 'We' – though she had attempted this before, notably in *The Waves* – also had a particular application at this time. As she began writing *Between the Acts*, she was still awaiting publication of *Three Guineas*, and she did so in a state of great anticipation and some dread. In the 'airy world of Poyntz Hall' she initially felt 'extremely little' by comparison with the feelings aroused in her in anticipation of *Three Guineas* being launched upon the world – 'What I'm afraid of,' she noted, 'is the taunt Charm and emptiness. The book I wrote with such violent feelings to relieve that immense pressure will not dimple the surface. That is my fear' (*D*, V, p. 141). Moreover, she felt yet more specifically that in *Three Guineas* she had taken the enormous risk of exposing *herself*, and she clearly anticipated shocked reactions to a point of view which she expected to be received as being quite outrageous: 'Also,' she noted, 'I'm uneasy at taking this role in the public eye – afraid of autobiography in public' (*ibid.*). But her total conviction in the wisdom of what she had said had inspired in her a tremendous, and uncharacteristic, feeling of strength and of resolution. Her fears were entirely outweighed, she assured herself, by the relief of having unburdened herself of her 'violent' feelings about the way in which society seemed to be run to male advantage. She could now, she felt, enjoy this moment of triumph: 'For having spat it out, my mind is made up. I need never recur or repeat. I am an outsider. I can take my way: experiment with my own imagination in my own way. The pack may howl, but it shall never catch me . . . I'm free' (*ibid.*).

'I am an outsider.' It was in this frame of mind that she began to plan a new novel, set in an English country house, with a terrace where nursemaids would walk, and a 'perpetual variety & change from intensity to prose' (*D*, V, p. 135). Very soon, she had resolved that it would in the end turn into a play, and this can be seen as a logical development of her determination, begun in *Three Guineas*, to give a rather more public performance of her views on society and 'the thing we do in the dark' than she had hitherto had the confidence to give. The discretions involved in writing Roger Fry's biography so soon after his death also undoubtedly played their part in this new resolve.

In addition, she began to prepare, alongside the manuscript, a collection of poems – some in metre, some in prose – collectively headed 'possible poems for P.H.'[2] Some of these anticipate the incantatory style of the poetry chanted by Isa in the published text, representing rather awkwardly expressed meditations on 'life', but what is striking about them is their essentially unpoetic quality. Again, as in *The Years*, she needed to find a mode in which to present a kind of commentary on action, and the poems may have served, at some level, the function of the chanting of a – here, invisible – chorus.

Much of the text which began as poetry has been transposed into narrative by the time it appears in the published draft. In the process, Woolf has toned it down: the 'message' of the poem, which is sometimes – as in the following passage – strikingly violent or crude –

has been 'civilised' somewhat, by the time it appears in narrative form. The following recitation, for example, originally formed part of the collection of 'possible poems for P.H.':

> Aren't you beautiful, life, with your many lamps shining,
> The rose and the red hot poker.
> But of course, as the poet says, There's a worm in the rose,
> And the papers say, A knife in the red hot poker.
> Aren't you dull, life, and tedious,
> With your basin of water, in which the last lodger washed his hands,
> When he stayed here; you know the story; it was in the papers:
> The man who killed the girl who came up from the country.
> He stripped her; then he killed her.
> For there's always a worm; or a knife; in the poker.[3]

The attempt to write poetry based on the imagery of worms and blades draws vivid attention to the fact that, for Woolf, these were essentially not 'poetic' images, revealing Woolf as either an astonishingly inept poet, or as a novelist struggling with an imagery which she cannot quite bring herself to accommodate within her prose. In the published text these warrior-flowers have been deleted – masculinity could not, it seems, ultimately be represented by poisonous or decaying flowers: it was not simply a question of turning the tables. Instead, Woolf supplies in the narrative the story they were unable, in the medium of poetry, to tell: that of male cruelty, which feeds upon the defencelessness of the female imagination, which it has so disingenuously gone out of its way to render defenceless.

In *Between the Acts*, the story is represented as newspaper reportage; told at one remove; and the symbolism of knives and worms has been erased:

> she took [*The Times*] and read: 'A horse with a green tail . . .' which was fantastic. Next, 'The guard at Whitehall . . .' which was romantic and then, building word upon word she read: 'The troopers told her the horse had a green tail; but she found it was just an ordinary horse. And they dragged her up to the barrack room where she was thrown upon a bed. Then one of the troopers removed part of her clothing, and she screamed and hit him about the face . . . (*BA*, p. 19)

It's 'fantastic'; it's 'romantic', and so she reads on. Woolf is interested, here, as in *The Years*, not only in the tall stories of men, but in the *process* by which they make themselves heard by women.

This deft translation enables the emergence of important themes, and reflects a masculine capacity to make up stories which cannot be taken at face value, since they appeal to and exploit the romantic expectations of women. The activity of reading the stories spun by men thus necessitates the forging of meaning piece by piece; a new process of interpretation (the continuation of the process Sara had begun on, in *The Years*). It is this wisdom that Miss La Trobe can be seen to be attempting to convey, through the medium of the pageant and in her ambitious aspirations regarding intended audience response, even though the attempt is presented by Woolf as pure slapstick farce: how, after all, could the unfortunate Miss La Trobe possibly have succeeded in an attempt which appears to have no precedent? The published version of the story read by Isa of male brutality, with its unpublished, suggestive moral ('For there's always a worm; or a knife in the poker') in fact establishes specific connections with the pageant, which depicts the Machiavellian nature of male desire through the ages, echoing its wry, punning moral in its title: 'Where there's a Will there's a Way' (*BA*, p. 109).

Between the Acts, then, begins to reflect the powerlessness of women confronted with the stories told by men, with their potentially disabling undercurrents, and shows women gradually and painfully beginning to grasp what it is that men actually *mean*. For it is in the interstices of this novel – 'between the acts' – that the unscrupulous intentions of men, veiled beneath layer upon layer of 'ceremony' and convention, are beginning to be depicted and explored. The lives of women, the novel seems to suggest, have long been subject to such narratives, functioning as raw material and shielded beneath a screen of story-telling, which now require a complicated and painful process of unveiling. In the process, it may be necessary to learn how to *disrupt* narrative; to seek different ways of telling.

On the face of it, it might seem, as one critic has suggested, as though *Between the Acts* represents a commitment on Virginia Woolf's part to realist narrative. It tells, after all, a straightforwardly mimetic story of a group of thoroughly English people on a thoroughly English day, and concentrates on the social notations implicit in the activities of the group. Woolf's registering of subjective experience within the novel has also been regarded as 'an entirely traditional part of the English novel.'[4]

But if it does own 'a certain looking-glass likeness to life' (as Woolf describes the role and function of the novel in *A Room of One's Own*,[5] it also reflects a contradictory intention, fitting Woolf's alternative description of the novel, in *A Room of One's Own*, as having an architectural structure 'built now in squares, now pagoda shaped, now

throwing out wings and arcades, now solidly compact and domed . . .'
(*ROO*, p. 71).

It has been suggested that in *Between the Acts* the contradiction between two 'shapes' or modes of narration is represented in the contradiction between a narrative continuum and the recurrence of certain images, motifs, phrases, which seem to *detach* themselves from this continuum,[6] in rather the same way as Isa's poetry detaches itself from the 'narrative' of her marriage.

But the novel also *parodies* this contradiction. Both the mirror and the architectural structure – here, in the imagery of Pointz Hall itself – are figured as instruments, respectively, of reflection and containment, and both are found to fall short. Miss La Trobe's mirror, intended as a prop reflecting the present day – the stage of history at which the pageant is concluded – fails as a mimetic device in two respects. Firstly, it moves the play away from the 'realist' tradition dependent on an omniscient narrator, focusing the post-realist importance of audience participation, or 'reader response', a device which fails because the audience fails to see what is required. Lucy Swithin has an inkling: asked to imagine an entire scene, she colludes: '"Imagine?" said Mrs Swithin. "How right! Actors show us too much. The Chinese, you know, put a dagger on the table and that's a battle. And so Racine . . ."' (*BA*, p. 104). Fortuitously, she picks up on the notion not only of the play's relative status within the wider context of other cultures and other literature, but also on the imagery of the dagger – suggestive of male aggression – which Woolf herself has deleted from the text. Like the plant on the table which had begun by suggesting a centrepiece for *The Waves*, this could have become symbolic, but remains obscure. Lucy Swithin's observation is inconclusive, providing a hint for the reader, but no clue as to how to follow it up.

Secondly, the mirror is itself exposed and parodied as a mimetic device, drawing attention, in the true modernist tradition, to the constituents of the work's construction in a style which also smacks of pantomime farce: a cheval glass has been rigged up, so that the audience can see themselves, but it proves too heavy: 'Young Bonthrop for all his muscle couldn't lug the damned thing about any longer.' He stops, and so do the rest of the stage hands carrying 'hand glasses, tin cans, scraps of scullery glass, harness room glass, and heavily embossed silver mirrors.' And the baffled audience is thus subjected to a view of itself, 'not whole by any means, but at any rate sitting still.' The clock stops 'at the present moment', and everyone looks away, except for Mrs Manresa, who brings out her own small glass and proceeds to powder her nose (*BA*, pp. 134–5).

The scene is reminiscent rather of the predictions for the novel offered by Woolf in the early piece, 'Mr Bennett and Mrs Brown', than of any of the more measured alternatives predicted in *A Room of One's Own*. In the earlier piece, Woolf had concluded her discussion of the limitations of the 'materialists' by suggesting that 'we must reconcile ourselves to a season of failures and fragments,' reflecting that, in any climate of change, 'the novel is bound to reach us in rather an exhausted and chaotic condition' (*CDB*, p. 117). In fact, here, almost every element of the fiction is reduced to parody: the clock has stopped 'at the present moment': in reality, of course, an impossibility. 'Reality' is presented in fragments, but this is because the stage hands are tired. Mrs Manresa, the only character capable of facing 'herself', duly holds her own mirror up to this newly depicted version of 'nature', but only with a view to arranging her painted, powdered image: elsewhere in the novel we have been told that 'her hat, her rings, her finger nails red as roses, smooth as shells, were there for all to see. But not her life history . . . nothing private; no strict biographical facts' (p. 33).

In rather the same way, Pointz Hall as a structure or framework representing containment – the house 'as' narrative structure – falls short, though it is clear from the early draft that Woolf originally invested in this as a serious possibility. Originally, the text was to be divided into 'rooms' and the action organised into sections headed, for example, 'The Garden', 'The Terrace', 'The Library'.[7] By the time she came to draft the published version of the text, she was clearly envisaging the possibility of parodying this idea: the house still functions as an 'architectural' structure or container, but its architectural features have little to do with its interiors: 'The Master . . . would bring gentlemen sometimes to see the larder – . . . Not to see the hams . . . , but to see the cellar that opened out of the larder and its carved arch' (pp. 27–8).

Carved arches, at Pointz Hall, are rendered incidental; in fact, despite its appearance, the house is relatively modern, and lacking in any substantial history: 'The Olivers, who had bought the place something over a century ago, had no connection with . . . the old families who . . . lay in their deaths inter-twisted, like the ivy roots, beneath the churchyard wall' (p. 9).

There is, within the house, historical *material*. As one reached the top of the staircase, for example, there was a portrait: 'a small powdered face, a great head-dress slung with pearls, came into view; an ancestress of sorts . . . and under a glass case there was a watch that had stopped a bullet on the field of Waterloo' (pp. 9–10). But the 'ancestress of sorts' turns out to be a fake. There is another portrait, we learn later, this time of a real ancestor, and his portrait is a conversation piece. But the stories which ensue are tedious and inconsequential – his picture tells a story of dogs and clergymen, in parody of typically English upper class pre-occupations and priorities, but the story does not appear to lead any-where. Further, the two subjects in the respective pictures are entirely unrelated, so there is no history of connection, and neither portrait gives any information about the lineage of the Olivers.

The portrait of a lady – bought by Oliver 'because he liked the picture' (p. 30) – appears to suggest something in the way of a different *kind* of story. In a manner characteristic of Woolf's early, 'aesthetic' prose, she 'led the eye up, down, from the curve to the straight, through glades of greenery and shades of silver' – the description is reminiscent of the prose of 'Kew Gardens' or 'A Haunted House' – but she is only a picture, a 'pretend' portrait, and the promised insight into the history of the household remains obscure.

The lady's picture represents, moreover, not only the absence of history, but the emptiness of the mimetic structure of the house: she leads the eye 'through glades of greenery and shades of silver . . . into silence. The room was empty.' The emptiness of the room is empha-sised, in a paragraph which harks back, in tone, to the 'Time Passes' section of *To the Lighthouse*: 'Empty, empty, empty; silent, silent, silent. The room was a shell, singing of what was before time was; a vase stood in the heart of the house, alabaster, smooth, cold, holding the still, distilled essence of emptiness, silence' (p. 31). In this sense she represents simply the power of illusion, and parodies the significance of an empty house as being evocative of the absence of living beings, and vital connections. Throughout the 'Time Passes' section of *To the Lighthouse*, what haunts is the ghost of Mrs Ramsay; here, in the piece of fake portraiture, the room the lady sits in is simply empty, even despite her presence: there is simply nothing there.

The lady represents something of a taunt: there is a sense in which she parodies the convenient illusion that women keep secrets, stand guard over the mysteries of life, that their silences are auspicious. Significant-ly, this is a myth from which Woolf's heroine in *Between the Acts*, Isa Oliver, seeks to *extricate* herself, rather than to endorse. For Woolf's subject matter here is not, as it was in *To the Lighthouse*, the exposure of conflicting masculine and feminine expectations, and the disingenuous-ness necessary for keeping conflicting differences in a fluid relation, but rather the complete dislocation and disruption – however obliquely this must be effected within the narrative – of this kind of 'arrangement'. Isa's concern is not to placate, but rather to pursue the difficult and sometimes baffling attempt to listen to her own voice, to explore the implications of her own point of view. Woolf's concern, here in *Between the Acts*, is primarily to explore the hypothesis she had put to Stephen Spender, that 'Difference of sex makes a different view.'

Difference of sex may also require a difference of style: a movement away from this tantalising imagery of green glades and silver shades. Isa Oliver, knowing full well that her fantasy-romance with the ravaged Haines cannot be contained within the narrative of her marriage, attempts to give this fantasy a formulation which will at once endorse its status as a secret, and allow her continued access to it. Listening to her father-in-law as he chants poetry, she thinks of Haines, and instantly the chanted words seem to her to describe the story of her imagined elopement:

> 'She walks like beauty in the night,' he quoted.
> Then again:
> 'So we'll go no more a-roving by the light of the moon.'   (*BA*, p. 8)

To Isa, the words seemed to make 'two rings', which floated them – herself and the oblivious Haines – downstream. But though the idea has, of itself, a certain cohesion, it is jarringly at odds with reality. As the fantasy is developed, she notices that 'his snow-white breast was circled with a tangle of dirty duck-weed, and she too, in her webbed feet was entangled, by the husband, the stock-broker' (*ibid.*).

For Isa, poetry *is* expressive of fantasy and desire, but it is contained by a prior narrative, which inscribes the history and continuation of her marriage. She longs for some passion, but can only envisage this as a possibility if she imagines it as extraneous to the framework of her everyday existence. Standing before her three-folded mirror, she contemplates (like the Pargiter sisters before her) different kinds of love: in the glass, she sees the phrase 'in love' – the only terminology at her disposal with which to describe her lonely passion for the un-suspecting Haines. Among the objects on the dressing table, she sees 'the other love', for her stockbroker husband. 'But what feeling was it that stirred in her now when above the looking-glass, out of doors, she saw coming across the lawn the perambulator; two nurses; and her little boy George, lagging behind?' (pp. 4–5).

The mirror reflects something very real, but secret: the expression of

her desire. The contents of the house reflect something more autonomous, more difficult to argue with: the tenacious narrative of life with
her husband. But then, out of the window – through the glass – she sees
a whole new, alternative narrative: the procession comprising all the
paraphernalia that surrounds the life of her child. How might he, this
extension of herself and living proof of the imminence of the future, fit
into the already complicated structure of the present?

She feels about for a language, an imagery, in which to describe this
third element, this unknown and yet fundamentally known quantity,
and produces an imagery which seems suggestive of a fusion between
the two conflicting landscapes of her passion for the farmer, and the
trappings of her marriage: 'Isolated on a green island, hedged about
with snowdrops, laid with a counterpane of puckered silk, the innocent
island floated under her window. Only George lagged behind' (p. 15).
Unlike Lily Briscoe, she cannot, by juxtaposing landscapes, comparing
stories, come to any conclusion, because such comparisons – even a
movement from sexual innocence to sexual experience – cannot take
account of George, who must be given an opportunity to tell his own
story: a story which cannot yet be known, let alone told.

Isa's capacity for procreation paradoxically prevents her from continuing, in the sense of being able to articulate her own voice, express
her own desire. There is a sense in which George, by virtue of his very
existence, determines the continuity of old, established patterns,
thereby fixing her firmly within the narrative of the past, so that old
Oliver 'was grateful to her, . . . for continuing' (p. 17). The scenario will
keep changing, but the narrative continuum remains the same, despite
her resistance to it: 'she loathed the domestic, the possessive; the
maternal. And he knew it and [teased her] on purpose . . . , the old
brute, her father-in-law' (p. 18). She can neither properly accommodate, nor properly escape this role, as the confusion between her poetic
and her domestic life indicates. Her poetry is held in check by her
domestic responsibilities, and her conviction in her motherhood, by
her poetry: as a result, it feels futile to try to keep any real account of her
life, because she seems to be so beholden to others and their constraining projections of her: 'The words weren't worth writing in the
book bound like an account book in case Giles suspected. "Abortive"
was the word that expressed her' (p. 16): she can never seem to find a
way of 'giving birth to' herself.

If Isa's search to express her own sexuality is presented as an 'abortive' struggle, so, too, on one level – though with an element of comic optimism tempered with despair – is that of the unfortunate Miss La Trobe. She has taken on a creative project of ludicrously ambitious proportions, which she sees through with a fortitude which is undeniably comic, but her own story is tragic, and there is a serious message in this send-up by Woolf of a perhaps ill-judged, certainly ill-fated lesbian attempt to achieve a new kind of integrity, presented from a new point of view and on new terms. If travesty is the keynote of the pageant itself, La Trobe's struggle is real, and the laughter Woolf allows us in *Between the Acts* is of the kind that ought, at least, to make us shift uncomfortably in our seats.

The demands of La Trobe's unflinching fidelity to her art can constitute an attempt to make sense of her dilemma, just as Isa's poetry can, up to a point, articulate hers, but they are also responsible for it: the demands of art are taxing and considerable, and the role played in the creative process by the artist's desire is an uneasy and constantly shifting one. If *Between the Acts* reflects the difference between traditionally apportioned male and female dynamics of continuity, it also distinguishes between sexuality and art which, like the men and women in this novel, stage a kind of running battle dependent for its continuity on an ongoing dialogue between the two. In *parodying* La Trobe's endeavour, Virginia Woolf not only makes a serious point in relation to her own project (the 'play within a play' *ought* to function in rather the same way as *The Mouse Trap* in *Hamlet*: in order to focus, in parody, the extreme seriousness of what is going on between the acts, and Woolf is appropriately employing, here, an accepted Renaissance device) – but she also shows up the poignancy of ridicule when it functions as a releasing reaction to events which culminate in failure and disappointment. Miss La Trobe's play *as it is here enacted* is clearly ludicrous, but her conception is not, and nor, moreover, is her own, extremely salient story: 'Since the row with the actress who had shared her bed . . . the horror and terror of being alone [had grown on her] . . . Nature had somehow set her apart from her kind. Yet she had scribbled in the margin of her manuscript: "I am the slave of my audience"' (p. 153). Here, couched behind the *partially* screening devices of comedy and travesty, are some of the terrors of the implications of artistic 'androgyny'.

What Miss La Trobe is attempting, in her idea to stage an Elizabethan drama with a modern implication, is ambitious and crystal-clear: she simply wants her play to change the way her audience sees things, to present 'a different view'. She is constrained, though (like the women in *The Years*), by lack of resources, lack of experience, and a total lack of comprehension or co-operation on the part of those she is valiantly attempting to address. Like Isa, she cannot change the preconceptions of others on the basis of her skimpy resources. What Isa expresses, in the process of making up her poetry, interrupting her father-in-law's reveries, confronting her image in the glass or – as it were – walking down Whitehall, is a 'splitting off of consciousness' which is, in fact, a baffled and impotent response to her own 'difference of view'.[8] The notion that 'difference of sex makes a different view', and the difference of style which results, are experienced as incapacity, inhibition, and a sense of oneself as 'abortive': here, in *Between the Acts*, expressed with a directness which implies anger as much as despair.

In this case, Isa's task, like Virginia Woolf's, must be to interpret that incapacity, and to intercept it: 'Where we know not,' chants Isa, 'where we go not, neither know nor care, . . . Flying, rushing through the ambient, incandescent, summer silent . . .' (p. 15). The woman writer, then, must find a way of writing herself into those breaks, to make some attempts to fill the gaps in her thinking ('The rhyme was "air". She put down her brush. She took up the telephone' (*ibid*.).) It is this challenge that Miss La Trobe can be seen to be taking up, in her attempt both to reflect the audience's dislocation from the action of the play, and also to reinstate a connection, to establish a *dialogue* which can be the only possible starting point for any kind of conception – Woolf's women, in this novel, are sick and tired of speaking into a void. A speaker requires an audience and Woolf clearly herself needed, in presenting her new novel in a new form (based on the play-poem idea) to find a different way of appealing to her audience with this story which she was becoming increasingly determined to tell.

But it is not only the women, in *Between the Acts*, who experience this sense of disconnection. William Dodge, in his miserable, unspoken confession to Lucy Swithin experiences it, and so does the irritable Giles. (' "I fear I am not in my perfect mind," Giles muttered . . . Words came to the surface – he remembered "a stricken deer in whose lean flank the world's harsh scorn had struck its thorn . . . For they are dead, and I . . . I . . . I," he repeated, forgetting the words, and glaring at his Aunt Lucy . . .' (p. 66)): so much for the idea of showing 'the fabric insensibly changing, without death or violence'.

Sexuality itself, perhaps, rather than specifically female desire, might then be responsible for creating these dislocations, these gaps in the continuity of life. If Woolf has hitherto been able to create a prose capable of indicating these gaps, veils, breaks in the continuity of 'being' which are yet suggestive of haunting desire ('those fumbling airs, that breathe and bend over the bed itself . . .' (*TL*, p. 144)), she is in this novel no longer content to do so in the abstract. Veils must be exposed as the wrappings and trappings of fakes; 'fumbling airs' simply waft through completely empty houses and are evocative of nothing, and desire, as experienced by both men and women, must be played out. To this end, the women in *Between the Acts* are in the business of *resisting* the kind of story-telling characteristic of Mrs Ramsay: both Isa and Miss La Trobe refuse to placate, would rather remain mute than go on telling stories. Not content to 'haunt' the interstices of Pointz Hall, they will find a way – willy-nilly – of coming out into the open, and/or of actually inhabiting the place. In *Between the Acts*, ghosts are out. Even the one the servants have invented, which is supposed to haunt the lily pond (of all places) is a fake; the relic dredged up only that of some sheep. A change in the 'fabric', the dawn of a new future – whatever that might mean – is in. This is 1938.

The problem with the future, of course, is that it cannot be formulated in advance. *Between the Acts* hovers on the brink of uncertainty and the prevailing mood is one of extreme instability, reflecting the world in which Woolf composed the novel. As she worked, she was living under the threat of a possible invasion by Hitler's troops: she and her Jewish husband had a suicide pact (they would gas themselves in the garage if the invasion occurred), and she feared for England's youth, particularly for her nephew, Quentin, who would probably be conscripted. She also desperately wanted to have the chance to go on developing her creative work, but the shape of things to come was desperately – and in the end, intolerably – unclear.

As La Trobe's pageant draws towards its end, it becomes clear that nobody, when the play is over, will have anywhere in particular to go. The home as a frame of reference is stale and outmoded, no longer offering solace or a stable base, but there is no real alternative. 'Home, gentlemen;' chivvies Budge, within the play, '. . . home, ladies, it's time to pack up and go home. Don't I see the fire (he pointed: one window blazed red) blazing ever higher? . . . That's the fire of 'Ome . . .' (p. 125). Mrs Lynn Jones obediently follows his gaze. But wasn't there, she muses, 'something – not impure, that wasn't the word – but perhaps "unhygienic" about the home? Like a bit of meat gone sour . . .' (p. 126). The smell of old meat which had permeated Abercorn Terrace, in *The Years*, is here re-invoked, and that particular theme of *The Years* endorsed: the home as a structure for regeneration is stale, anachronistic;

the insistence on the power and potency of the 'family seat' is an idea which is falling into decay.

From this point of view, the idea of a resident ghost becomes even more untenable, as the language Woolf uses to describe the lily pond in which 'a lady' is supposed to have drowned suggests. In the imagery of water, falling petals and fleets of boats in which Woolf might have reconciled her male character, North's vision of the 'heart of darkness' in *The Years* with her own vision of the possibility of finding a new way of describing sexuality, she depicts, once again, the abortiveness of that endeavour:

> Water, for hundreds of years, had silted down into the hollow, and lay there four or five feet deep over a black cushion of mud . . . Silently, [the fish] manoeuvred in their water world, . . . a petal fell, filled and sank. At that the fleet of boat-shaped bodies paused; poised; equipped; mailed; then with a waver of undulation off they flashed.
> It was in that deep centre, in that black heart, that the lady had drowned herself . . . (*BA*, pp. 35–6)

It was a sheep's bone that had been recovered, not a lady's, but the servants refused to believe this, and went on believing in the lady's ghost. And so none of them would walk by the lily pond at night, and 'the flower petal sank; the maid returned to the kitchen' (*ibid.*). It is impossible to re-educate those who persist in clinging to old, super- stitious beliefs, and the falling petal which always signifies, in Woolf's work, a moment of movement towards new understanding, a possible new appropriation of a 'difference of view', here simply sinks. There *is* a 'deep centre', a 'black heart', which might have been a site of origina- tion: the moment is not without possibilities: the fleet of bodies (those of fish, presumably, but they are nevertheless very much alive) is 'poised; equipped; mailed', but they simply flit hither and thither, with no direction. Everything is very much in motion, here, it is a potential site for change, but Woolf must somehow, if she is to capitalise on this, find a way not simply of 'floating' her petals, but of constructing, as she had attempted to do in the early stages of the composition of *The Waves*, a centrepiece capable of coming into flower.

Between the Acts hovers, throughout, on the edge of this possibility: that Woolf will, in this final novel, tear the veil of her aesthetic, 'ghostly' prose – the prose of 'Kew Gardens' and 'A Haunted House' – and reveal in its place the seeds of another story. But the power of this technique of 'floating' is considerable, and the possibility of its removal creates the possible danger of discovering in its place an arid, bleak scenario, unrelieved by surface elegance, such as that which, for

Stephen Spender and others, had characterised *The Years*. There may well be something 'behind' the gaps of Isa's – and Virginia Woolf's – poetic prose, but equally, those gaps, if exposed, might yield insights which prove to be intolerable. This is a possibility of which Isa, for one, is constantly reminded. Turning aside from her poetry, engaging, instead, in the kinds of linguistic exchange which characterise the conversation of her in-laws (the phrase, of course, neatly sums up the constraints of her situation) she faces, most immediately and evidently, the problem of living without the consoling imagery of illusion: they are a hundred miles from the sea (or is it, as her father-in-law claims, only thirty-five?) and yet to Isa it seems 'as if the land went on for ever and ever' (pp. 25–6). There might never be any escape.

To live without illusion may mean living without passion. In the imagery of fishing which, elsewhere in Woolf's work, represents a challenge to the woman artist to maintain her 'different view' in the face of patriarchal expectations, Isa recalls her first meeting with her disagreeable, irresistible husband. She had first met Giles in Scotland, fishing, each from their respective rocks. Her line, like that of the woman novelist in 'Professions for Women', had got tangled, but Isa, unlike the woman novelist, had not been constrained by the voice of 'Reason': she had 'watched him with the stream rushing between his legs, casting, casting – until, like a thick ingot of silver bent in the middle, the salmon had leapt, had been caught, and she had loved him' (p. 39). Released from the constraints of Victorian censorship, Isa has leapt from the frying-pan into the fire, and submitted to, rather than defied, her expectations regarding heterosexual love: as a result, she has simply been sucked into the traditional domestic and familial structures and entered the house of in-laws merely by a slightly modernised route. Now she can no longer properly hear her own voice: she cannot even complete a poem, having relinquished full access to the imagery of her own creative vision, which now lies buried deep, as it were, beneath the mud.

In the presence of Giles and the earnestly flirtatious Mrs Manresa, it is no surprise that she feels imprisoned. Her feelings of entrapment are expressed in the form of a sudden, urgent desire for water – something fluid: – 'A beaker of cold water, a beaker of cold water,' she repeated, and saw water surrounded by walls of shining glass' (p. 52). Water surrounded by glass, glass surrounded by water, figure in one, reversible image the 'abortive' endeavour of *Between the Acts* and also, in a sense, sum up the dilemma running through the whole of Virginia Woolf's writing practice. Water is releasing, but it is contained in glass, which has both reflective and screening properties. Isa experiences all this, by now, in the terrible imagery of blunt arrows: 'Through the bars of the prison, . . . blunt arrows bruised her; of love, then of hate . . .' (*ibid.*). They might have been capable of piercing the veil of her almost intolerable frustration, but are not even sufficiently sharp to shatter the screen of her emotional confusion. All she can feel is the numbing effects of continued self-denial, rather than the ultimately more satis- factory, though painful, cutting edge of self-revelation. The Olivers are miles from the sea, which might have reflected the more violent and ruthless rhythms of nature; the glass in which she continues to gaze frames only infinitely receding versions of the same ideal: of romantic love, which might still, she dreams, represent the power to subvert the male-female dialectic which both sustains and undermines it.

Does *Between the Acts* offer, then, after all, no release from the debilitating constraints on self-expression? The fragmented narrative which takes place between the acts of the pageant exposes throughout the novel the extent to which the integrity of desire is sacrificed to the more visible, more socially acceptable continuum of historical consis- tency. In the interludes of the play we learn of William Dodge's homo- sexuality, La Trobe's lesbianism, Isa's fantasies about the 'ravaged' Haines, and Giles' barely concealed hankering after a bit on the side with the 'wild child of nature', Mrs Manresa. Desire, in *Between the Acts*, is accompanied by irritation, frustration and rage, since to act it out would necessitate transgression, and the breaking of rules set up supposedly in the interests of continuity. It offers the possibility of a new line of development, a new kind of continuum, but one the future of which is necessarily unknown, and there is no way out of the double bind, since to ignore its dictates is to submit to emotional and ultimately social paralysis, as Dodge's unspoken confession illustrates: he has been bullied at school; his child is not his own; he is a 'flickering, mind-divided little snake in the grass' (p. 57), but he cannot say any of this: it is an unpalatable story, of the kind he knows better than to tell, so 'he said nothing; and the breeze went lolloping along the corridors, blowing the blinds out' (p. 57) for all the world as if we were back in the narratives of 'Kew Gardens,' 'A Haunted House' or even *Mrs Dalloway*, where the choice was clear: frigidity or madness.

    Between the Acts, then, reflects the agony of having a story it seems impossible to tell, but it also contains – and therefore does manage to release the germs of – such stories, reflecting also some of the discoveries Woolf was beginning to make in the process of drafting her own memoirs, for the project she began on during this time, 'A Sketch of the Past'. She began the 'Sketch' with the idea to write 'not exactly diary. Reflections. That's the fashionable dodge' (*D*, V, p. 229) and this discovery of an oblique angle by means of which to approach the writing of autobiography may have bequeathed William Dodge his name. The writing which evolved out of the 'dodge' enabled her to retrieve 'moments of being' from the 'cotton wool' of the past by 'listening in' to herself as she wrote 'without stopping to find [her] way' (*op. cit.*), and Dodge, too, is on some level aware that the only way of inhabiting the present fully by exorcising the paralysing effects of the past was by lifting the veil of the numbing tactic which keeps everything under wraps, or behind glass. However, like Virginia Woolf, he cannot hope to finish the story which begins to emerge because he cannot be sufficiently sure of his audience to take the risk of telling it.

Isa, with her secret poetry, faces the same problem: her innermost thoughts can never be expressed, so she can never properly use the past as a way of reinterpreting the present. Lucy Swithin, with her inter-mittent monologue on the primeval, goes further, in her way, by attempting to align the past with the present and by having developed a method of simply thinking aloud, but the problem is that no one *listens* to her, which means that, in effect, her thoughts become as 'abortive' as anybody else's. La Trobe, by contrast, may well be onto something, with her ambitious project to use literature to highlight the past in relation to the present, but the script is appalling, the props are disastrous and the cast is a joke. These are the only materials, however, to which La Trobe has access. Who knows how significant an artist, if she had ever been taken remotely seriously, she might have become?

The increasing focus away from the narrative of events taking place between the acts towards the pageant itself, and the emphasis on La Trobe's complete fidelity to her project, re-focuses the part played in the emerging fiction of *Between the Acts* by Virginia Woolf herself, not least because in her determination to break new artistic ground, her compulsion to innovate and her intense personal involvement in her work, her character, Miss La Trobe, has much in common with her. At this time, for Woolf, the boundaries between styles of writing and styles of identity were for the first time becoming blurred: one of her struggles was to allow a story about *herself* to emerge, in 'A Sketch of the Past', while still needing, nevertheless, to find ways of regulating the potentially dangerous imagery which was beginning to emerge. The distinction between herself and her characters was perhaps becoming less clear than ever before, her authorial anonymity was being called into question, and the 'scattered parts' of Virginia Woolf seemed dangerously as though they might at any moment be reassembled into a shape or whole over which she might not have complete control.

One of the effects of this process was that the idea for a book to follow *Between the Acts*, which came to her just as she began to finish the novel, seems, unusually for her, to have come to her more or less entire – almost as though it was something that had already been written. On 23 November 1940, she recorded that, having just 'this moment' finished 'The Pageant – or Poyntz Hall?' – she was already turning her mind to thoughts towards a completely new project. 'Anon, it will be called', she resolved. And she described an incident which reads oddly, in relation to her writing practice and the place she usually allocated it within the domestic sphere: 'The exact narrative of this morning', she notes, should refer to the interruption by her housemaid, Louie, 'holding a glass jar, in whose thin milk was a pat of butter. Then I went in with her to skim the milk off: then I took the pat & showed it to Leonard. This was a moment of great household triumph' (*D*, V, p. 340).

She continues, without a break, 'I am a little triumphant about the book. I think its an interesting attempt in a new method. I think its more quintessential than the others. More milk skimmed off. A richer pat, . . .' (*ibid.*). This conjunction of concerns, and the uncharacteristically shared imagery for domestic and writing life is (as I have already suggested, in relation to 'A Sketch of the Past') peculiar to this final stage of Woolf's life and writing; it also suggests an overlap with her character Isa, for whom the languages of writing and domestic life are inextricably fused. But the passage is also indicative of another change: it is as though the 'richer pat' of the idea spanning both the just completed and the newly conceived book, have already been allocated to the finished project. The book which was to follow would comprise that which remained when the cream of the idea had been skimmed off; for the first time, Woolf's drafts for a new book – the 'Anon' which was never to be completed – represent more or less exactly the 'cotton wool' of what has already been written. *Anon*, Woolf's final, unfinished and unpublished work, represents, in large measure, her attempt to outline the theory behind Miss La Trobe's already enacted play.

The holograph notes for *Anon* dated September 1940 record the origins of this enterprise, which was suggested to her by talking to Duncan and Vanessa about the differences between literature and painting. She would next write, she notes, a book 'explaining literature from our common standpoint to painters.' She would begin, she resolved, by taking 'a very old anonymous poem'. She would distinguish between 'the actual scene', or setting, and issues such as 'the patron; society; . . .' and it was to be chronological. The focus would be on 'the inevitability of the creative interest', and she emphasises the need to find the right form: '*Evolve the form*' (emphasis Woolf's). The rest of this fragment is in note form: 'The great house. Fill England with people. Take samples. Book of art and of the outer pressure': the problem of reconciling creativity with the 'outer pressure' of *The Years* was still to be resolved. 'Keep a running conversation upon the external', she reminds herself. And again, she would somehow find a way of moving forwards into the future: 'The "modern" . . . the growth of articulation . . .'[9]

She has just described, here, the main emphasis of the narrative of *Between the Acts*. It is all there: the setting of the scene, home, patronage, the strict chronology, the importance of form, the great house, England, the audience, and the 'running conversation upon the external'. Central to that novel is of course the notion that 'the "modern" . . . the growth of articulation' has its basis in the origins of the English literary tradition: the pageant opens on a small, anonymous girl, who takes up her position and begins her solemn prologue, in the form of a 'very old anonymous poem': 'Gentles and simples, I address you all' (*BA*, p. 59).

But there is also another conjunction at stake here, one that cannot necessarily be read quite as literally as the conjunction between *Anon* and *Between the Acts*, except in that single, emphasised instruction, '*Evolve the form.*' It is also the case that a version of the project suggested in these early notes towards *Anon* which applied to Woolf *herself* had begun to emerge as 'A Sketch of the Past', the work in which she was attempting to enact the lifting of constraints on her own process of self-expression. *Between the Acts*, and, in turn, *Anon*, can both be seen to reflect the discovery Woolf was making, in 'A Sketch of the Past': that it might, by focusing on individual moments and by means of a 'fashionable dodge', prove possible to somehow go right back to the origins of current reflection, and eventually work back into the 'deep centre' which is the only conceivable stone left unturned; the 'real' source of creative energy: Virginia Woolf's 'black heart'.

Anon takes as its starting point, as does 'A Sketch of the Past', the attempt to identify the origins of the process upon which it is based. Recalling Miss La Trobe's attempt to take the audience right back to the beginning of the English literary tradition, the two simultaneous drafts relating to *Anon* take as their starting point the attempt to identify the point in history at which English literature began to be read. The two drafts, which relate chronologically and conceptually to the idea for this book, which would trace the development of English literature, are entitled *Anon* and *The Reader* – material for one or the other is sometimes indistinguishable and the two drafts, which were both revised many times, overlap. Both reveal the importance for Woolf of the literature of the Elizabethan Age, the period with which La Trobe begins her pageant. A particularly brief and succinct draft of *Anon* begins,

> Anon died round about 1477. It was the printed book with the authors name attached that killed him. (After that the audience was separate from the singer.) And with anon died that part of the song that the audience sang, the voice that supplied the story, filled in the pauses, and added sometimes a nonsensical chorus. After that the song was attached to the singer.[10]

This donnish attempt to begin at the beginning is uncharacteristic of Woolf: it is as though, this time, she was absolutely determined not to let anything 'escape'.

The connection with La Trobe's pageant is clear: she, too, is trying to get back to the beginning, and to revive an ancient tradition, by getting her audience to re-compose the 'orts [*sic*], scraps and fragments' of the pageant into a story; to '[fill] in the pauses.' By urging them to appreciate their relationship with the action of the play, she hopes to persuade them to participate fully in the performance. But she is faced with the difficulty of appealing to a 'modern' audience, an audience which simply wants to be told the point of the story, so that it can rest assured that it has benefited from the performance and continue to go about its business more or less undisturbed.

Virginia Woolf might have anticipated a similar set of problems regarding likely audience response to her own composition, had she lived to tell the 'whole' story, and the fragment which remains presents material which has vital bearing on her thoughts relating to the notion of anonymity. There is a strong sense running through the 'Sketch' that 'the voice that supplied the story' has for a long time been silenced, can no longer be heard – there seems to have been, for a long time, no one to tell – and if one cannot imagine telling a story there becomes, all too soon, a sense in which there is no recoverable story to tell. The process of writing fiction, which became Virginia Woolf's *modus vivendi*, is at once a vehicle for a partial release of censored recollections and feelings, and also yet another practice which tended to re-confirm her sense of isolation and impotence in relation to her own 'black heart', which so often cast her into a mood which she could only describe as 'non-being', and which triggered feelings of bleak anonymity.

She went on attempting to turn this to her advantage: 'to use writing as an art, not as a method for self-expression' (*op. cit.*), but at the same time as this tactic enabled her to achieve integration of a kind, it tended also to function as yet another distancing technique. She bequeathed, in *Between the Acts*, this practice – with all its paradoxes, ambivalences and double binds – to Miss La Trobe, who in a sense represents the modern-day Anon ('Very little was actually known about her': 'with that name she wasn't presumably pure English', which, it is hinted, presumably accounts for her 'passion for getting things up' (p. 46)). The modern Anon cannot carry the status of the ancient Anon, however, who has been deleted from history by the emergence of the printed book: the physical appearance of Miss La Trobe, her earnestness and her strangeness, all contribute to her difficulties in being taken seriously. As a result of her ambivalence regarding the status and nature of her own position – *vis-à-vis* both the audience and the text – La Trobe can never quite establish access to 'the inner voice, the other voice' which, she perceives, should have made a connection between the audience and the play. There is a particular voice – which would take the place, in a modern performance, of the original, unified voice of Anon – which she cannot seem to make heard, and when the voice of the Chorus becomes inaudible and La Trobe's power to exert control over the performance of her creation eventually begins to desert her, the cows in a neighbouring field – surely, the ultimate indignity – seem capable of making a noise which is every bit as significant, as far as the audience is concerned, as anything in La Trobe's play:

> suddenly, as the illusion petered out, the cows took up the burden. One had lost her calf . . . From cow after cow came the same yearning bellow. The whole world was filled with dumb yearning. It was the primeval voice sounding loud in the ear of the present moment . . . The cows annihilated the gap; bridged the distance; filled the emptiness and continued the emotion. (*BA*, pp. 103–4)

It is, here, as though nature has taken over from art: there is nothing in art that can take the place of the 'primeval' voice which Woolf seeks so consistently throughout the story of *Between the Acts* to find a way to release; or rather, no way of creating this particular, plangent and desperate appeal by means of the printed word. What is being expressed here – as it were quite fortuitously, or by default – is a pure, unexpurgated expression of loss: its cutting edge, its plangency, and its potential as an idea which, could it only be sufficiently strongly expressed, would demonstrate its potential as a force enabling release.

What follows this passage in the narrative of *Between the Acts* is, from this point of view, no less strategically placed. When the cows cease their bellowing, there is an awkward moment of silence during which those in the audience lower their heads, consult their programmes and learn that the director now 'craves [their] indulgence'. Due to lack of time, a scene, it seems, has been omitted, and La Trobe appeals to the audience to consult the programme notes and attempt to visualise the expurgated material. Significantly enough, in the overall context of Woolf's work, what has been omitted is the conclusion, in which old Lilyliver's dastardly plot to cheat his young niece of her inheritance is uncovered; the young beauty is reunited with her lover, and the two young lovers 'fly together', leaving the older generation alone together (p. 104).

The conclusion to 'Where There's A Will There's A Way' is, therefore, felicitous. Unlike the unfortunate Isa, the young Flavinda will be released from the constraints and jealousies of her elders and 'fly', together with her young lover, presumably off into the future, with no familial strings attached. The audience, moreover, seems willing to make the relevant effort to picture the scene ('"That's very wise of her," said Mrs Manresa' (p. 104)). But the problem is that, judicious though this ending may be, no one in the audience will be able to get the full measure of it unless it is actually played out. La Trobe has been so anxious to 'get everything in' that she has edited out the most significant moment in the play, so that the audience is here more or less called upon to supply the entire story.

The audience, then, is placed in the position of a Bernard or a North, but without any of their prior knowledge: it is the audience who must now bear the weight of the challenge to sum up, or provide a conclusion to a drama it could not possibly have invented. The audience must thus function here, for La Trobe as for Virginia Woolf, as the 'other' in a dialogue which must somehow present 'a different view' by creating, in a newly invented form, the possibility of entering into an argument on a new level – a level on which it might be possible to speak without the interruption of all the old prohibitions and censors – 'Reason'; the 'Angel in the House'; the 'men [who] would be shocked' – and to stage a discussion in which it might finally be possible for 'She' to come out from beneath her 'semi mystic' veils and speak in a different, more audible voice. This audience, however, is simply not equipped to do all this.

Both La Trobe and Virginia Woolf, however, make a striking and valiant attempt, and the model of the Elizabethan drama provides, within *Between the Acts*, an opportunity which Woolf had earlier envisaged and commented on, in an essay entitled 'Notes on an Elizabethan Play', in which she describes the capacities of the Elizabethan drama, in contrast to the constraints of the novel form. In that piece, she had compared Ford's play, *'Tis Pity She's A Whore*, with Tolstoy's *Anna Karenina*, noting that the heroine of the play, Annabella, is 'always at the height of her passion'. She compares 'the long leisurely accumulated novel' with 'the little contracted play', noting that in the novel, emotion is 'all split up, dissipated and then . . . slowly and gradually massed into a whole', whereas the play, which 'after all, is poetry', can achieve moments of intensity of which the novel would never be capable. She supplies, in support of her argument, a phrase of 'astonishing beauty': 'With all her reality, Anna Karenina could never say, 'You have oft for these two lips / Neglected cassia'.[11] That striking and poignant appeal is presumably a statement which Virginia Woolf would desperately have liked to be able to make in her fiction: a statement expressive of the heady ruthlessness and powerfully determining capacity of desire where it can be fully, unconditionally and candidly expressed. She would, perhaps, have liked to make such a statement in place of that other, terrible phrase, expressive only of the incapacitating silence of shock and prohibition: 'I feel nothing whatever.'[12] The two phrases are poles apart, and the contrast between 'being' and 'non-being' is here sharply suggested, but the real tragedy is that those two phrases, one of which simply represents the 'other face' of the statement implicit in the other, can never be reconciled.

Between the Acts does, in fact, alternate between statements not entirely dissimilar to these; does indeed express these very polarities, moving, for example, between Isa's flights of imagination and Dodge's impotent, inexpressible confession. But Isa, locked into the *forms* of marriage for which Ford's Elizabethan girl has a fundamental disregard, has lost access to the kind of energy – an energy which cannot flourish in a context of disingenuousness – which would enable her to put her fantasies into play.

As a result, we see Virginia Woolf here in her holograph notes for *The Reader* and *Anon* persisting with the ultimately abortive attempt to offer a completely comprehensive historical context for her discovery, valiantly attempting to give 'factual' credence to the notion that stories such as Isa's, and even La Trobe's, dependent as they are on the interplay of an audience or 'other' schooled only in tolerance and misinterpretation, cannot hope – at least, not at this point in the course of history – to be able to tell. Like 'the story of' Woolf's ongoing attempt to find a form for the story which, as she had once resolved, should 'all be told on one occasion' – the story, simply, of the effect of a difference of sex on a different view – such stories can only be told in fragments, or in euphemisms: 'She' is 'semi mystic, very profound'; she has an alabaster shell, a black heart. In her notes for *Anon* she is already caught up in a network of euphemisms, and about to become entangled in a story which – to the extent that she would ever be able to tell it – she has already, in *Between the Acts*, courageously and ingeniously told.

One possibility remains, at the close of *Between the Acts*: that is, the notion of blind faith in the future as suggestive of new possibilities, as envisaged by Lucy Swithin. Though Pointz Hall is hundreds of miles from the sea, though the story attached to the lily pond is pure fiction, Lucy focuses on the pond, at the close of the novel, as a possible vessel of hope for the future of the human race. In her reflections, she takes us back into the imagery of Woolf's early experimental work: she observes the fish, which seldom came to the surface of the water, as they 'slid on, in and out between the stalks, silver; pink; gold; splashed; streaked; pied' (p. 148) and we are positioned, as readers, in the same relation to the water as to the flower bed in 'Kew Gardens' of which this passage is reminiscent.

'Fish had faith,' 'reasons' Lucy (p. 149). 'They trust us because we've never caught 'em.' But that is simply greed, remonstrates her brother. Their beauty he interprets as sex, and to Lucy's question, 'Who makes sex susceptible to beauty?' he simply has no answer. 'Silenced, she returned to her private vision; of beauty which is goodness; the sea on which we float': the note of romantic optimism is reminiscent of the kinds of 'consolation' characteristically offered by Mrs Ramsay, who has also, to all intents and purposes, given up the fight.

There is some dialogue about sex being initiated here, but Lucy, questioning the connection between sex and beauty, desire and the capacity to reflect, is soon silenced. Perhaps, then, the only answer resides somewhere in a rather muddy notion that beauty, sexuality, creativity can only now, in the face of all we know about individual psychology and social and political history, be interpreted in the light of 'a different view' which, at least for the time being (here, 1938) remains obscure. The source of potency, the conclusion to *Between the Acts* seems to suggest, is in ourselves, not in our connections with others. As Lucy returns, defeated in her attempt to make new connections, to her 'private vision; of beauty which is goodness; the sea on which we float', the reader may be reminded of Rachel Vinrace, seated mutely at the piano: Virginia Woolf has come full circle.

Ultimately, *Between the Acts* can pave the way – Virginia Woolf was right – only for the germination of another work of art: another novel, another play: a story which 'shall all be told on one occasion,' but at some time in the future, when 'the audience' is better equipped to respond to changes which, in 1938, were only just beginning to unfold. For Miss La Trobe, as for Virginia Woolf, 'another play always lay behind the play she had just written' (p. 50). At the close of the novel, Isa and Giles Oliver begin to enact another drama, as yet simply a gleam in the eye of Miss La Trobe – an 'impossible' fictitious occurrence: like the lady in the portrait, a trick. Miss La Trobe, dropping her suitcase in at the kitchen window, and so avoiding, at least for the time being, the defeat implicit in returning home, anticipates the possibility of another play by herself; another novel by Virginia Woolf:

> 'I should group them,' she murmured, 'here'. It would be midnight; there would be two figures, half concealed by a rock. The curtain would rise. What would the first words be? The words escaped her.   (*BA*, p. 152)

Here are Giles and Isa again, posed as if attendant on some new ceremony: a rite, perhaps, of initiation. This time the same rock, rather than the 'his' and 'hers' from which they had once fished, obscures them. La Trobe continues,

> It was strange that the earth, with all those flowers incandescent . . . – should still be hard. From the earth green waters seemed to rise over her. She took her voyage away from the shore, and, raising her hand, fumbled for the latch of the iron entrance gate.   (*BA*, pp. 152–3)

Even in a world newly lit with an array of incandescent flowers, even in a vision which tells the story of everything up and out, everything on fire and in flower, the 'earth' from which such a vision springs will not be re-defined: the *context* for such a vision is immoveable, unchangeable, and the visionary poet, the visionary dramatist, the visionary novelist, is branded as an 'outsider': she is out there on her own. As the curtain rises, man and woman are about to speak; the *real* 'facts' of life, perhaps, are about to be discussed, even enacted, and this time from within the context of a 'different view'. But such a story cannot (yet) take place in the form of a drama by Miss La Trobe. Even the framework of Virginia Woolf's fiction cannot contain it.

Conclusion

A curious sea side feeling in the air today . . . Everyone leaning against the
wind, nipped & silenced. All pulp removed . . . And Nessa is at Brighton, &
I am imagining how it wd be if we could infuse souls . . . L. is doing the
rhododendrons . . .   (*Diary*, V, p. 359)

What was at stake for Virginia Woolf was the difficulty and challenge of
writing with a difference. Woolf herself articulated her differences with
her Edwardian predecessors, in 'Modern Fiction' and 'Mr Bennett and
Mrs Brown'; her differences with the Victorian patriarchy surface in
The Pargiters and then *The Years* as well as in *A Room of One's Own*;
and the differences between canonical readings of Woolf and new
feminist readings have begun to highlight the extent to which her
writing seems to have represented an opportunity for her to grapple
with her differences with herself, as well as to 'use writing as an art . . .'.

To the extent that Woolf's writing is feminist, it is so because she
attempts to re-formulate meaning within fictitious forms, rather than
because she harboured any long-term strategies for political change;
nor do I think she had any clear sense of working within an easily
definable context of political oppression until the emergence of the
poets of the 1930s, and ultimately she found the politics of the 'young
poets' and its infiltration into poetry indefensible. It drove her to
despair, not recuperation. She had no Marxist persuasions. She lacked
the strategic skills as well as the constitution of a 'guerilla fighter',
though her 'Victorian skirts' must of course, at least in some measure,
be held accountable for this lack.[1] 'The style of Mrs Woolf' was crucial
to her as a mainstay in her life and in her writing, and the persona of Mrs
Woolf acted as a counter to her always potentially debilitating sense of
anonymity. Her writing was a way of achieving integration, even if her
sense of personal integrity always seemed to her to fall short of full
expression. Her style functioned as a bond between the continua of life

171

and writing, and focused the relationship and interaction between the two. She wrote 'about' *writing*, and was not afraid to explore, and sometimes to exploit, the level of *invention* integral to the creative process.

In her writing practice, she uncovered feminist issues and offered revisionary perspectives. But she was in no sense a leader of women, nor did she offer any practicable strategy in women's defence. In the preceding chapters, I have attempted to point towards some fundamental reasons why this seems to me to be the case. It is impossible to sum up, on Virginia Woolf's behalf, a 'position' which she herself was ultimately unable to arrive at. I could only go on illustrating aspects and examples of her endeavour.

In the Summer of 1926, for example, she made a diary entry which is as provocative an illustration as I can find of her *in*ability to occupy a feminist position: she notices 'two resolute, sunburnt, dusty girls, . . . with packs on their backs, . . . tramping along the road in the hot sunshine at Ripe.' Her first reaction is to condemn them: her instinct, she records, 'at once throws up a screen' and she passes them off as 'in every way angular, awkward and self-assertive'. She resolves to stop erecting screens '& get at the thing itself, which has nothing whatever in common with a screen.' However, she adds, 'the screen making habit . . . is so universal, that probably it preserves our sanity.' If we did not have this device, she surmises, 'we might, perhaps, dissolve utterly. But screens are in the excess,' she concedes, 'not the sympathy' (*D*, III, p. 104).

In the final analysis, she not only screened herself from her own 'black heart', she also attributed this method of self-protection to others, so that she maintains an illusion, at least, of collectivity. The screen protected her from loss of control, as became apparent when she began tentatively to remove it in the process of writing *Between the Acts* and 'A Sketch of the Past'. Her writing, she had once remarked, was the only forum in which she dared lure herself 'out of the little circle of safety, on and on, to the whirlpools',[2] and if the little circle of safety were removed, she would 'go under' (*ibid.*). Eventually she did go under, propelled by feelings of inadequacy, confusion, constraints on self-expression and the unhappy sense that she had never, by contrast with Vita, been a 'real woman'.[3] In the end, she took her own life in an attempt – so she put it to herself and to him – to spare her husband the burden of having to live with someone miserably unable to reconcile the differences within herself. The suicide's gesture of self-effacement is perhaps the most ambiguous it is ever possible to make. By the same token, she set a dubious precedent for contemporary feminists who seek to identify in her work any kind of blueprint for change. Her writing represents, above all, the ultimately irreconcilable co-existence of gender-related dilemmas, and it is in the original artistic expression of this delicately fused conjunction of concerns that she distinguished herself as a woman writer.

It becomes possible, then, to make some judgements about Virginia Woolf. She suffered considerable tragedy, a network of losses which her work reflects and repeats while at the same time screening, from Woolf as from her readers, both the sources and the full implications of loss. Hers was a creativity which was fractured, interrupted, ultimately withheld. In which case, how can we make judgements about the writing which comes to be seen as a product of this network of distressing conjunctions?

Her writing practice, seen in this light, becomes a way of telling stories and of exploring historical continua which can only be partially understood. The writing, then, comes to reflect the mixture of pleasure and despair which Woolf experienced with each novel's composition; to be 'about' the potential for enormous powers of creativity and inventiveness, the ability to perceive hidden connections and to formulate insights, but it is a writing necessarily impeded by loss and by the debilitating effects of censorship – personal, social, historical – at practically every level, and exacerbated by the writer herself.

Her celibacy informed her writing. She could not get to the bottom of this, since the problem of sexuality was at the source of the problematic which fused history, aesthetics and her intermittent attempts to formulate a theory of gender (as in *A Room of One's Own*, 'Professions for Women' and *Three Guineas*). These attempts were always abortive; always at some level distressing. What was at stake, of course, was the 'black heart' of her own creativity, so it is little wonder that with the publication of each novel she feared the exposure of her dilemma, and that each exposure would further incapacitate her. She had good reason to be anxious. The appearance of each work constituted, from this point of view, not a celebration but rather the exposure of her damaged creativity: with each artistic achievement she 'celebrated', however unconsciously, her creative incapacity.

She focused compulsively, and not surprisingly, on the depiction of objects with beautiful surfaces, on form and colour, which initially served to detract from any analysis of 'the depths'; paid sustained attention in her work to the descriptions of shapes and objects which glimmer and gleam and reflect: in their lights and shapes some access to pleasure seems to be being proposed, but is as quickly dispersed. In 'A Mark on the Wall', for example, what promises to emerge as history is, after, merely a trick of the light: the object under observation is not a source but a *transparency* which focuses, not the source of subjectivity but 'herself' as transmitter or burning glass.

The surfaces she describes mirror her own function as a creative artist, reflecting always, rather than penetrating, her dilemma, and protecting always some vestige of herself from this endeavour, because 'Suppose the looking-glass smashes, the image disappears, and the romantic figure . . . is there no longer, but only that shell of a person which is seen by other people – what an airless, shallow, bald, prominent world it becomes! A world not to be lived in' ('A Mark on the Wall', *HH*, p. 38).

There is no penetrating the 'great space of life'[4] which would ensue: the great space vacated by her mother and intruded on by early, traumatic sexual experiences, the space which should have contained narratives about sexuality, even narratives explaining loss; the space which remained, however, empty. Empty, that is, of the kinds of narrative which would have explained or given Virginia Woolf access to the source of her own dilemma and enabled her to inhabit her own 'heart', but crowded with kaleidoscopic images which seem to offer visions which, when observed very closely, are seen to function only as distractions. Such images seem to offer access to aesthetic pleasure, but never to its source.

Ultimately, the activity of reading the work of Virginia Woolf necessitates accompanying her to the 'dark places' and understanding how these resist illumination or closure; it involves exposure to a conjunction of interrupted history, screened sexuality and inexpressible loss which may well strike a chord of familiarity with some readers. It may even be that women readers will read Woolf's work with a special sense of recognition. But if her work has a particular poignancy in these regards, it is probably to do with the courage and conviction with which she went on believing – in her writing practice if not in other aspects of her life – that she might ultimately be capable not only of describing but also of illuminating the *source* of these experiences and dilemmas.

Virginia Woolf set herself the impossibly complex task of re-telling in fiction a story she had never really been able to tell herself: she lacked the framework as well as the vocabulary she would have needed to represent fully the conjunction of impeded sexuality with chronic and debilitating loss. These are aspects of a common dilemma, of course, but the particular designs they compose in the history and writing of Virginia Woolf are her own: unique, as well as crucially important, to her. This particular vision – of a story now composed of gleams and glimmers of light, now obscured by partial or total darkness – was all she had to go on. It was her own: the particular, fractured design which represented her own subjectivity, her own creativity. She did not want to – could not – make it whole, or conclusive, without losing her fundamental sense of its *shape*: its contrasts of light and shade, its ever-fluctuating rhythms. She wrote it exactly as she perceived it, though she experimented, from time to time, with different methods and forms. The attempt to offer a theory of the writing which ensued, to cast light on the dark places, to fill the empty spaces with new, enlightened narratives, cannot really serve to penetrate the exact nature of the mind of Virginia Woolf. We can only experience for ourselves, through the activity of reading her writing, both the light and the dark places of a peculiarly innovative, sensitive and fundamentally honest mind at work, and make whatever deductions we can.

Even that will not suffice as an ending, though. It seems too bleak, as though, yet again, the exact imagery, the colours and shapes, the fluctuating rhythms, the highly tuned energy of Virginia Woolf's writing have all been suddenly passed over, or left out. Only these can finally serve to offer a – however unsatisfactory – conclusion. Here, then, is one of the last examples of her writing: the last few paragraphs of her final Diary entry, made four days prior to her suicide. She notes,

> A curious sea side feeling in the air today. It reminds me of lodgings on a parade at Easter. Everyone leaning against the wind, nipped & silenced. All pulp removed.
> This windy corner. And Nessa is at Brighton; & I am imagining how it wd be if we could infuse souls.
> Octavia [Wilberforce]'s story. Could I englobe it somehow? English youth in 1900.
> Two long letters from Shena & O. I cant tackle them, yet enjoy having them.
> L. is doing the rhododendrons . . .   (*D*, V, p. 359)

It is all still there: everyone silenced, emptied; her sense of estrangement from her sister; her strong and fundamental desire for connection, translated into an abstraction: the problem of 'infusing souls'. An aesthetic problem ensues: how might she 'englobe' Octavia's story. How might she re-write history. There *are* correspondences, promises of connection, but she will keep them at arm's length: 'cant tackle them'. And perhaps one of the most poignant images of all throughout this restless fluctuation, this coming and going from abstract to concrete, these alternating rhythms of pleasure and distress: the presence of that other largely anonymous figure who accompanied her right up to the end: the silent figure of Leonard Woolf, stooping among the flowers. At the end, though, even 'L.' could not fathom the complex and daunting mind of Virginia Woolf, its shifts from flights of brilliance to shrouded and impenetrable darkness.

Notes

Introduction

1. For Virginia Woolf's own account see 'A Sketch of the Past', in *Moments of Being*, edited by Jeanne Schulkind (London: Triad/Panther, 1978), pp. 78–80; also '22 Hyde Park Gate' in *Moments of Being*, pp. 163–80 (p. 180). See also Louise DeSalvo, *Virginia Woolf: The impact of Childhood sexual abuse on her life and work* (Boston: Beacon, 1989 and London: The Women's Press, 1989) which appeared just as this book was about to go to press.
2. See Quentin Bell, *Virginia Woolf: A biography*, vol. I: *Virginia Stephen, 1882–1912* (London: Triad/Paladin, 1976), pp. 11–27.
3. See Monks House Papers, III, University of Sussex Library.
4. See Quentin Bell, *Virginia Woolf: A biography*: vol. II: *Mrs Woolf*, 1912–1941 (London: Triad/Paladin, 1976), p. 2.
5. Gayatri C. Spivak, 'Unmaking and Making in *To the Lighthouse*', in Ginet, Borker and Furman (eds.), *Women and Language in Literature and Society* (New York: Praeger, 1980).
6. For contemporary critiques of Woolf's 'aestheticism' see the reactions of the 'Scrutineers', collected in Robin Majumdar and Allen McLaurin (eds.), *Virginia Woolf: The Critical Heritage* (London: Routledge, 1975), spanning the period 1919 (from the publication of 'Kew Gardens') to 1922 (to the publication of *Jacob's Room*). For feminist critiques of Woolf's work see for example Jane Marcus (ed.), *New Feminist Essays on Virginia Woolf* (London: Macmillan, 1981) and Jane Marcus (ed.), *Virginia Woolf: A feminist slant* (Nebraska: University of Nebraska Press, 1983). For a fuller analysis of the critical reception of Virginia Woolf's work see Sue Roe, *Virginia Woolf, Writing and Gender* Ph.D. thesis, 1988; held in the Library of the University of Kent at Canterbury).
7. Wilfrid Mellers, review of *The Years* in Robin Majumdar and Allen McLaurin (eds.), *Virginia Woolf: The Critical Heritage* (London: Routledge, 1975), pp. 74–5.
8. Virginia Woolf reviewed Dorothy Richardson's *Revolving Lights* in the *Times Literary Supplement* on 19 May 1923, and paid special attention to the ways in which Richardson experimented with perspective within narrative form. Her central character, Woolf noted, was 'aware ... of the atmosphere of the table rather than of the table; ... Therefore she adds an element to her perception of things which has not been noticed before'. The review is printed in *Virginia Woolf: Women and writing*, introduced by Michèle Barrett (London: The Women's Press, 1979). See also my discussion of the connections between Woolf's and Richardson's work, in Part I, above. Note also the symbolic function of the tea table in Woolf's work. It appears in 'A sketch of the Past' (*MB*, p. 158) as the Victorian symbol of the contrived (and disingenuous) relationship between the subject and society (see p. 56 above). In *The Voyage Out* Woolf attempted to point up its constraints, in *Night and Day* she parodied it. It is in *Jacob's Room* that she for the first time dispenses with it. The problem of what to put in its place (how to offer a

new definition of the subject) ensues, and Woolf is still working along these lines in *The Waves* (see Chapter 4 above). For reasons of space and cohesion, and with some regret, I have omitted from the present text my work on *Jacob's Room* in this regard, but the reader may like to be referred to my introduction to the new Penguin edition of *Jacob's Room* (Penguin, forthcoming).

Part 1: *Virginia Woolf's writing practice*

1. The critical reactions to Woolf's early 'experimental' writing are collected in Robin Majumdar and Allen McLaurin (eds.), *Virginia Woolf: The Critical Heritage* (London: Routledge, 1975 [hereafter referred to as *CH*], and span the period 1919–1922, from the publication of 'Kew Gardens' to that of *Jacob's Room*, during which period she began to be recognised as an innovator. For a good analysis of Virginia Woolf's visual imagination and her interest in the techniques of painting, see C. Ruth Miller: *Virginia Woolf: The frames of art and life* (London: Macmillan, 1988).
2. Virginia's Woolf's literary criticism offers countless examples of this tendency. See, for example, Virginia Woolf, 'Notes on D. H. Lawrence', *The Moment and Other Essays* (London: Hogarth, 1981; first published 1947), pp. 79–82.
3. Virginia Woolf, 'Craftsmanship', *The Death of the Moth* (London: Hogarth, 1981); first published, London, 1942, pp. 126–132.
4. Letter from Roger Fry to Virginia Woolf, 18 October 1918, Monks House Papers, III (University of Sussex).
5. See, for example, Virginia Woolf, 'Freudian Fiction', *Contemporary Writers* (New York: Harcourt Brace, 1976; first published, London, 1965), pp. 152–4, for Woolf's 1920 review of J. D. Beresford's novel, *An Imperfect Mother*. Woolf complained that the science of psychoanalysis had interfered with the artistic composition of the novel and remarked that 'all the characters have become cases'. (p. 153).
6. See Virginia Woolf, 'The Tunnel', *Contemporary Writers* (New York: Harcourt Brace, 1976; first published, London, 1965), pp. 120–2. Woolf's 1919 review of Dorothy Richardson's novel, *The Tunnel*, originally appeared in *The Times Literary Supplement*, 13 February 1919, and is reprinted in Virginia Woolf, *Women and Writing*, edited by Michèle Barrett (London: The Women's Press, 1979), pp. 188–91.
7. MSS. D, i, p. 5 (British Library), cited in Lyndall Gordon, *Virginia Woolf: A writer's life* (Oxford: Oxford University Press, 1984), pp. 194–5.
8. Virginia Woolf, *Diary*, II, p. 186, 26 July 1922: 'On Sunday L. read through Jacob's Room . . . I have no philosophy of life he says; my people are puppets'.
9. Virginia Woolf, *The Waves*, Holograph Notes, unsigned, dated 15 June 1930–30 January 1931, p. 1 (dated 3 November 1930): Henry W. and Albert A. Berg Collection, The New York Public Library, Astor, Lenox and Tilden Foundations.
10. Virginia Woolf, *Mrs Dalloway*, Holograph Notes, unsigned, dated 9 November 1922–2 August 1923, p. 2: Henry W. and Albert A. Berg Collection, The New York Public Library, Astor, Lenox and Tilden Foundations.
11. Virginia Woolf, *To the Lighthouse: The original holograph draft*, transcribed and edited by Susan Dick (London: Hogarth, 1983), Appendix A, p. 48.
12. *Ibid.*
13. Roger Fry, *Vision and Design* (London: Chatto, 1928), p. 310.
14. Virginia Woolf, *Mrs Dalloway*, Holograph Notes, unsigned, dated 9 November 1922–2 August 1923, p. 2: Henry W. and Albert A. Berg Collection, The New York, Public Library, Astor, Lenox and Tilden Foundations.
15. Woolf's notes on the Choephori of Aeschylus appear on the verso pages of her Holograph Notes on *Mrs Dalloway* (*ibid.*). Henry W. and Albert A. Berg Collection,

The New York Public Library, Astor, Lenox and Tilden Foundations.

16. Virginia Woolf, *Mrs Dalloway*, Holograph Notes, *op. cit.*, p. 7 (dated 7 May 1923). Henry W. and Albert A. Berg Collection, The New York Public Library, Astor, Lenox and Tilden Foundations.

17. Virginia Woolf, *Mrs Dalloway*, Holograph Notes, *op cit.*, p. 9 (dated 18 June 1923). Henry W. and Albert A. Berg Collection, The New York Public Library, Astor, Lenox and Tilden Foundations.

18. Virginia Woolf, *Mrs Dalloway*, Holograph Notes, *op. cit.*, p. 10 (dated 22 July 1923). Henry W. and Albert A. Berg Collection, The New York Public Library, Astor, Lenox and Tilden Foundations.

19. Virginia Woolf, '*The Waves: The two holograph drafts*', transcribed and edited by J. W. Graham (London: Hogarth, 1976), Draft I, p. 2.

20. Virginia Woolf, *Pointz Hall: The earlier and later typescripts of Between the Acts*, edited, with an introduction, annotations and an afterword, by Mitchell A. Leaska (New York: University Publications, 1983), p. 33.

21. Virginia Woolf, '*Pointz Hall: The earlier and later typescripts of Between the Acts*', edited, with an introduction, annotations and an afterword, by Mitchell A. Leaska (New York: University Publications, 1983), pp. 33; 43; 48.

22. Virginia Woolf, '*Pointz Hall: The earlier and later typescripts of Between the Acts*', edited, with an introduction, annotations, and an afterword, by Mitchell A. Leaska (New York: University Publications, 1983).

23. Victoria Glendinning, *Vita: The life of V. Sackville-West* (London: Weidenfeld & Nicolson, 1983), pp. 153–6 gives details of Vita's journey to Persia in 1926. Vita left for Persia on 20 January 1926 and was still en route on 27 February, the date on which Virginia was imagining 'the moon which is risen over Persia'.

24. The 24 volumes of Diary span the years 1895–1941. Those covering the period 1915–1941 are edited by Anne Oliver Bell and Andrew McNeillie (London: Hogarth, 1977–1984) in five volumes. Those covering the period 1895–1915 are held in the Berg Collection.

25. See Brenda R. Silver, *Virginia Woolf's Reading Notebooks* (Princeton: Princeton University Press, 1983), p. 116. See also Virginia Woolf, *Diary*, V, pp. 251–2; 248, for evidence that Woolf was reading Freud during December 1939.

26. See Brenda R. Silver, *Virginia Woolf's Reading Notebooks* (Princeton: Princeton University Press, 1983), p. 115. See also Virginia Woolf, *Diary*, V, p. 266.

27. Brenda R. Silver, *Virginia Woolf's Reading Notebooks* (Princeton: Princeton University Press, 1983), p. 115. See also Virginia Woolf, *Diary*, V, p. 266–7; and '*The Leaning Tower*', *The Moment and Other Essays* (London: Hogarth, 1981; first published, London 1947), pp. 105–25.

28. This 'phase' in Virginia Woolf's life might be seen to roughly correspond to Lacan's 'symbiotic' phase. (For a succinct and useful discussion of the 'symbiotic' phase and its correspondences with Lacan's 'Imaginary', see K. K. Ruthven, *Feminist Literary Studies: An introduction* (Cambridge: Cambridge University Press, 1984), pp. 93–102, though I am disinclined to suggest here that any sustained comparison, even were this possible, would throw further light on the vagaries of Virginia Woolf's writing practice. The reverse might even be the case. Virginia Woolf's accounts might serve to alert us to the *symbolic* status of Lacan's 'mirror', for example.

29. Leonard Woolf, *Downhill All The Way: An autobiography of the years 1919 to 1939* (London: Hogarth, 1975 (first published, 1971)), pp. 168–9: '[Freud] was extraordinarily courteous in a formal, old-fashioned way – for instance, almost ceremoniously he presented Virginia with a flower.' Cf. Phyllis Rose, *Woman of letters: A life of Virginia Woolf* (London: Routledge, 1978), p. 272: 'Freud gave Virginia Woolf a narcissus (which need not have been meant as a comment on her character)'; and Stephen Trombley, *All That Summer She Was Mad: Virginia Woolf and her Doctors* (London: Junction Books, 1981), p. 182: 'On 28 January 1939, the Woolfs visited the ailing Freud in Hampstead. Canny to the end, Freud presented Virginia with a narcissus.'

30. Virginia Woolf, *Diary*, II, pp. 298–9, 5 April 1924.

31. Hermione Lee discusses this passage in detail in Hermione Lee, 'A burning glass:

reflection in Virginia Woolf', in Eric Warner (ed.), *Virginia Woolf: A centenary perspective* (London: Macmillan, 1984), pp. 12–17.
32. See *Virginia Woolf: Moments of Being*, Jeanne Schulkind (ed.), (London: Triad/Panther, 1978), p. 137: 'Why should our lives have been so tortured and fretted by . . . the lash of a random and unheeding flail?' The survival of Julia and Stella, she surmises, would have ensured a 'normal and natural' continuity.
33. See *Virginia Woolf: Moments of Being*, Jeanne Schulkind (ed.), (London: Triad/Panther, 1978), p. 107: '"When I see mother, I see a man sitting with her" . . . was it true? . . . certainly, . . . when [Stella] . . . made me visualize my mother, I seemed to see a man sitting bent on the edge of the bed.'
34. See Virginia Woolf, *Diary*, V, p. 293, 7 June 1940: 'It struck me that one curious feeling is, that the writing "I" has vanished. No audience. No echo. Thats part of one's death . . . it is a fact – this disparition of an echo.'
35. See Leonard Woolf, *The Journey Not the Arrival Matters: An autobiography of the years 1939 to 1969* (London: Hogarth, 1973; first published, 1969), pp. 93–4, where Virginia Woolf's three suicide notes (two to Leonard and one to Vanessa) are quoted in full.
36. See Elizabeth Hardwick, *Seduction and Betrayal: Women and literature* (New York: Vintage Books, 1975), p. 141.
37. See Phyllis Rose, *Woman of Letters: A life of Virginia Woolf* (London: Routledge, 1978), p. xvii, paraphrasing E. L. Doctorow (quotation not cited).

Part II: Virginia Woolf's later novels, Chapter 1

1. See Virginia Woolf, *Diary*, II, p. 317: 'I see already the Old Man' (17 October 1924). The connection with Leslie Stephen is verified in a later entry, in *Diary*, III, p. 3: 'I'm always conceiving stories now . . . – for instance The Old Man (a character of L.S.)' (6 January 1925).
2. See Part I, p. 25 above.
3. Septimus Smith had used language in this way: Sir William Bradshaw had detected 'A serious symptom to be noted on the card.' Virginia Woolf: *Mrs Dalloway* (London: Penguin, 1972), p. 106.
4. See, for example, Herbert Marder, *Feminism and Art: A study of Virginia Woolf* (Chicago and London: University of Chicago Press, 1968), p. 35; Michael Rosenthal, *Virginia Woolf* (London: Routledge, 1979), p. 104; Kate Millett, *Sexual Politics* (London: Hart Davis, 1971), pp. 139–40; Barbara Hardy, *The Appropriate Form: An essay on the novel* (London: Athlone Press, 1964), p. 76.
5. Jane Lilienfeld, 'Where the spear plants grew: the Ramsays' marriage in *To the Lighthouse*', in Jane Marcus (ed.), *New Feminist Essays on Virginia Woolf* (London: Macmillan, 1981), pp. 148–69 (p. 165).
6. John Mepham, 'Figures of desire: narration and fiction in *To the Lighthouse*', in Gabriel Josipovici (ed.), *The Modern English Novel* (London: Open Books, 1976), pp. 149–85; Erich Auerbach, 'The brown stocking' in *Mimesis: The Representation of Reality in Western Literature*, translated by William Trask (Princeton University Press, 1953), Chapter 20.

Chapter 2

1. Mary Jacobus, 'The Difference of View', in Jacobus (ed.), *Women Writing and Writing about Women* (London: Croom Helm, 1979), pp. 10–21.
2. The difference for Woolf between writing (fiction) and writing 'about' ('facts') is well documented in the *Diaries*. See for example *Diary*, III, p. 239: 'I should be tackling Mary Wollstonecraft. I am in the thick of my four Herald articles, thus cutting into my Moths

(. . .) & hope to be quit of it all by August 14th & then go down step by step into that queer region.' (5 August 1929).
3. See John Mepham, 'Trained to silence', *London Review of Books*, 20 November–4 December 1980, pp. 21–3.
4. Woolf's attitude to her atheism is always ironic and playful. See for example *Letters*, I, p. 63: 'Once when our singing mistress asked me why I hung up my stocking on Christmas Eve, I said it was to celebrate the crucifixion (or however you spell it – not *fiction* I am sure – but the x looks so peculiar)' (27[?] December 1902, to Violet Dickinson). I lack the space here to develop an examination of the extent to which Woolf's atheism, established by her parents and unquestioned by her, may have contributed to her sense of dislocation, discussed in this chapter. Certainly, this was a possibility put to her by her 'fat religious cousin [Dorothea Stephen]', who tried to prove 'that certain sections of her soul are alive and afloat while ours [the Stephen children's] are "atrophied"'. See Virginia Woolf, *Letters*, I, p. 85 (7[?] July 1903), to Violet Dickinson. Fat religious Dorothea may have had a point: certainly, her use of language echoes that employed by Woolf to describe her periods of despair, the illnesses which she believed to be 'partly mystical': see Virginia Woolf, *Diary*, III, p. 287 (16 February 1930): 'Something happens in my mind. It refuses to go on registering impressions. It shuts itself up. It becomes a chrysalis. I lie quite torpid,' (*ibid.*).
5 Virginia Woolf, 'Professions for women', *The Death of the Moth* (London: Hogarth, 1981; first published, London 1942), pp. 149–54. Also in Virginia Woolf, *Women and Writing*, edited by Michèle Barrett (London: The Women's Press, 1979), pp. 57–63. The essay is based on Woolf's speech to the London/National Society for Women's Service on 21 January 1931. The typescript of the unabridged speech (including Woolf's annotations) is reprinted in Virginia Woolf, *The Pargiters*, edited by Mitchell A. Leaska (New York: Harcourt Brace, 1977), pp. xxvii–xliv. Woolf followed Ethel Smyth on this occasion, admitting that this made her feel 'rather like an idle and frivolous pleasure boat lolloping along in the wake of an ironclad' (*The Pargiters*, p. xxvii), but it was nevertheless the case that Ethel tended to bring out Virginia's brazen side: see their correspondence on the subject of a 'womans autobiography' cited in Part I, p. 43 above.
6. See Note 3 above.
7. For an excellent discussion of the relationship, for Woolf, between chastity and class, see Lillian S. Robinson, 'Who's afraid of a Room of One's Own?' in Louis Kampf and Paul Lauter (eds.), *The Politics of Literature: Dissenting essays on the teaching of English* (New York: Pantheon, 1972), pp. 254–411.
8. See also Virginia Woolf, *Moments of Being*, Jeanne Schulkind (ed.) (London: Triad/Panther, 1978), p. 79: 'This did not prevent me from feeling ecstacies and raptures spontaneously and intensely and without any shame or . . . guilt, so long as they were disconnected with my own body.' Also p. 48 above.

Chapter 3

1. See Virginia Woolf, *Diary*, III, p. 157: 'Vita should be Orlando' (20 September 1927). See also Virginia Woolf, *Letters*, III, pp. 428–9; 443, for letters from Woolf to Vita Sackville-West relating to *Orlando*.
2. Winifred Holtby, *Virginia Woolf: A critical memoir* (Chicago: Academy Press, 1978; first published, London, 1932).
3. See Sandra Gilbert, 'Costumes of the mind', in Elizabeth Abel (ed.), *Writing and Sexual Difference* (Brighton: Harvester Wheatsheaf, 1982), pp. 193–219: '*Orlando*, a work that is nominally about a trans-sexual, depicts trans-sexualism through sardonic costume changes rather than through actual physical transformations . . . Her trans-sexual, she argues, is no more than a transvestite.' (pp. 206–7). See also Elaine Showalter, *A Literature of their Own* (London: Virago, 1978; first published, Princeton, 1977), p. 291. For Showalter, androgyny is celebrated in the 'tedious high camp of *Orlando*', in contrast to

A Room of One's Own, where Woolf presents an 'ambivalent solution to the conflict of wishing to describe female experience at the same time that her life presented paralyzing obstacles to such self-expression.'

4. See Virginia Woolf, *Between the Acts* (London: Granada/Panther, 1978), pp. 147–9, also pp. 167 below.
5. The subject of Vita Sackville-West's 'free' marriage to Harold Nicolson is well documented in Nigel Nicolson, *Portait of a Marriage* (London: Weidenfeld and Nicolson, 1973). See also Victoria Glendinning, *Vita: The life of V. Sackville-West* (London: Weidenfeld and Nicolson, 1983). Glendinning gives details of an unfinished play by Vita, entitled *Marriage,* which charts the heroine's desire to be 'a whole person by [herself], not just half of a composite person' (pp. 117–18).
6. Gillian Beer, 'Virginia Woolf and pre-history', in Eric Warner (ed.), *Virginia Woolf: A centenary perspective* (London: Macmillan, 1984), p. 121.

Chapter 4

1. Quoted in J. J. Wilson, 'Why is *Orlando* difficult?', in Jane Marcus (ed.), *New Feminist Essays on Virginia Woolf* (London: Macmillan, 1981), pp. 170–84 (p. 179).
2. Virginia Woolf, *Diary,* III, pp. 176–7, 18 March 1928.
3. Virginia Woolf, *Diary,* III, p. 131, 14 March 1927.
4. Virginia Woolf, *Diary,* III, pp. 156–7, 20 September 1927.
5. See Note 1 to Chapter 3, above.
6. The Woolfs published Freud's *Collected Papers* in four volumes, thence establishing The Hogarth Press's connection with the International Psycho-Analytic Library.
7. See Brenda R. Silver, *Virginia Woolf's Reading Notebooks* (Princeton: Princeton University Press, 1983), pp. 115–16. See also Virginia Woolf, *Diary,* V, pp. 248, 252 for evidence that Woolf was reading Freud during December 1939. By 11 February 1940 she was noting, 'I think there's something in the psycho-analy[s]is idea', in connection with her essay 'The Leaning Tower': see *Diary,* V, pp. 266–7; also 'The Leaning Tower' in *The Moment and Other Essays* (London: Hogarth, 1981; first published, London, 1947), pp. 105–25.
8. Of *Orlando,* Woolf had noted, 'Anyhow I'm glad to be quit this time of writing "a novel"; & hope never to be accused of it again . . . Something abstract poetic next time – I don't know.' *D,* III, p. 185, 31 May 1928.
9. W. H. Mellers, review, *Scrutiny,* June 1937, pp. 71–5, reprinted in *CH,* pp. 395–9 (p. 396).
10. M. C. Bradbrook, 'Notes on the style of Mrs Woolf', *Scrutiny,* May 1932, pp. 33–8, reprinted in *CH,* pp. 308–13 (p. 311).
11. Elizabeth Hardwick, *Seduction and Betrayal: Women and literature* (New York: Vintage Books, 1975), pp. 141–2.
12. Virginia Woolf, *The Waves: The two holograph drafts,* transcribed and edited by J. W. Graham (London: Hogarth, 1976).
13. Madeleine Moore, *The Short Season Between Two Silences: The mystical and the political in the novels of Virginia Woolf* (Boston, London and Sydney: Unwin Hyman, 1984), pp. 122–6.

Chapter 5

1. Virginia Woolf spoke to the London branch of the National Society for Women's Service on 21 January 1931. The text of the speech is transcribed and reprinted in *The Pargiters* (New York: Harcourt Brace, 1978; first edition 1977), edited with an introduction by Mitchell A. Leaska, pp. xxvii–xliv.

2. Virginia Woolf, *Diary*, IV, p. 6.
3. Virginia Woolf, *Diary*, IV, p. 233.
4. Ethel Smyth was also a vigorous campaigner for women's rights. For a biographical note, see *Diary*, IV. p. 367.
5. Virginia Woolf, 'Professions for women', *The Death of the Moth* (London: Hogarth, 1981; first published, London, 1942), pp. 149–54. The novelist begins as 'a girl in a bedroom with a pen in her hand' (p. 149), but as the essay develops she becomes 'a fisherman lying sunk in dreams on the verge of a deep lake with a rod held out over the water.' (p. 152).
6. Virginia Woolf, *Three Guineas* (London: Penguin, 1979; first published, London, 1938), p. 85: 'the enormous professional competence of the educated man has not brought about an altogether desirable state of things in the civilized world'. The strategy offered by *Three Guineas* as a whole is that of organising an alternative society of women – the 'Outsiders' Society' – in order to restore to society the life of the senses.
7. Virginia Woolf, 'Modern Fiction', *The Common Reader*, I (London: Hogarth, 1984; first published, London, 1925), p. 150.
8. Jane Marcus, '*The Years* as Greek Drama, Domestic Novel, and Götterdämmerung', *Bulletin of the New York Public Library*, vol. 80, Winter 1977, no. 2, pp. 276–301.
9. Caroline Emilia Stephen, Virginia Woolf's aunt. Woolf refers to *Light Arising: Thoughts on the Central Radiance* (1908) in *Letters*, I, p. 331, in a letter of 13 May 1908 to Violet Dickinson: 'It is a gloomy work I know, all gray abstractions, and tremulous ecstacies, and shows a beautiful spirit.' The description is characteristic of Rachel Vinrace, in *The Voyage Out*, but I have not been able to document any specific connection.
10. Virginia Woolf, *Night and Day* (London: Penguin, 1975; first published, London, 1919), pp. 106–7: ' "What is nobler", [Mrs Hilbery] mused, . . . than to be a woman to whom everyone turns, in sorrow or difficulty? How have the young women of your generation improved upon that, Katherine? I can see them now, sweeping over the lawns . . . , in their flounces and furbelows, so calm and stately and imperial (. . .), as if nothing mattered in the world but to be beautiful and kind. But they did more than we do, I sometimes think. They *were*, and that's better than doing." '
11. Virginia Woolf *Three Guineas* (London: Penguin, 1979; first published, London, 1938), p. 130: 'Broadly speaking, the main distinction between us who are outside society and you who are inside society must be that whereas you will make use of the means provided by your position – leagues, conferences, campaigns, great names, and all such public measures as your wealth and political influence place within your reach – we, remaining outside, will experiment not with public means in public but with private means in private.'
12. *ibid.*
13. See Martine Stemerick: *From Clapham to Bloomsbury: Virginia Woolf's Feminist Rebellion* (Hemel Hempstead: Harvester Wheatsheaf, forthcoming), pp. 3–5 (pagination refers to the typescript).
14. See Victoria S. Middleton, '*The Years:* A deliberate failure', *Bulletin of the New York Public Library*, vol. 80, Winter 1977, no. 2, pp. 158–171 (p. 158).
15. Quentin Bell, *Virginia Woolf, II* (London: Triad/Paladin, 1976; first published, London, 1972), p. 187.
16. Mitchell A. Leaska, 'Virginia Woolf, The Pargeter: A reading of *The Years*', *Bulletin of the New York Public Library*, vol. 80, Winter 1977, no. 2, pp. 172–210.
17. See Note 8 above.
18. It is of course possible that in her depiction of the sirens Woolf was evoking – consciously or unconsciously – an indirect reference to the Sirens in Greek drama. I cannot, however, uncover any evidence in support of this hypothesis.
19. Virginia Woolf, 'On Not Knowing Greek', *The Common Reader*, I (London: Hogarth, 1984; first published, London, 1925), pp. 23–38 (p. 38).
20. Leonard Woolf, in his edition of Virginia Woolf, *A Writer's Diary* (London: Triad/Panther, 1978; first published, London, 1953), attributes Virginia Woolf's diary entry of 20 January 1931 ('I have this moment, while having my bath, conceived an entire new book') to the eventual composition of *Three Guineas* (p. 162). Mitchell A. Leaska, in *The*

Pargiters, claims that the entry refers to *The Years*. Anne Olivier Bell, in her note on the entry in *Diary*, IV, p. 6, claims it as the genesis of both *Three Guineas* and *The Years*.

Chapter 6

1. Virginia Woolf, *Pointz Hall: The earlier and later typescripts of Between the Acts*, edited, with an introduction, annotations and an afterword by Mitchell A. Leaska (New York: University Publications, 1983).
2. Virginia Woolf, *Pointz Hall: The earlier and later typescripts of Between the Acts*, edited, with an introduction, annotations and an afterword by Mitchell A. Leaska (New York: University Publications, 1983), Appendix D, pp. 557–61.
3. Virginia Woolf, *Pointz Hall: The earlier and later typescripts of Between the Acts*, edited, with an introduction, annotations and an afterword by Mitchell A. Leaska (New York: University Publications, 1983), p. 559.
4. J. Hillis Miller, *Fiction and Repetition: Seven English novels* (Oxford: Basil Blackwell, 1982), p. 208.
5. Virginia Woolf, *A Room of One's Own* (London: Penguin, 1963; first published, London, 1928), pp. 79–84.
6. See Note 4 above.
7. See Part I, p. 32 above.
8. Virginia Woolf, *A Room of One's Own* (London: Penguin, 1963; first published, London, 1928), p. 96: 'Again if one is a woman one is often surprised by a sudden splitting off of consciousness, say in walking down Whitehall, when from being the natural inheritor of that civilization, she becomes, on the contrary, outside of it, alien and critical.' I discuss this passage in Part II, Chapter 2 above.
9. Virginia Woolf, Holograph reading notes entitled 'Notes for reading at random', Holograph notebook, dated 18 September 1940, p. 4 (Berg Collection). Henry W. and Albert A. Berg Collection, The New York Public Library, Astor, Lenox and Tilden Foundations.
10. Virginia Woolf, *Anon*: typescript fragment, unsigned, dated 24 November 1940, with the author's ms. corrections (26 pp.), p. 3. Henry W. and Albert A. Berg Collection, The New York Public Library, Astor, Lenox and Tilden Foundations.
11. Virginia Woolf, 'Notes on an Elizabethan Play', *The Common Reader*, I (London: Hogarth, 1984) first published, London, 1925), pp. 48–57 (pp. 52–3).
12. See Virginia Woolf, *Diary*, II, pp. 298–9; see also Part I, p. 54 above.

Conclusion

1. Jane Marcus, *New Feminist Essays on Virginia Woolf* (London: Macmillan, 1981), p. 1.
2. Joanne Trautmann Banks (ed.), *Congenial Spirits: The selected letters of Virginia Woolf* (London: Hogarth, 1989), p. 154. Quoted but not cited in Victoria Glendinning, 'Cry Woolf on the rocks' (*The Times*, 20 July 1989, p. 19).
3. Virginia Woolf, *Diary*, III, p. 52: 'There is her maturity & full breastedness: her being so much in full sail on the high tides, where I am coasting down backwaters; her capacity I mean to take the floor in any company, to represent her country, to visit Chatsworth, to control silver, servants, chow dogs; her motherhood (. . .) her being in short (what I have never been) a real woman.' (21 December 1925).
4. Virginia Woolf, *The Voyage Out* (London: Penguin, 1970; first published, London, 1915), p. 217. Quoted above as epigraph to Part II.

Bibliography

Works by Virginia Woolf

Between the Acts (London: Hogarth, 1941; Penguin, 1953; Granada/Panther, 1978).

Books and Portraits: Some further selections from the literary and biographical writings of Virginia Woolf. Edited and with a preface by Mary Lyon (London: Hogarth, 1977; Triad/Panther, 1979; New York: Harcourt Brace, 1977).

The Captain's Death Bed and Other Essays (London: Hogarth, 1950; New York: Harcourt Brace, 1978).

Collected Essays, edited by Leonard Woolf, 4 vols. (London: Chatto, 1966, 1967).

The Common Reader: First Series (London: Hogarth, 1925; New York: Harcourt Brace, 1925; revised edition, edited and introduced by Andrew McNeillie, London: Hogarth, 1984).

The Common Reader: Second Series (London: Hogarth 1932; New York: Harcourt Brace, 1932; revised edition, edited and introduced by Andrew McNeillie, London: Hogarth, 1986).

The Complete Shorter Fiction of Virginia Woolf, edited by Susan Dick (London: Hogarth, 1985).

Congenial Spirits: The Letters of Virginia Woolf, selected and edited by Joanne Trautmann Banks (London: Hogarth, 1989).

Contemporary Writers: Essays on Twentieth Century books and authors by Virginia Woolf with a Preface by Jean Guiguet (London: Hogarth, 1965; New York: Harcourt Brace, 1976).

The Death of the Moth (London: Hogarth, 1981, first published, 1942).

The Diary of Virginia Woolf, 5 vols., edited by Anne Olivier Bell and Andrew McNeillie (London: Hogarth, 1977, 1978, 1980, 1982, 1984).

Flush: A Biography (London: Hogarth, 1933; New York: Harcourt Brace, 1976).

Freshwater: A Comedy, edited and with a preface by Lucio P. Ruotolo (New York and London: Harcourt Brace, 1976).

Granite and Rainbow: Essays by Virginia Woolf (London: Hogarth, 1958; New York: Harcourt Brace 1975).

A Haunted House and Other Stories (London: Hogarth, 1944; Penguin, 1973; New York: Harcourt Brace 1972).

Jacob's Room (London: Hogarth, 1922; Penguin, 1965).

A Letter to a Young Poet (London: Hogarth, 1932; reprinted in *The Death of the Moth* (London: Hogarth, 1981 first published, 1942).

The Letters of Virginia Woolf, 6 vols., edited by Nigel Nicolson and Joanne

Trautmann (London: Hogarth, 1975, 1976, 1977, 1978, 1979, 1980).
The Letters of Vita Sackville-West to Virginia Woolf, edited by Louise DeSalvo and
     Mitchell A. Leaska (London: Hutchinson, 1984).
The London Scene: Five Essays by Virginia Woolf (London: Hogarth, 1982; first
     published, New York: Frank Hallman, 1975).
A Moment's Liberty: The shorter diary, abridged and edited by Anne Olivier Bell,
     introduction by Quentin Bell (New York: Harcourt Brace, 1990).
The Moment and Other Essays (London: Hogarth, 1981; first published, 1947).
Mrs Dalloway (London: Hogarth, 1925, Penguin, 1964, 1966).
Mrs Dalloway's Party: A short story sequence by Virginia Woolf, edited, with an
     introduction by Stella McNichol (New York and London: Harcourt Brace,
     1975).
Night and Day (London: Duckworth, 1919, Penguin, 1969, 1971).
Orlando (London: Hogarth, 1928; Penguin, 1942, 1963).
Roger Fry (London: Hogarth, 1940; London: Peregrine, 1979).
A Room of One's Own (London: Hogarth, 1928, Penguin, 1945, 1963).
Three Guineas (London: Hogarth, 1938; Penguin, 1979).
To the Lighthouse (London: Hogarth, 1927; Penguin, 1964, 1965).
The Voyage Out (London: Duckworth, 1915; Penguin, 1970, 1972).
The Waves (London: Hogarth, 1931; Penguin, 1951, 1964, 1966).
Women and Writing, introduced by Michèle Barrett (London: The Women's Press,
     1979).
A Writer's Diary, Being Extracts from the Diary of Virginia Woolf, edited by
     Leonard Woolf (London: Hogarth, 1953; Triad/Panther, 1978).
The Years (London: Hogarth, 1937, Penguin, 1968; Granada/Panther, 1977).

Posthumously published draft material by Virginia Woolf

The Pargiters, The Novel – Essay Portion of The Years, edited, with an introduction
     by Mitchell A. Leaska (New York and London: Harcourt Brace, 1977).
Pointz Hall, The Earlier and Later Typescripts of Between the Acts, edited, with an
     Introduction, annotations and an Afterword, by Mitchell A. Leaska (New
     York: University Publications, 1983).
Melymbrosia, An Early Version of The Voyage Out, edited with an Introduction by
     Louise DeSalvo (New York: The New York Public Library, 1982).
Moments of Being: Unpublished autobiographical writings, edited, with an
     Introduction and Notes by Jeanne Schulkind (London: Chatto and Windus,
     1976; Triad/Panther, 1978; New York: Harcourt Brace, 1976; revised and
     enlarged edition: London: Hogarth, 1985).
To the Lighthouse: The original holograph draft, transcribed and edited by Susan
     Dick (London: Hogarth, 1983).
The Waves: The two holograph drafts, transcribed and edited by J. W. Graham
     (London: Hogarth, 1976).

Bibliography

Kirkpatrick, B. J., *A Bibliography of Virginia Woolf* (Oxford: Oxford University
     Press, 1980; first published, 1957).

Biography

Bell, Quentin, *Virginia Woolf: A biography: Vol. I: Virginia Stephen, 1882–1912* (London: Triad/Paladin, 1976; first published, Hogarth, 1972).
Bell, Quentin, *Virginia Woolf: A biography: Vol. II: Mrs Woolf, 1912–1941* (London: Triad/Paladin, 1976; first published, Hogarth, 1972).
Gordon, Lyndall, *Virginia Woolf: A writer's life* (Oxford: Oxford University Press, 1984).
Love, Jean O., *Virginia Woolf: Sources of madness and art* (California and London: University of California Press, 1977).
Pippett, Aileen, *The Moth and the Star: A biography of Virginia Woolf* (Boston and Toronto: Little, Brown and Co., 1953).
Rose, Phyllis, *Woman of Letters: A life of Virginia Woolf* (London: Routledge, 1978).

Bloomsbury, and related titles

Ackroyd, Peter, *T. S. Eliot* (London: Hamish Hamilton, 1984).
Anand, Mulk Raj, *Conversations in Bloomsbury* (London: Wildwood House, 1981).
Annan, Noel, *Leslie Stephen: His thought and character in relation to his time* (London: MacGibbon and Kee, 1951).
Annan, Noel, *Leslie Stephen: The godless Victorian* (London: Weidenfeld & Nicolson, 1984).
Anscombe, Isabelle, *Omega and After: Bloomsbury and the decorative arts* (London: Thames and Hudson, 1982).
Bell, Clive, *Civilization and Old Friends*. Two volumes in one (Chicago: University of Chicago Press, 1973; first published as *Civilization*, London, 1928; *Old Friends, London, 1956*).
Bell, Quentin, *Bloomsbury* (London: Futura/Omega, 1974; first published, 1968; new edition, Weidenfeld & Nicolson, 1986).
Bell, Quentin and Garnett, Angelica, *Vanessa Bell's Family Album* (London: Jill Norman and Hobhouse, 1981).
Bell, Quentin 'Where Bloomsbury Flowered', in Rosenthal, A. M. and Gelb, Arthur (eds.), *The Sophisticated Traveller: Beloved cities of Europe* (New York: Villard Books, 1984).
Dangerfield, George, *The Strange Death of Liberal England* (London: Granada/Paladin, 1983; first published, 1935).
Deacon, Richard, *The Cambridge Apostles: A history of Cambridge University's elite intellectual Secret Society* (London: Robert Royce, 1985).
Edel, Leon, *Bloomsbury: A house of lions* (London: Hogarth, 1979).
Eliot, T. S., *After Strange Gods: A primer of modern heresy* (London: Faber, 1934).
Fry, Roger, *Vision and Design* (Chatto, 1920).
Gadd, David, *The Loving Friends: A portrait of Bloomsbury* (London: Hogarth, 1974).
Garnett, Angelica, *Deceived with Kindness: A Bloomsbury childhood* (London: Chatto/Hogarth, 1984).
Garnett, David, *Great Friends: Portraits of seventeen writers* (London: Macmillan, 1979).

Gathorne-Hardy, Robert (ed.), *Ottoline at Garsington: Memoirs of Lady Ottoline Morrell, 1915–1918* (London: Faber, 1974).
Glendinning, Victoria, *Vita: The life of V. Sackville-West* (London: Weidenfeld and Nicolson, 1983).
Halperin, John, 'Bloomsbury and Virginia Woolf: another view', *Dalhousie Review*, vol. 59, no. 3.
Holtby, Winifred, *Women and a Changing Civilization* (Chicago: Academy Press, 1978; first published, New York, 1935).
Johnstone, J. K., *The Bloomsbury Group: A study of E. M. Forster, Lytton Strachey, Virginia Woolf, and their Circle* (London: Secker and Warburg, 1954).
Kennedy, Richard, *A Boy at the Hogarth Press* (London: Penguin, 1978; first published, 1972).
Lee, Hermione (ed.), *The Hogarth Letters* (London: Chatto, 1985).
Lehmann, John, *Thrown to the Woolfs: Leonard and Virginia Woolf and the Hogarth Press*, introduction by Phyllis Rose (New York: Holt, Rinehart, 1978).
Lehmann, John, *Virginia Woolf and her World* (London: Thames and Hudson, 1975).
Lewis, Percy Wyndham, *Men Without Art* (London: Cassell, 1934).
Llewelyn Davies, Margaret (ed.), *Life as We Have Known It* by Co-operative Working Women, with an introduction by Virginia Woolf (London: Virago, 1977, first published, Hogarth, 1931).
Marcus, Jane (ed.), *Virginia Woolf and Bloomsbury: A centenary celebration* (Indiana: Indiana University Press, 1985; Basingstoke: Macmillan, 1987.).
Meisel, Perry and Kendrick, Walter (eds.), *Bloomsbury/Freud: The letters of James and Alix Strachey 1924–1925* (London: Chatto and Windus, 1986).
Nicolson, Nigel, *Portrait of a Marriage* (London: Weidenfeld and Nicolson, 1973).
Partridge, Frances, *Memories* (London: Robin Clark, 1982).
Rosenbaum, S. P. (ed.), *The Bloomsbury Group* (Toronto and Buffalo: University of Toronto Press, 1975).
Spalding, Frances, *Vanessa Bell* (London: Weidenfeld and Nicolson, 1983).
Spater, George and Parsons, Ian, *A Marriage of True Minds: An intimate portrait of Leonard and Virginia Woolf* (London: Cape and Hogarth, 1977).
Spender, Stephen, *The Destructive Element* (London: Cape, 1935).
Stephen, Sir Leslie, *Mausoleum Book*, with an introduction by Alan Bell (Oxford: Clarendon Press, 1977).
Woolf, Leonard and Strachey, James (eds.), *Virginia Woolf and Lytton Strachey: Letters* (London: Hogarth, 1956).

Critical books on Virginia Woolf

Bazin, Nancy Topping, *Virginia Woolf and the Androgynous Vision* (New Brunswick, New Jersey: Rutgers University Press, 1973).
Bennett, Joan, *Virginia Woolf: Her art as a novelist* (Cambridge: Cambridge University Press, 1945).
Blackstone, Bernard, *Virginia Woolf: A commentary* (London: Hogarth, 1949).
Bowlby, Rachel, *Virginia Woolf: Feminist Destinations* (Oxford: Basil Blackwell, 1988).
Clements, Patricia and Grundy, Isobel, *Virginia Woolf: New critical essays* (London: Vision Press, 1983).
Daiches, David, *Virginia Woolf* (London: Nicholson and Watson, 1945).

Defromont, Françoise, *Virginia Woolf: Vers la Maison du Lumière* (Paris: Editions des Femmes, 1985).

DeSalvo, Louise, *Virginia Woolf: The impact of childhood sexual abuse on her life and work* (London: The Women's Press and Boston: Beacon Press, 1989).

Di Battista, Maria, *Virginia Woolf's Major Novels: The fables of Anon* (New York and London: Yale University Press, 1980).

Fleishman, Avrom, *Virginia Woolf: A critical reading* (Baltimore: Johns Hopkins University Press, 1975).

Fox, Alice, *Virginia Woolf and the Literature of the English Renaissance* (Oxford: Clarendon Press, 1990).

Freedman, Ralph (ed.), *Virginia Woolf: Revaluation and continuity* (Berkeley and London: University of California Press, 1980).

Gorsky, Susan Rubinow, *Virginia Woolf* (Boston: G. K. Hall, 1978).

Guiguet, Jean, *Virginia Woolf and her Works*, translated by Jean Stewart (London: Hogarth, 1965).

Hafley, James, *The Glass Roof: Virginia Woolf as novelist* (Berkeley and Los Angeles: University of California Press, 1954).

Hardy, Barbara Nathan, *The Appropriate Form: An essay on the novel* (London: Athlone Press, 1964).

Holtby, Winifred, *Virginia Woolf: A critical memoir* (London: Wishart, 1932, reprinted, Chicago: Academy Press, 1978).

Kelly, Alice van Buren, *The Novels of Virginia Woolf: Fact and vision* (Chicago and London: Chicago University Press, 1971).

Leaska, Mitchell A., *The Novels of Virginia Woolf: From beginning to end* (London: Weidenfeld & Nicolson, 1977).

Lee, Hermione, *The Novels of Virginia Woolf* (London: Methuen, 1977).

McLaurin, Allen, *Virginia Woolf: The echoes enslaved* (Cambridge: Cambridge University Press, 1973).

Love, Jean, *Worlds in Consciousness: Mythopoetic thought in the novels of Virginia Woolf* (California: University of California Press, 1970).

Marcus, Jane (ed.), *New Feminist Essays on Virginia Woolf* (London: Macmillan, 1981).

Marcus, Jane (ed.), *Virginia Woolf: A feminist slant* (Nebraska: University of Nebraska Press, 1983).

Marder, Herbert, *Feminism and Art: A study of Virginia Woolf* (Chicago and London: University of Chicago Press, 1968).

Meisel, Perry, *The Absent Father: Virginia Woolf and Walter Pater* (New Haven and London: Yale University Press, 1980).

Miller, Ruth, *Virginia Woolf: The frames of art and life* (London: Macmillan, 1988).

Moody, A. D., *Virginia Woolf, 'Writers and Critics'* (Edinburgh : Oliver and Boyd, 1963).

Moore, Madeleine, *The Short Season Between Two Silences: The mystical and the political in the novels of Virginia Woolf* (Boston, London and Sydney: Allen and Unwin, 1984).

Naremore, James, *The World Without a Self: Virginia Woolf and the novel* (New Haven and London: Yale University Press, 1973).

Nathan, Monique, *Virginia Woolf* (London and New York: Evergreen Books, 1961, first published, Paris: Seuil, as *Virginia Woolf Par Elle-même*).

Pinkney, Makiko Minow, *Virginia Woolf and the Problem of the Subject: Feminine writing in the major novels* (Brighton: Harvester, 1987).

Poole, Roger, *The Unknown Virginia Woolf* (Brighton: Harvester, 1982, first published, Cambridge, 1978).

Poresky, Louise A., *The Elusive Self: Psyche and spirit in Virginia Woolf's novels* (London and Toronto: Associated University Presses, 1981).

Richter, Harvena, *Virginia Woolf: The Inward Voyage* (Princeton: Princeton University Press, 1970).

Rosenman, Ellen Bayuk, *The Invisible Presence: Virginia Woolf and the mother-daughter relationship* (Baton Rouge and London: Louisiana State University Press, 1986).

Rosenthal, Michael, *Virginia Woolf* (New York: Columbia University Press, 1979).

DeSalvo, Louise, A., *Virginia Woolf's First Voyage: A novel in the making* (London: Macmillan, 1980).

Schlack, Beverly Ann, *Continuing Presences: Virginia Woolf's use of literary allusion* (Pennsylvania and London: The Pennsylvania State University Press, 1978).

Spilka, Mark, *Virginia Woolf's Quarrel with Grieving* (Lincoln, Nebraska and London: University of Nebraska Press, 1980).

Stemerick, Martine, *From Clapham to Bloomsbury: Virginia Woolf's feminist rebellion* (Hemel Hempstead: Harvester Wheatsheaf (forthcoming)).

Trombley, Stephen, *All That Summer She was Mad: Virginia Woolf and her doctors* (London: Junction Books, 1981).

Warner, Eric (ed.), *Virginia Woolf: A centenary perspective*, foreword by Quentin Bell (London: Macmillan, 1984).

Zwerling, Alex, *Virginia Woolf and the Real World* (California: University of California Press, 1986).

Books containing chapters on Virginia Woolf

Auerbach, Erich, *Mimesis: The representation of reality in Western literature*, translated by Willard Trask (Princeton: Princeton University Press, 1953).

Blanchot, Maurice, *The Sirens' Song*, edited by Gabriel Josipovici (Brighton: Harvester, 1982).

Daiches, David, *The Novel and the Modern World* (Chicago: University of Chicago Press, 1973, first published, 1960).

Dowling, David, *Bloomsbury Aesthetics and the Novels of Forster and Woolf* (London: Macmillan, 1985).

Edel, Leon, *Stuff of Sleep and Dreams: Experiments in literary psychology* (New York: Harper & Row, 1982).

Forster, E. M., 'Virginia Woolf', The Rede Lecture (Cambridge: Cambridge University Press, 1941). Collected in *Two Cheers for Democracy* (London: Penguin, 1965, first published, 1951).

Gloversmith, Frank, 'Autonomy Theory: Ortega, Roger Fry, Virginia Woolf' in Gloversmith, Frank (ed.), *The Theory of Reading* (Brighton: Harvester, 1984).

Hardwick, Elizabeth, *Seduction and Betrayal: Women and literature* (New York: Vintage Books, 1975).

Hillis Miller, J., *Fiction and Repetition: Seven English novels* (Oxford: Basil Blackwell, 1982).

Josipovici, Gabriel, *The Mirror of Criticism: Selected reviews, 1977–1982* (Brighton: Harvester, 1983).

Kampf, Louis and Lauter, Paul (eds.), *The Politics of Literature: Dissenting essays on the teaching of English* (New York: Pantheon, 1972).

Lodge, David, *Language of Fiction* (London: Routledge, 1966).

Mepham, John, 'Figures of Desire: Narration and Fiction in *To the Lighthouse*' in Josipovici, Gabriel (ed.), *The Modern English Novel: The reader, the writer and the work* (London: Open Books, 1976).

O'Faolain, Sean, *The Vanishing Hero: Studies in novelists of the Twenties* (London: Eyre and Spottiswoode, 1956).

Ozick, Cynthia, *Art and Ardor: Essays* (New York: E. P. Dutton, 1984).

Rigney, Barbara Hill, *Madness and Sexual Politics in the Feminist Novel: Studies in Brontë, Woolf, Lessing and Atwood* (Wisconsin: University of Wisconsin Press, 1978).

Roe, Sue (ed.), *Women Reading Women's Writing* (Brighton: Harvester, 1987).

Savage, D. S., *The Withered Branch: Six studies in the modern novel* (London: Eyre and Spottiswoode, 1950).

Showalter, Elaine, *A Literature of their Own: British women novelists from Brontë to Lessing* (London: Virago, 1978, first published, Princeton and London: Princeton University Press, 1977).

Spivak, Gayatri C., 'Unmaking and making in *To the Lighthouse*', in Ginet, Borker and Furman (eds.), *Women and Language in Literature and Society* (New York: Praeger, 1980).

Watney, Simon, 'The connoisseur as gourmet: The aesthetics of Roger Fry and Clive Bell' in Jameson, Frederic *et al.*, *Formations of Pleasure* (London: Routledge, 1983).

Feminist criticism/critical theory relating to Virginia Woolf

Bradbrook, Muriel, *Women and Literature 1779–1982: The collected papers of Muriel Bradbrook, II* (Brighton: Harvester, 1982).

'Bulletin of the New York Public Library: Virginia Woolf issue', vol. 80, Winter 1977, no. 2 (The New York Public Library, Astor, Lenox and Tilden Foundations).

'Bulletin of research in the Humanities (continuing the Bulletin of the New York Public Library): Virginia Woolf issue, II, vol. 82. Autumn 1979, no. 3 (The New York Public Library, Astor, Lenox and Tilden Foundations).

Diamond, Arlyn and Edwards, Lee R. (eds.), *The Authority of Experience: Essays in feminist criticism* (Amherst: University of Massachusetts Press, 1977).

Ellmann, Mary, *Thinking About Women* (London: Virago, 1979).

Gilbert, Sandra M. and Gubar, Susan, *The Madwoman in the Attic: The woman writer and the Nineteenth-Century literary imagination* (New Haven and London: Yale University Press, 1979).

Humm, Maggie, *Feminist Criticism* (Brighton: Harvester, 1986).

Jacobus, Mary (ed.), *Women Writing and Writing About Women* (London: Croom Helm, 1979).

Keohane, Nannerl O., Rosaldo, Michelle, Z. and Gelpi, Barbara C., *Feminist theory: A critique of ideology* (Brighton: Harvester, 1982, first published, Chicago: University of Chicago Press, 1981).

Lazarre, Jane, *On Loving Men* (London: Virago, 1981, first published, N.Y.: The Dial Press, 1980).

Marks, Elaine and De Courtivron, Isabelle, *New French Feminisms: An anthology* (Brighton: Harvester, 1981, first published, Massachusetts: University of Massachusetts Press, 1980).

Millet, Kate, *Sexual Politics* (London: Hart-Davis, 1971).

Mitchell, Juliet and Rose, Jacqueline, *Feminine Sexuality: Jacques Lacan and the École Freudienne*, translated by Jacqueline Rose (London: Macmillan, 1982).

Mitchell, Juliet, *Psychoanalysis and Feminism* (London: Allen Lane, 1974).

Moers, Ellen, *Literary Women* (London: W. H. Allen, 1977).

Moi, Toril, *Sexual/Textual Politics: Feminist literary theory* (London and New York: Methuen, 1985).

Radcliffe Richards, Janet, *The Sceptical Feminist: A philosophical enquiry* (London: Routledge, 1980).

Rose, Phyllis, *Writing of Women: Essays in a renaissance* (Connecticut: Wesleyan University Press, 1985).

Ruthven, K. K., *Feminist Literary Studies: An introduction* (Cambridge: Cambridge University Press, 1984).

Showalter, Elaine, *A Literature of their Own* (London: Virago, 1978: first published, Princeton: Princeton University Press, 1977).

Showalter, Elaine (ed.), *The New Feminist Criticism: Essays on women, literature and theory* (New York: Pantheon, 1985).

Spacks, Patricia Mayer, *The Female Imagination* (New York: Avon, 1975, first published, 1972).

Spender, Dale (ed.), *Feminist Theorists: Three centuries of women's intellectual traditions* (London: The Women's Press, 1983).

Spender, Dale, *Man Made Language* (London: Boston and Henley: Routledge, 1980).

Stimpson, Catharine R. and Person, Ethel Spector (eds.), *Women: Sex and sexuality* (Chicago and London: University of Chicago Press, 1980).

Stubbs, Patricia, *Women and Fiction: Feminism and the novel 1880–1920* (Brighton: Harvester, 1979).

Critical theory relating to Virginia Woolf

Derrida, Jacques, *Writing and Difference*, translated by Alan Bass (Chicago: University of Chicago Press, 1978).

Eagleton, Terry, *Literary Theory: An introduction* (Oxford: Basil Blackwell, 1983).

Heath, Stephen, *The Sexual Fix* (London: Macmillan, 1982).

Kristeva, Julia, *Desire in Language: A semiotic approach to literature and art*, edited by Roudiez, Leon S. (New York: Columbia University Press, 1980).

Selden, Raman, *A Reader's Guide to Contemporary Literary Theory* (Brighton: Harvester, 1985; revised edition, 1989).

Other related material

Abel, Elizabeth (ed.), *Writing and Sexual Difference* (Brighton: Harvester, 1982, first published, Chicago, 1980).

Beauman, Nicola, *A Very Great Profession: The woman's novel, 1914–39* (London: Virago, 1983).

Bell, Anne Olivier, *Editing Virginia Woolf's Diary* (Oxford: The Perpetua Press, 1989).

Benjamin, Walter, *Illuminations*, edited by Hannah Arendt and translated by Harry Zohn (Fontana/Collins, 1973, first published, Frankfurt: Suhrkamp Verlag, 1955).

Carpenter, Edward, *The Art of Creation: Essays on the self and its powers* (London: Allen and Unwin, 1904).

Leaska, Mitchell A. and Phillips, John (eds.), *Violet to Vita: The Letters of Violet Trefusis to Vita Sackville-West* (London: Methuen, 1989).

Majumdar, Robin and McLaurin, Allen, *Virginia Woolf: The Critical Heritage* (London: Routledge, 1975).

Noble, Joan Russell (ed.), *Recollections of Virginia Woolf* (London: Penguin, 1975; first published, 1972).

O'Brien, Edna, *Virginia* (London: Hogarth, 1981).

Sackville-West, V., *The Land* (London: Heinemann, 1926).

Silver, Brenda (ed.), *Virginia Woolf's Reading Notebooks* (Princeton: Princeton University Press, 1983).

Stephen, Mrs Leslie, *Notes from Sick Rooms*, with an introduction by Constance Hunting (Maine: Puckerbrush Press, 1980, first published privately, London, 1883).

Woolf, Leonard, *Sowing: An autobiography of the years 1880 to 1904* (London: Hogarth, 1960).

Woolf, Leonard, *Growing: An autobiography of the years 1904 to 1911* (London: Hogarth, 1961).

Woolf, Leonard, *Beginning Again: An autobiography of the years 1911 to 1918* (London: Hogarth, 1964).

Woolf, Leonard, *Downhill All the Way: An autobiography of the years 1919 to 1939* (London: Hogarth, 1967).

Woolf, Leonard, *The Journey Not the Arrival Matters: An autobiography of the years 1939 to 1969* (London: Hogarth, 1969).

Select related articles on Virginia Woolf

Bennett, Arnold, 'Is the novel decaying?' *Cassell's Weekly*, 28 March 1923, p. 47 (reprinted in *The Critical Heritage*, pp. 112–14).

Bodenheim, Maxwell, review of *Jacob's Room*, *Nation*, 28 March 1923, pp. 368–9 (reprinted in *The Critical Heritage*, pp. 110–11).

Bradbrook, M. C., 'Notes on the style of Mrs Woolf', *Scrutiny*, May 1932, pp. 33–8 (reprinted in *The Critical Heritage*, pp. 308–13).

Courtney, W. L., review of *Jacob's Room*, *Daily Telegraph*, 10 November 1922, p. 4 (reprinted in *The Critical Heritage*, pp. 103–5).

Davies, Russell, 'The heavenly dialogue of Mrs Woolf and Mr Joyce', *The Sunday Times*, 31 January 1982, p. 43.

Dinnage, Rosemary, 'The last act', *The New York Review of Books*, 8 November, 1984, pp. 3–4.

Forster, E. M., 'Visions', *Daily News*, 31 July 1919, p. 2 (reprinted in *The Critical Heritage*, pp. 68–70).

Forster, E. M., review of *The Voyage Out*, *Daily News and Leader*, 8 April 1915, p. 7 (reprinted in *The Critical Heritage*, pp. 52–5).

Glendinning, Victoria, 'Cry Woolf on the rocks', *The Times*, 20 July 1989, p. 19.

Gordon, Lyndall, 'The unmated soul', *Times Literary Supplement*, 27 December 1985, p. 1479.

Grosskurth, Phyllis, 'Between eros and thanatos', *Times Literary Supplement*, 31 October 1980, pp. 1225–6.

Halperin, John, 'Bloomsbury and Virginia Woolf: Another view', *Dalhousie Review*, vol. 59, no. 3.

Harrington, Henry R., 'The central line down the middle of *To the Lighthouse*', *contemporary literature*, xxi, 3.

Heilbrun, Carolyn G., 'Virginia Woolf in her fifties', *Twentieth Century Literature*, vol. 27, Spring 1981, no. 1.

Juranville, Anne, 'La figure de la mère chez Virginia Woolf', *Psychoanalyse à l'Université*, Revue trimestrielle, tome 7, no. 26, Mars 1982, pp. 219–49.

Kiely, Robert, 'The years of maturity', *The New York Times Book Review*, 11 July 1982, pp. 3–23.

Kristeva, Julia, 'Oscillation du "pouvoir" au "refus"', an interview by Xavière Gauthier, *Tel Quel*, Summer 1984, reprinted in Marks and de Courtivron (eds.), *New French Feminisms* (Brighton: Harvester, 1981), pp. 165–7.

Leavis, F. R., 'After *To the Lighthouse*', *Scrutiny*, X, 3, 1942, pp. 297–8.

Leavis, Q. D., 'Caterpillars of the Commonwealth unite', *Scrutiny*, September 1938, pp. 203–14 (reprinted in *The Critical Heritage*, pp. 409–19).

Leavis, Q. D., 'Leslie Stephen: Cambridge critic', *Scrutiny*, 7, no. 4, March 1939, pp. 406–7.

Lee, Hermione, 'With Towser and Potto', *Times Literary Supplement*, 21 December 1984, p. 1480.

Lipking, Joanna, 'The Manx cat again', *Virginia Woolf Miscellany*, Fall 1984, no. 23.

Mansfield, Katherine, review of *Night and Day*, *Athenaeum*, 21 November 1919, p. 1227 (reprinted in *The Critical Heritage*, pp. 79–82).

Mellers, W. H., 'Mrs Woolf and life', *Scrutiny*, VI, 1, 1937, pp. 71–5.

Mellers, W. H., review of *The Years*, *Scrutiny*, June 1937, pp. 71–5, reprinted in *The Critical Heritage*, pp. 395–9.

Mepham, John, 'Trained to silence', *London Review of Books*, 20 November–4 December 1980, pp. 21–3.

Middleton Murry, John, 'Romance', *Nationa di Athenaeum*, 10 March 1923, p. 882 (reprinted in *The Critical Heritage*, p. 109).

Morris, Feiron, review of 'Mr Bennett and Mrs Brown', *Criterion*, January 1925, pp. 326–9 (reprinted in *The Critical Heritage*, pp. 134–7).

Muir, Edwin, review of 'Mr Bennett and Mrs Brown', *The Nation and Athenaeum*, 6 December 1924, p. 370 (reprinted in *The Critical Heritage*, pp. 133–4).

Roe, Sue, 'Paradoxes of design', *Times Literary Supplement*, February 3–9, 1989, p. 100.

DeSalvo, Louise, 'Lighting the cave', *Signs*, vol. 8, no. 2, 1982.

Troy, William, 'Virginia Woolf', *Symposium* (Concord, New Hampshire), January–March 1932, pp. 53–63 and April–June 1932, pp. 153–66 (reprinted in *The Critical Heritage*, pp. 314–15).

Troy, William, review of *The Years*, *Nation* (New York), 24 April 1937, pp. 473–4 (reprinted in *The Critical Heritage*, pp. 392–4).

Unsigned review of *Jacob's Room*, *Yorkshire Post*, 29 November 1922, p. 4 (reprinted in *The Critical Heritage*, pp. 107–8).

Unsigned review of 'Kew Gardens', *Times Literary Supplement*, 29 May 1919, p. 293 (reprinted in *The Critical Heritage*, pp. 66–7).

Unsigned review of 'The Voyage Out', *Times Literary Suppplement*, 1 April 1915, p. 110 (reprinted in *The Critical Heritage*, pp. 49–50).

Vigne, Marie-Paule, 'Réflexions autour d'un thème: Virginia Woolf et l'eau' in Colloque de Cerisy (Direction Jean Guiguet), *Virginia Woolf et le groupe de Bloomsbury* (Paris: Union Générale d'Editions, 1977).

West, Rebecca, review of *Jacob's Room*, *New Statesman*, 4 November 1922, p. 142 (reprinted in *The Critical Heritage*, pp. 100–2).

Archival materials

Monks House Papers, University of Sussex.

Henry W. and Albert A. Berg Collection, The New York Public Library, Astor, Lenox and Tilden Foundations.

Note on Virginia Woolf's works

I normally cite in the above bibliography only the first British edition and the edition consulted throughout.

Index

Notes
1. All references are to Virginia Woolf and her writings, unless otherwise indicated.
2. Fictional characters are shown in inverted commas.
3. Only the titles of Virginia Woolf's writings are given. Other titles are subsumed under the names of authors.